THE LOST JOURNALS

OF CHARLES S. ARMSTRONG:

From Arkport, New York to Aspen, Colorado

1867-1894

CHRISTIAN J. BUYS

D1603052

WESTERN REFLECTIONS PUBLISHING COMPANY®

Montrose, CO

First Edition
Printed in the United States of America

Library of Congress Catalog Card Number 2002100712

ISBN 1-890437-66-2

Front cover photograph: Charles S. Armstrong (left) and two fishermen friends pose in front of Armstrong's cabin on Castle Creek. (Author's collection)

Back cover photograph: Charles S. Armstrong embarks on a camping and fishing trip. (Author's collection)

Cover and text design by Laurie Goralka Design

Western Reflections Publishing Company®
P.O. Box 1647
Montrose, CO 81402
www.westernreflectionspub.com

To
Amy E. Buys and C.R. Taylor
and
Matthew E. Buys and Beth A. Buys

"Charlie Armstrong always stood as a man among men, and was one of the pioneer builders of the West. As a surveyor he was recognized as an outstanding figure in that profession."

Front page of *The Aspen Times*, Friday, November 23, 1928

CONTENTS

ACKNOWLEDGMENTS

Jack and Joyce Howe of Arkport, New York, welcomed me—a complete stranger—into their home, willingly shared their Arkport and Hornellsville archival material, and took me on a tour of Charles S. Armstrong's early environs. Marion Springer, researcher in the Stueben County Historian's Office in the Magee House in Bath, New York, directed me to numerous resources, patiently answered *all* my questions about Stueben County history, and graciously reviewed portions of the manuscript. Mark Buremann, Director of The Carroll Mansion, home of the Leavenworth County Historical Society in Leavenworth, Kansas, personally found key resources and images related to Armstrong's sojourns in early Leavenworth. Debra Bates-Lamborn, of First City Photo in Leavenworth, went out of her way to obtain permission (from David Phillips) to rephotograph a stereocard of the Continental Hotel, where Armstrong served as a night clerk, for inclusion in this book. Thanks also to Laurie Goralka Casselberry for her exemplary art direction, design, and production.

Su Lum of Aspen, Colorado, directed me to Jony Larrowe of El Jebel, Colorado, who shares my interest and enthusiasm for Charles S. Armstrong's journals. Jony personally guided me to Armstrong's second cabin site, told me of his obituary notice, which I had been unable to find, and shared several images included in this book. More recently, Jony introduced me to Russell Holmes who as a young boy stayed with his father in Armstrong's cabin during the summer of 1933. Thus, Su and Jony helped make this book complete.

Larry Fredrick, a good friend and knowledgeable Aspen historian, enthusiastically shared his archival material, found Armstrong's grave site, uncovered a key 1884 Pitkin County map, and directed me to numerous early sources related to Armstrong's journals. He also reviewed most of the material included in this book. Beth VanKuiken Buys, my wife, and Su Lum contributed substantial and insightful editorial suggestions. Rita Eisenheim also carefully reviewed and improved several portions of the original manuscript.

Lisa Hancock, Curator of Collections at the Aspen Historical Society, always seemed to know instantaneously the location of anything I needed in the Aspen Historical Archives. Barbara Dey, reference librarian in the Stephen Hart Library of the Colorado Historical Society, efficiently directed me to numerous early business directories and resources with information pertinent to Armstrong. Trevor Washko, Lynne Mace, and Isabel Mace freely shared their extensive knowledge of Aschoft history.

My two close friends, Bill Ellicott and Scott Strain, accompanied me (more often guided me) on numerous trips into the high country in search of various "Armstrong locations." During these trips they politely listened to me drone on about minutia related to Armstrong's journals. For that, I owe them both a sincere thank you. Scott Strain, Ben Bennett, Dom Popish, Russell Holmes, Bill Venner, Linda Gustafson, and Trevor Washko helped me, either directly or indirectly, locate several regional sites familiar to Armstrong. By combining diligence and creativity, Scott Strain produced a wonderful map of numerous claims that Armstrong surveyed. Barbara Bost, another close friend, provided support for this book through her "behind the scenes" help and deep appreciation of Colorado history. Amy Buys, my daughter, and C.R. Taylor, her fiancee, provided invaluable technical computer assistance.

I also want to acknowledge Leo Stambaugh for discovering, preserving, and realizing the potential historical value of Armstrong's journals. Lastly, a special thanks to my good friends and publishers, P. David and Jan Smith, for their support and encouragement throughout this project.

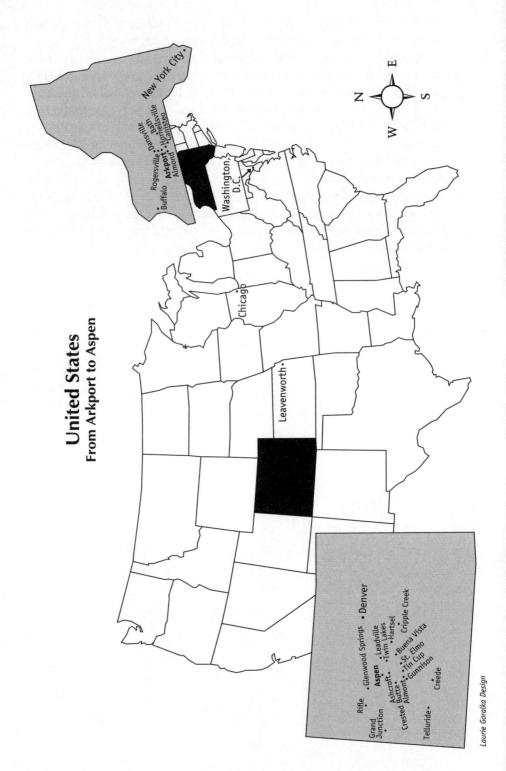

United States
From Arkport to Aspen

New York City

Rogersville• •Dansville
Bath
•Hornellsville
Arkport• •Canisteo
Almond•
Buffalo•

Washington, D.C.

Chicago•

Leavenworth•

Rifle•
Grand
Junction
•Glenwood Springs •Denver
Ashcroft•• •Leadville
Butte• •Twin Lakes
Crested •Almont• •Hartsel
Buena Vista
•St. Elmo
•Tin Cup
•Gunnison
•Cripple Creek

Telluride•
•Creede

N
W — E
S

Laurie Goralka Design

Ashcroft Region 1880s*

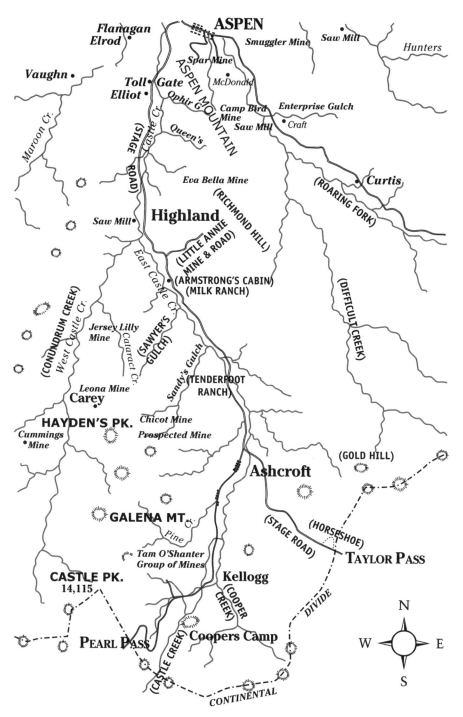

Flanagan
Elrod •

Vaughn •

Toll • Gate
Elliot •

ASPEN

Smuggler Mine   • Saw Mill

Hunters

Spar Mine

ASPEN MOUNTAIN

McDonald

Enterprise Gulch

Camp Bird
Mine
Saw Mill

• Craft

Ophir Gulch

(STAGE ROAD)

Castle Cr.

Queen's

Eva Bella Mine

Maroon Cr.

Saw Mill •

Highland

(LITTLE ANNIE MINE & ROAD)

(RICHMOND HILL)

(ROARING FORK)

• Curtis

East Castle Cr.

(ARMSTRONG'S CABIN)
(MILK RANCH)

(CONUNDRUM CREEK)

West Castle Cr.

Jersey Lilly
Mine

Cataract Cr.

(SAWYER'S GULCH)

Sandy's Gulch

(TENDERFOOT
RANCH)

(DIFFICULT CREEK)

Leona Mine
Carey

HAYDEN'S PK.

Cummings
• Mine

Chicot Mine

Prospected Mine

(GOLD HILL)

Ashcroft

GALENA MT.

Pine

Tam O'Shanter
Group of Mines

Kellogg

(STAGE ROAD)

(HORSESHOE)

TAYLOR PASS

CASTLE PK.
14,115

(COOPER CREEK)

DIVIDE

PEARL PASS

(CASTLE CREEK)

Coopers Camp

N

W   E

S

CONTINENTAL

Laurie Goralka Design

* {Based on 1884 map of Pitkin County. Locations in parentheses added by author.}

MAPS   v

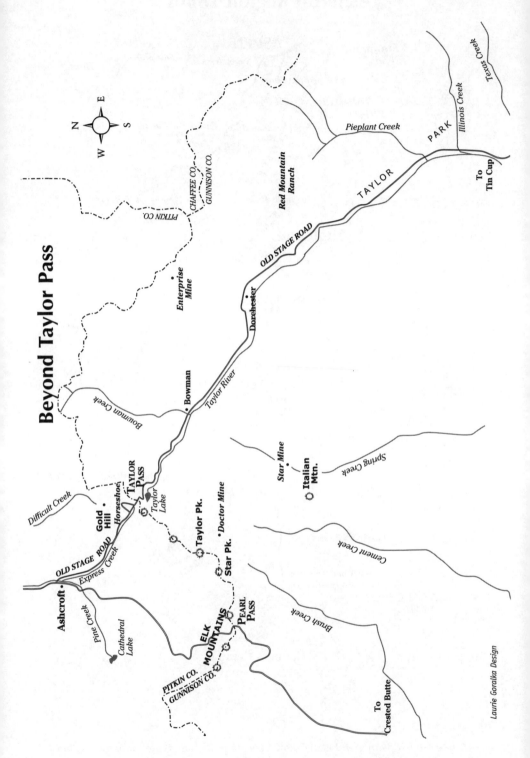

Beyond Taylor Pass

N E S W

Texas Creek
Illinois Creek
TAYLOR PARK
Pieplant Creek
To Tin Cup
OLD STAGE ROAD
Red Mountain Ranch
CHAFFEE CO.
GUNNISON CO.
PITKIN CO.
Enterprise Mine
Dorchester
Taylor River
Bowman
Bowman Creek
Star Mine
Italian Mtn.
Spring Creek
TAYLOR PASS
Taylor Lake
Horseshoe
Difficult Creek
Gold Hill
Taylor Pk.
Doctor Mine
Star Pk.
Cement Creek
OLD STAGE ROAD
Express Creek
Ashcroft
Pine Creek
Cathedral Lake
ELK MOUNTAINS
PEARL PASS
Brush Creek
PITKIN CO.
GUNNISON CO.
To Crested Butte

Laurie Goralka Design

Regional Map of Contemporary Aspen

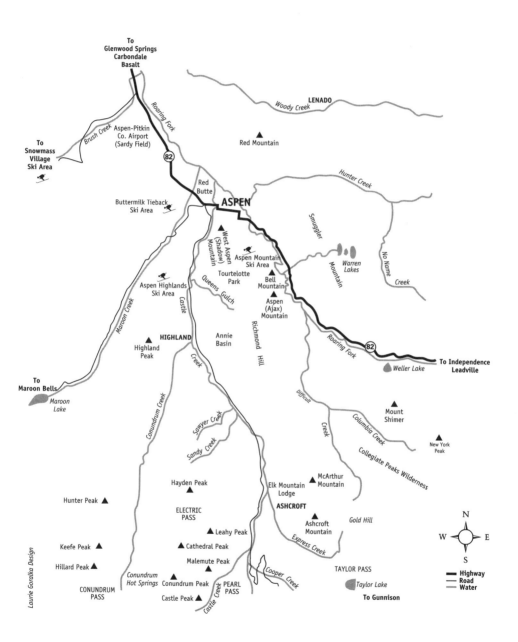

Mining Claim Locations
From the Survey Notes of
Charles S. Armstrong

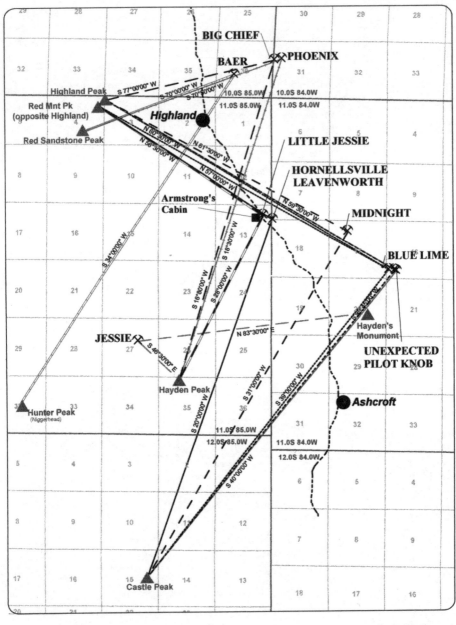

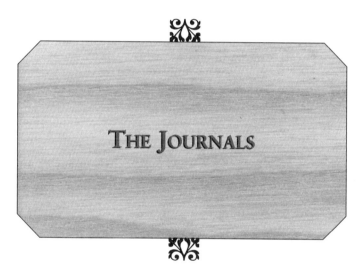

THE JOURNALS

In the early spring of 1999, after a research session at the Colorado Historical Society in Denver, Colorado, I stopped to see a friend, Leo Stambaugh, in Georgetown. Georgetown sits high on the eastern slope of the Rockies. Grand Junction, Colorado, my home, is on the other side of Continental Divide near the border of eastern Utah. I had called Leo earlier to ask for permission to photograph some of the Aspen artifacts in his store and his small, yet impressive, museum. I hoped to use some of the images in my upcoming Aspen pictorial history book. Leo graciously agreed to let me photograph any item that caught my eye. After I finished photographing a few artifacts, he asked me if I wanted to look at something else. Behind the counter, on a stool, sat a cutoff cardboard box. From it protruded a set of small dusty journals and a listing pile of curled, faded photographs. "What's this?" I inquired. A soft-spoken gentleman, Leo almost apologized. From the shoddy appearance of the materials I could understand why. He responded, "It's a set of old diaries from the Aspen area." He also shared his feeling that someone should delve into them, and that they might be of historical significance.

I stared at the pocket-sized journals for a moment, then began to shuffle carefully through them like a deck of cards. Several of the covers had ornate handwritten dates from the 1890s and early 1900s. Better yet, a few of the calf-hide covers carried captivating folk art. If the content of these journals, I conjectured aloud, actually focused on Aspen, I could at least photograph this primitive, yet appealing art. It would add a personal dimension to my pictorial Aspen book. "Sure," Leo concurred, "just take them with you and return them when you're done." At first I hesitated, but I finally agreed to do so. I did not want to take all nineteen journals, so I selected a few with the most decorative covers and three of the plain ones with tattered covers. I had no clue about their significance. I also borrowed several of the most intriguing photographs.

A few days later I began browsing through the journals. I selected one with a soft, reddish-colored cover and no date. Within minutes I found myself mesmerized by what I was reading. Could this be? In 1887 a man named Charles S. Armstrong had written almost daily accounts of his life while living in a small log cabin near Highland along Castle Creek in the foothills south of Aspen. Accounts of prospecting, trapping, fishing, gardening, and a myriad of other activities, including drinking, leapt from the pages. He described the stagecoaches and prospectors who regularly passed by his cabin, and his visits to Aspen, Ashcroft, and beyond. Comments were made on the weather, birds, animals, fellow prospectors, Indians, and local and national politics.

My heart began to race. Quickly, I reached for the other journals, searching for an even earlier date. There was none, so I picked out a heavily worn journal with an ornate "1912" drawn on the cover. I searched for two events: the fire that gutted the Wheeler Opera House (in Aspen) and the sinking of the *Titanic*. Sure enough, Armstrong mentioned both. I was hooked. Here was a stunning set of personal commentaries from someone living during one of the most fascinating eras in the West. They allowed me a glimpse of history through the eyes of someone living it! I spent the next several evenings reading every word of each journal.

Then I began to hope. If the journals that I had left behind in Georgetown—the ones without the cover dates and folk art—*happened* to start before 1887 and *happened* to describe this young man's trip to Aspen, well, it would be special, very special. I moved up a planned trip to Denver, stopping in Georgetown to pick up the remaining journals. They were even better than I had dared imagine. Charles S. Armstrong began his first journal—a small, plain black one that I had passed over as unremarkable—in 1867 in Arkport, New York. He scribbled his last entry in 1926 in Aspen, Colorado. A record spanning nearly sixty years! Better yet, some of his most detailed and poignant descriptions focused on his journey west— from Arkport, New York, to Leavenworth, Kansas, to Denver, Colorado, then on to Leadville, and ultimately, to nascent Aspen. A true Aspen pioneer, Armstrong huddled in his tent in May 1880 and wrote impressions of his arduous trip over Hunter's Pass (present-day Independence Pass) into the Roaring Fork Valley. As he passed through "Aspen and Roaring Fork City," he observed that there were no houses, only tents. These entries alone took my breath away. I began to realize what a find this was.

I still, however, did not fully appreciate the rarity of these journals. It took Duane Smith, perhaps Colorado's finest historian, and P. David Smith, a publisher of Colorado history, author, and mining historian, to enlighten me. During a casual after-dinner conversation one beautiful spring evening in Ouray, Colorado, I described the journals. I inquired about the existence of other personal accounts similar to these, because I had had no success finding them in various archives in Colorado. They stared at me incredulously. Surely I knew, they said, that several "49'ers" had kept journals on their way to the California goldfields in the mid-nineteenth century (I did know that), as had immigrants trekking over the Oregon Trail and numerous combatants in the Civil War (I knew that, too). And surely I knew, they continued, that keeping personal diaries seemed to be the order of day for Victorian-era women and men (I did not know that). But a miner, or prospector, keeping a diary spanning several decades? Such men were not the type. In fact, neither Duane nor P. David knew of any Colorado miner's journal. A few sets of miners' letters existed, but these correspondences seldom continued for more than a year or two. "No," P. David deliberated, "I know of no such journals, or at least none have surfaced." Duane nodded in agreement.

We talked about how troublesome it would be for an early prospector, or miner, to keep a daily journal in primitive and difficult living conditions. Add to this the considerable motivation necessary to maintain such a personal ledger over six decades. It would be almost too much to ask—until now. Then I told Duane and P. David that Armstrong drew in his journals and kept photographs, too.

After learning of the rarity of the journals, I decided to make the title of my book, *Historic Aspen in Rare Photographs, Featuring the Journal of Charles S. Armstrong.* I wove several "Armstrong entries" throughout my pictorial history of Aspen. After publication, Armstrong's entries attracted more attention and interest than any of the photographs, or the typical—though still intriguing—Colorado mining-town history. Since these popular entries and images represented only a small fraction of Armstrong's journals, drawings, and photographs, I considered putting Armstrong's journals in print.

First I began the task of transcribing all nineteen journals onto my computer. The final transcription amounted to over 1,100 pages. Charles S. Armstrong penciled in his first journal entry on January 1, 1867, at the age of nineteen in Arkport, New York, and his last on May 8, 1926, at the age of seventy-eight in Aspen, Colorado.

On a broad psychological plane, Armstrong's journals capture the quintessential urge of a young man in nineteenth-century America to "Go West." On a more personal level, this unique written record allows one to become intimately acquainted with one of the thousands of fortune seekers who poured into the West, most of whom had neither the time, nor inclination, nor ability to write about their remarkable experiences. Moreover, I often felt like I was part of Armstrong's personal odyssey. His words also helped me understand and participate in, albeit vicariously, an incredible American era that passed in a moment, never to be possible again. Historians necessarily focus on generalities: wars, fiscal policies, ethnic groups, westward movements, inventions, social trends, disasters and, among others, technological advances. Charles put a singular human face on many of these—from his attitudes toward Indians to the Spanish-American War.

I came to know Charles personally as well: his kindnesses, moods, perceptiveness, self-criticism, strengths, weaknesses, foibles, and dreams. For over thirty years he lived south of Aspen in two small log cabins (one after the other), that he built himself. Now when I hike by dilapidated log cabins in the high country, they seem more human, more alive. Each one has its own story to tell, like Armstrong's.

During the year I spent transcribing his journals, I could hardly wait until the next evening, or weekend, when I found time to sit in silence in front of my computer and lose myself once again in Armstrong's world—a world far distant from our current high-tech, cyberspaced, frenetic reality. Yet Charles often drove me to distraction with months of succinct pedestrian entries, only to write something perceptive, humorous, circumspect, or wicked. I noticed more than anything else how in tune he was with the seasons, and the effect they had upon his psyche and behavior.

When I was about halfway through transcribing the journals, I knew I had to follow Armstrong's path. To this end, I drove from Aspen, Colorado, to Leavenworth, Kansas, where Armstrong boarded the train to Denver in the spring of 1880. From Leavenworth, I drove east to his childhood home in Arkport, New York. Each summer I have driven and hiked to several of his favorite Colorado haunts. The images and information that resulted from these trips appear in this book.

During the course of my transcriptions, I discovered that one of the later journals was missing—leaving a gap from November 6, 1899, to May 17, 1901. Thus, I was thrilled to discover that the Aspen Historical Society's archives held a complete transcription of the missing journal. One winter, while working with this archival "Armstrong" folder, I noticed a handwritten note among the papers. It was written by a person named Su Lum, who had copied the original journal for a friend. I asked the Aspen Historical Society's Curator of Collections, Lisa Hancock, if she knew Su Lum. She did. Lum, a writer, lived in Aspen and worked at the *Aspen Times*. The next day I called Su from my home in Grand Junction. I introduced myself and told her the purpose of my call. She responded as though she knew me.

"Do I know you?" I inquired as politely as possible.

"No, but I know you. In fact, my daughter just lent me your Aspen book, the one you gave her. I was just looking at it."

Small world. Her daughter turned out to be Hillery McCallister. Hillery and her husband Bruce, owners of the Western Hardware Antique Mall in Leadville, Colorado, have been friends of mine for several years. Indeed, I had just given them a copy of my new Aspen pictorial book, because they had graciously allowed me to use one of their Aspen photographs.

Su told me that the "missing" journal belonged to a woman by the name of Jony Larrowe, who had also lived in Aspen. Su knew that Jony had moved "down valley," toward Carbondale. She volunteered to find Jony's phone number. True to her word, two days later Su called me with the number.

I immediately called Jony Larrowe, who now lives in El Jebel, about twenty miles north of Aspen. Sure enough, a friend of Jony's had given her the turn-of-the-century calf-hide journal in the early 1970's because she had expressed an interest in it, and even written about its fascinating contents. When I asked Jony where her friend had obtained the journal, she told me that in the mid-1960s her friend's son, Eric Johnson, had retrieved the journal from the Aspen dump.

Jony also knew things about Charles S. Armstrong that I did not. I had been unable to locate his final resting place, either in the cemetery over-looking Arkport or on any of the three Aspen archival cemetery lists (Red Butte, Aspen Grove, and Ute). I scoured numerous 1926 *Aspen Times* for a notice of his death after his last journal entry on May 8, 1926. Nothing. Next I searched through the 1927 Aspen newspapers. Still nothing. My wife (Beth), my daughter (Amy), and I searched the Masonic section of the Red Butte Cemetery in Aspen, where Armstrong had helped lay to rest many of his Masonic mates. Again, nothing. We wondered if his headstone remained, or might be one of those with the name weathered away.

A few months later, I found "Charles Armstrong" listed in several Colorado State Business Directories (in the Stephen H. Hart Library at the Colorado Historical Society) as "county surveyor" (which he was) and "civil engineer" from 1925 through 1928. In 1929, he last appeared as a "civil engineer." I concluded that Armstrong was unable to continue writing in his journals after May 8, 1926, because of rheumatism, failing eyesight, and probably a stroke. I determined to search the *Aspen Times* from 1928 through 1929, although based on my previous dealings with State Directory listings, I knew they often lagged a year or more behind. Jony Larrowe saved me the trouble. Although she no longer had a copy of his obituary, she told me that she had read it. Armstrong died on November 20, 1928, nine days before his 81st birthday. Further, he was buried in the Masonic section in the Red Butte Cemetery in Aspen. Jony had speculated, too, that the harsh elements must have worn Armstrong's name off one of the modest headstones.

A few months before this book went to press, Larry Fredrick, a friend and local Aspen historian, solved the mystery. During a conversation with a member (Stoney Davis) of the Red Butte Cemetery Board, Larry learned about the existence of a "Plot Book." Upon examination of this book, he discovered that Armstrong's final resting place is "Plot 7, Lot B, of Block 12." The headstone is gone.

Armstrong's long-time, second cabin site by Castle Creek between Highland and Ashcroft had also eluded me. I narrowed my search to about a one-mile stretch, but my attempt to find the precise location proved frustrating and fruitless. Once again, Jony knew something I did not. She had a photograph of Armstrong's cabin from a 1935 *Denver Post*. With that in hand, and with directions from long-time Aspen miner Russell Holmes, who in the 1930s had stayed with his father *in* Armstrongs'cabin, Jony had found Armstrong's exact cabin site almost two decades ago. The Forest Service, she lamented, burnt it in the late 1930s: they deemed it an eyesore and wanted to keep the squatters out. Within a month after I first spoke to

Jony, she graciously guided me (I called it my "pilgrimage") to Armstrong's second cabin site, where he penned most of his journals.

Still, there was something missing that would have made this book complete: a photograph of Armstrong. Besides, I really wanted to know what he looked like. Sometimes I thought he must have been slender—from his strenuous treks in the high country. Other times I pictured him as plump and fluffy—from his drinking episodes. For no apparent reason I envisioned him with a neatly trimmed mustache and full shock of hair. Yet after two years of research in photographic archives in Colorado, Kansas, and New York, I came to believe that no image of Armstrong existed.

Then, at the last moment, serendipity intervened. During December 2001, while reviewing the final version of this first volume, I received an e-mail from Leo Stambaugh. Leo had "run across some things that had become separated from the other Armstrong material." These "things" turned out to be a wallet with Armstrong's name on it with five photographs inside. A few days later Leo graciously sent me the wallet and photographs. In one photograph, probably taken in the early 1900s, three men posed proudly with their fishing poles in front of Armstrong's cabin along Castle Creek. I turned over the faded, brittle photograph. One the back Armstrong had written, "Me, Tom, Boyd." So there he was, the "older" man sitting on his bench in front of his cabin. I had my photograph of Charles S. Armstrong. Charles did not write anything on the back of the next photograph. He didn't have to. It was Charles again, this time standing beside one of his "jacks." What else could I ask for? These images of Armstrong now grace the front and back covers of this volume.

As for the layout of this book, I struggled with it for several weeks. First I pored through numerous books containing personal journals, diaries, and lengthy letters. None of the layouts satisfied me. In their attempts to document details (especially in academic theses), the editors, in my judgment, sacrificed an intimate "feel" for the writer. Next I decided to print similar entries in several different formats. That made my decision easier. Although I value the information contained in footnotes and notations, I found that no matter where I placed them—within a sentence, at the bottom of the page, or even directly across the page—they ruined the pace and rhythm of Armstrong's writing. Even small footnote numbers placed high at the end of sentences distracted me, and they certainly never appeared in Charles's journals. Thus, my prime consideration became letting Armstrong's journals flow as naturally as he wrote them.

To this end, his accounts are presented here with minimal annotation. I have reluctantly added some punctuation, capitalization, and paragraphing for ease of reading. Most spelling "errors," and there are a plethora of them, remain. I corrected a few obvious slips, errors, and thoughtless repetitions. If I could not decipher a word or name, I duly noted this with a question mark placed in brackets. I also felt it necessary, even at the cost of including more brackets, to include definitions for a few archaic words and some unfamiliar terminology. Moreover, since I agree with William Unrau (1979) "that punctuating and syntax for a particular period are of more than casual interest," few major editorial changes have been made. I also had to remind myself that English was not as standardized in the mid-1800s as it is now. Lastly, Charles mentions over 1,000 individuals in his set of 19 journals. I wish I had the time to search archival resources for all of them, and to tell their life stories as well. For now, most of them appear in name only.

At the beginning of each chapter I include a section entitled, "Historical Setting and the Man." Here I do two things. I briefly set the historical stage by pointing out certain people, events, and places of particular relevance to Armstrong, or of special historical interest. Then, as a psychologist, I analyze Charles the man by examining his words, thoughts, and actions.

After Su Lum finished reading the Armstrong entries in my pictorial Aspen book and a transcription of one of his early journals, she sent me a letter. Her words, and many of her keen insights into Armstrong's psyche, helped motivate me to complete this first volume:

> *I encourage you to proceed with the Armstrong diaries—if ever a book was waiting there for someone to publish it, this is it! While some parts may seem mundane or boring, it is the OVERALL effect that brought the one journal I read come to life: I loved reading about what he ate (what he grew, trapped, shot and bought), his interest in the news of the world, the weather patterns, the resolutions he made (and broke), and his ART . . . . (doodles and droodles that revealed the real person more than the accounts).. . . . In this day of dietary correctness and obsession with prevention, he consumed quantities of animal fats, smoked, drank, lived a long life and then BANG. His penultimate entry was lucid, his final entry was the end. I'm surprised you couldn't find out what happened to him [I have since], but let us hope that that was IT [it was not]. Isn't that how all of us would hope to go? . . . . ONWARD to a book on the journals!*

CHAPTER 1
AT HOME IN ARKPORT
1867

HISTORICAL SETTING AND THE MAN

C harles S. Armstrong entered this world in Arkport, New York, on November 29, 1847. A potato famine had just ravished Ireland, Marx and Engels were about to issue *The Communist Manifesto,* Liberia became the first black republic in Africa, and revolutions simmered in France, Germany, and Italy. In the United States, President James Knox Polk presided over 22,000,000 Americans spread over twenty-six states and several vast "unexplored," though certainly occupied, territories. Nine out of ten U.S. citizens lived in rural areas. No one had even conceived of a state named Colorado, let alone the mining town of Aspen: Armstrong's ultimate destination.

During the 1840s, the young, burgeoning republic of the United States simmered with promise, prosperity, and energy. It was also fraught with contradictions. Thousands of covered wagons headed west over the Oregon Trail to the promised land of the Pacific Coast. Along the way they cut deeper and deeper ruts through pristine prairies, high deserts, and mountain passes. In the late 1840s this human surge turned into a tidal wave with the discovery of gold in California. Clever and wondrous inventions, from the telegraph to the sewing machine, bolstered the country's confidence even more. The 1840s also cast a pall over the human spirit. The expansion west reeked of illegal land grabs from, among others, Native Americans. And, too, much of the nation's prosperity came at the cost of immigrants' grinding poverty, brutal exploitation of child labor, and nearly ubiquitous enslavement of African-Americans. Welcome to your world, Charles Armstrong.

By the time Armstrong, at age nineteen, penned his first journal entry on January 1, 1867, the world had changed dramatically. The British had created the Dominion of Canada, Russia had sold Alaska to the United States, the Mexicans had executed Emperor Maximillan, the Dual Monarchy of Austria-Hungary had been born, and among an array of other dizzying technological breakthroughs fueled by the Industrial Age, Alfred Nobel had invented dynamite. In the United States, President Andrew Johnson, the first president to be impeached, presided over almost 40,000,000 people in 35 states and several territories (including Colorado Territory) still trying to recover and cope with the horrors of a monstrously bloody and divisive Civil War. Precious minerals started to pour out of the Rockies. Modest child labor laws were enacted and the institution of slavery was legally abolished. Tentacles of iron rails began spreading rapidly west.

Did all this affect a young man in rural, western New York? It did, and it did not. Events playing out on the world stage often garnered Armstrong's attention at local "Lyceums," or public programs. Polygamy among the Mormons, rejuvenating the devastated American South, and the foreboding power of the Turkish Empire drew bare mention in his first journal.

Of course, young Charles wrote the most about his immediate geographic and social realms in Arkport, and nearby Hornellsville, in western New York. By 1770, the Iroquois, Seneca, and Erie nations, already decimated by European diseases, warfare, and the onslaught of "western pioneers," had ceded (lost) most of the land in western New York. In 1797, pioneer Christopher Hurlbut, who served in the Continental Army directly under the command of George Washington, purchased 637 acres in what is now Arkport in the Canisteo Valley. This rich farmland astride the Canisteo River soon attracted new settlers. The Canisteo River, which meanders southeastwardly through the village of Arkport, ultimately flows into Chesapeake Bay. In 1800, the New York State Legislature officially designated the Canisteo River as a "public highway" for shipment of goods.

Residents of the valley became known for building wooden "arks," thus the name "Arkport." They loaded them with farm products, usually wheat, and floated them down the Canisteo to the more populous Chesapeake Bay area. There the enterprising farmers sold their goods, then dissembled the arks and sold the timber at a tidy profit as well. Once the Erie Canal opened in 1825 the river trade faded fast. By 1830, Arkport still claimed to be a

CHRISTOPHER HURLBUT HOUSE, ARKPORT, N.Y.
ERECTED 1804

Armstrong's father rented a home from Myron Hurlbut, the eldest son of Arkport, New York pioneer Christopher Hurlbut (above). Built in 1804, Christopher Hurlbut's original home still stands. (Clayton, 1879; Courtesy of Joyce and Jack Lowe)

Christopher Hurlbut served in the Continental Army directly under the command of General George Washington (above). (Harper's Weekly, *February 27, 1869)*

well-established frontier community, but it was barely that. As for Arkport's dreams of growth and prosperity, a steady exodus of young settlers to Ohio, Indiana, Illinois, and Michigan kept its population consistently below 1,000.

Three miles south of Arkport, the town of Hornellsville (now Hornell) was "set off" from the town of Canisteo in 1821. Although no one could have imagined it in 1821, in 1851 the first Erie Railroad engine chugged its way into a jubilant Hornellsville. Better yet, the town had miraculously captured the coveted Erie Railroad's primary maintenance facilities. The massive engine shops alone could handle twenty steam engines at once. Thus, Hornellsville's size and economic fortunes suddenly and forever outstripped Arkport, its sleepy northern neighbor.

In 1867, journal entries indicate that Charles—like thousands of other young men throughout the rural eastern United States—judged his life to be comfortable, nonprofitable, and "smothe." Smooth to the point of being maddeningly monotonous. Like the majority of folks in Arkport and the rest of the United States, the Armstrongs (his father, John, his mother, Roxanne, and his younger sister, Roxie) grew most of their own food and traveled by horseback. Seasonal cycles of agricultural living dictated the pace and focus of their daily activities. In winter Charles worked long hours in his father's blacksmith shop for little, if any, pay. He spent his leisure time reading books, attending church and school (possibly in nearby Rogersville), and weather permitting, visiting his Uncle Rile. During fall he worked for wages at harvest time. In the spring and summer he helped with the garden, worked in his father's "Shop," hunted with his dog, took hikes, attended a "maple sugar party," and enjoyed the company of friends. Life had a regular tempo to it, albeit too slow and mundane for Charles—a young man with dreams and aspirations. Highlights for Charles proved to be trapping and fishing in the Marsh Ditch (dug to reclaim farmland from a large marsh), socializing at the local "Corner's" tavern, watching plays and circuses in nearby Hornellsville, enjoying a rare "glorious" dance, and secretly harboring, perhaps, a first love.

Charles made one reference to attending an evening "Survey School," an institution one would not normally expect to find in a small rural community like Arkport. Most likely Christopher Hurlbut, the founder of Arkport, had a hand in establishing the school. According to one biographical source (Clayton, 1879), the elder Hurlbut was "of more than usual education; a good mathematician and a practical surveyor." Whatever the school's origin, the surveying skills Charles acquired would prove critical to his future in Colorado.

There are intriguing details in this first journal that lead one to interesting insights about the immediate post Civil War period. For example, Charles mentioned being paid in shillings, indicating that English money was still being accepted in rural New York as legal tender. That he earned only $1.25 for a day's hard labor suggests why he yearned for greener monetary pastures. He worked on Christmas Day, affirming that in the 1860s the holiday had yet to reach the extraordinary status it enjoys today. It is also apparent that his father, John Armstrong, could not save enough money to purchase his own farm: he rented a place from Myron Hurlbut, Christopher Hurlbut's eldest son.

There's more, much more. Almost every journal page contains details about life and times in the late 1860s in sleepy rural villages like Arkport—psychological breeding grounds for the mentality of "Go West Young Man." Today the tendency is to either glorify these times, or to be grateful that they are long gone. As for myself, I lean toward a little of both.

What about Charles's psychological side? What do the journals reveal about his personality, familial relations, attitudes toward women, and social attitudes? Before I can give those answers, I need to discuss the concept of projective personality tests. In clinical psychology, therapists employ projective tests to uncover clients' inner cognitions and emotions. The most popular is the Rorschach test, more commonly known as the "inkblot test." Ambiguous stimuli (inkblots) are presented to the clients who tell the psychologist what they "see." The assumption is that clients will project (thus, the word "projective") their inner thoughts and feelings onto the ambiguous images, in this case, inkblots. The psychologist interprets the clients' perceptions, often using them to open up sensitive and important psychological realms for discussion. While this may sound like psychological mumbo jumbo to some people, many reputable clinical psychologists trust the validity of projective techniques.

Clearly, Charles is our inkblot. Our tendency is to see what we want to see in his journals. With this in mind, I had several colleagues and friends read portions of Armstrong's first journal. They often agreed on various aspects of his personality, but they also "saw" things in Charles that I did not. Moreover, they were all inclined to extrapolate beyond what he wrote, making inferences and judgments about his personality and behavior. I find this tendency to go beyond the words fascinating. I do not want to do a disservice to Charles or his memory by over-analyzing what he wrote, or did not write. I will, however, try to look realistically at the man through his words and actions. As a psychologist, I find it fascinating to speculate about his upbringing and personality. But first let's take stock of his contemporary social environment.

Charles's social milieu doesn't require clinical training to interpret. He lived in a small, comfortable community anchored by family and church. The Hurlbut family clearly served as the benevolent patriarchs of the Arkport community. Charles spent most of his time helping his father in their blacksmith "Shop," attending school, working for the Hurlbuts during fall harvest, and pursuing his favorite pastimes—hunting, fishing, and trapping. Regular town meetings, school (even at twenty years old), evening "Singing School," and Lyceums provided more formal opportunities for social interchanges. Informally, barn-raisings, maple sugar parties, dances, and local tavern banter bound together even more tightly the already intimate community. The cliche', "everyone knew everyone's business," fit. Although local gossip and social news attracted some of Charles's attention, he did not fixate on it.

Charles carefully watched the weather, like everyone else. The quality of their lives depended on, among other climatic vicissitudes, a good growing season. (Today huge urban enclaves are totally cut off from the agrarian life. Despite appearances, near-perfect farm products do not grow in shiny plastic bags in giant grocery stores.) Numerous references to "very cold days" made me shiver for Charles. Yet his "good" and "first rate" sleighing comments evoked idyllic images of horse-drawn sleighs with jangling bells being whisked across miles of wintry snowfields.

Surely some social status accompanied Charles's position of trust as treasurer of the local Lyceum, although he did not make a big deal of it. I dearly wish he would have elaborated on the Lyceums' topics such as "Polygamy in Utah," "The War & the South," and Myron Hurlbut's "First-Rate" discussion of the "Turkish Empire." In this regard I thought of Neal Postman's provocative book, *Amusing Ourselves to Death*. Postman divides our cognitive and epistemological capacities into "print-culture" and "television-culture" eras. He contends that people in the nineteenth-century (print-culture) had a far greater capacity to "engage in rational public discourse and reasoned public affairs." That is, the citizens of Arkport, including young Charles S. Armstrong, *really* listened to and *really* understood contemporary political debates and issues because they had often *read* about them at length. Today, Postman contends, our cognitive capacities for meaningful public discourse and acquiring in-depth knowledge have fallen victim to random twenty-second television "news bits" meant to entertain rather than inform ("television-culture"). When was the last time Americans listened intently to, and prepared for, a series of three-hour presidential debates like those between Lincoln and Douglas? Anyway, I can visualize Charles sitting there at the regular local Lyceums in rural Arkport, New York, listening attentively to in-depth presentations and discussions of contemporary nineteenth-century issues.

As I have stated previously, I yearned for more lengthy entries. Unfortunately, something simple led to Charles's abbreviated comments in his 1867 journal. Limited diary space. The "Pocket Diary" presented to him as a Christmas gift by William Hurlbut, Christopher's second eldest son, allotted only enough space (2 1/2" x 1") between printed dates for about six lines with six words each. Fortunately, Charles bought larger, opened-ended journals throughout the rest of his life.

Some of Arkport's social mores come to light in the "misunderstanding" between a male teacher and one of the female students at Charles's school. Apparently an exchange of amorous poetry ended with the student leaving school. Drinking alcoholic beverages was far from forbidden. Several times Charles went up to the Corner's "Tavern" in the evening. He wrote that the blacksmith, Jerry Rym, got so drunk one cold evening in January that he "layed down" and "both feet and hands froze." In December he mentioned Rym getting drunk again, then trying to pick a fight. A Quaker Charles was not.

Charles's upbringing and its subsequent effect on his personality is not as easily discernable as his mid-nineteenth-century social environment. My sense, as I examine the inkblot, is that familial determinants of Charles's personality took center stage early in his childhood, then stayed with him the rest of his life. To begin with, only one mention of his mother throughout the year strikes me as incongruous. His single dispassionate entry reads: "Mother was worse & I did not get away till to [sic] late." Worse from what? Now consider what he did *not* write about his mother. Not a single mention of her warmth. Not a hint of her emotional or behavioral support. No favorite meals. No special treats. No specially made clothes. Nor is there a single word about her home duties, hobbies, or social activities. Would not a son, albeit one turning twenty years old, who lives at home, mention *some* of these motherly attributes? Add to this his father buying him clothes and Charles doing, what appears to be, the family washing. It all points to a mother with problems. Was she incapable of giving emotional support? Did she suffer from clinical depression before the syndrome had a name? Had she struggled with a traumatic childbirth? Roxie, his younger sister and only sibling, was born ten years after Charles. Would not there have been children in between? Or maybe some neuromuscular disease partially incapacitated her? Whatever the explanation, there is simply no sense of a nurturing home, hearth, and haven. This leads me to conclude that Charles and his mother did not have a normal mother-son relationship. Indeed, he seems to have been looking out for himself psychologically and physically since an early age.

Perhaps I go too far. After all, Charles did not wax emotionally about his father, either. All his entries about his father, a blacksmith and carriage maker, seem matter of fact, even when his father bought him an expensive suit. He attended a Lyceum with his father, but he never mentioned fishing or hunting with him. (Perhaps his father had more to do than most husbands?) Nor did he ever mention his father's Civil War service. (I did not know that John Armstrong had participated in the Civil War until I saw, "C 161 Regt. N. Y. Vols.", engraved on his headstone in the Arkport Cemetery.) Charles's relationship with his father centered on, as one might expect, work and more work. It is notable that he never complained about it. He wrote about going to church and the circus with his younger sister Roxie, but once again there is no sign of a close emotional bond with her. That he omitted any mention about family members' birthdays, including his own on November 29, suggests an emotionally segmented family as well. Plus, Charles, by himself, regularly visited his Uncle Rile. Perhaps it afforded him social interactions and interpersonal opportunities not available in his home.

To this point I have focused on the atypical and negative, a common tendency in psychologists. Now I want to stress that Charles showed no signs of clinical abnormality. To the contrary, he struck me as intelligent, perceptive, well read and well educated for his time, and, in my judgment, about as normal as one can get. Was he emotionally distant? Somewhat. Was he an emotional zombie? No. Certainly he spent time alone, but he never mentioned being lonely. As for his attitudes toward his family, *not once* did he utter a bad word about his mother, father, sister, or anyone else for that matter. He reserved his criticism for himself, in particular his monotonous and "smothe" life, covertly suggesting that he needed to get on with his own life and career. His rare words of praise—nothing wrong in that— fell upon a non-family member.

Charles enjoyed socializing. Like most young adults, his social activities occurred away from home. Lyceums, dances, school, maple sugar parties, barn raisings, tavern talk, church, circuses and theaters in Hornellsville, and work during harvest, gave him ample opportunity to fulfill his social needs. As for young women, he thoroughly enjoyed their infrequent company. On May 6, the day after he walked Grace Holzman home, he bought himself a pair of five-dollar boots. On May 8 his father was out of town and he wrote "May 8" in bold letters in the front and back of his pocket diary as well as scrolled a redundant "Mmmmaaaay mmmaaayyy 888th May 8th May 8th 1867" across the exact date. Suggestions regarding the meaning of these clues include Charles making a major resolution, meeting the girl of his dreams, his first kiss, or even losing his virginity: the inkblot phenomenon personified. I would guess first kiss.

Soon he stopped writing in his diary, then after sporadic entries in July and August, he began writing again in September. At this point, he was infatuated from afar with someone else, referred to as "L." On September

18, he complained that "I dont progress much." On September 19, he again wrote "L not progressing." During the next few weeks he wrote, "Saw her thats all," "Favorable. but dont progress," "Not any progress," "[She] was here this afternoon hot. me no good," "Saw L but I did not speak," and so forth. Throughout this period there was never any mention of love, secret lusts, marriage, or even the possibility of a meaningful relationship. On October 10, he attended at dance and had a "Glorious time!" He took Grace Holzman (his former heartthrob and "dasher"), and his friend Sime took Leib. Is "Leib" the "L" of his new infatuation? That we will never know, because he never mentioned her, or Grace, again.

With church playing a pivotal community role in Arkport and in Charles's social life, I am surprised that he was not more "religious." Here, once again, I am going to make infer-ences based on what he did not write. Not once did Charles mention prayer,

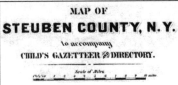

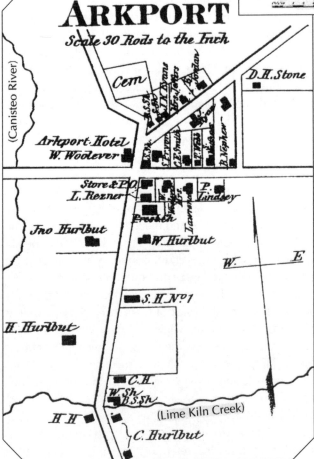

For almost thirty years, this was Armstrong's world. Charles's father, John, never owned property so the family name did not appear on this map. The "Corners" that Charles frequently mentioned was, and still is, the central crossroads in rural Arkport. John Armstrong also rented a blacksmith shop that could be sig-nified by the let-ters "B.S. Sh" by the creek (Lime Kiln) at the bottom of the map. (Atlas of Steuben County New York, 1873)

God, the Bible (although he did read the "Ledgers," which may have been "a book of the Bible in English"), or the content of a single sermon (other than praising a guest preacher) of which he must have heard plenty. Yet we know several of the Lyceum topics. For some reason the organized religion of Charles's youth did not seem to have left an imprint on his personal life. One hint regarding the genesis of Charles's religious neutrality is that he helped his father work in the shop on Sunday, so perhaps his father served as a model for moderation in orthodox matters.

William Hurlbut gave Charles Armstrong his first journal (shown here) on Christmas day, 1866. (Armstrong's journals)

I doubt Charles would have kept this first diary had not William Hurlbut presented it to him as a Christmas gift in 1866. As Charles hinted, he sometimes had trouble motivating himself to get going, especially when things were going "smothe." (His motivation, or lack thereof, will become more of an issue in future journals.) To help combat his self-perceived tendency toward laziness, he cut out a small newspaper article entitled, "YOUNG MAN, PAY ATTENTION!" and glued it on the inside cover of his diary. It reads: "Don't be a loafer; don't call yourself a loafer; don't keep a loafer's company; don't hang about loafing places. Better work for nothing and board yourself, than to sit arround corners with your hands in your pockets . . . . Quit droning and complaining; keep busy and mind your chances."

For the next decade Charles did not keep a diary. But, as you will see in the next chapter, between 1867 and 1877 Charles kept busy as well as "minded his chances" to head west. In fact, he made it as far as

Leavenworth, Kansas, in the early 1870s. Although in 1877, at the age of thirty, he would once again find himself back home in Arkport, New York.

Now it is a pleasure to present this first journal penned by Charles S. Armstrong. It takes some patience and effort to become comfortable with his writing style. At first his entries seem too brief, awkward, and mundane. Once one gets into the rhythm of reading his entries, however, numerous historical and personal gems present themselves. Indeed, his first journals constitute an archetypical record that document the quintessential urge of young Americans to go west. Moreover, Charles's firsthand accounts of his subsequent sojourn will ultimately connect two vastly different geographies, centuries, and lifestyles. It is also a personal, timeless journey that we all take, one way or another.

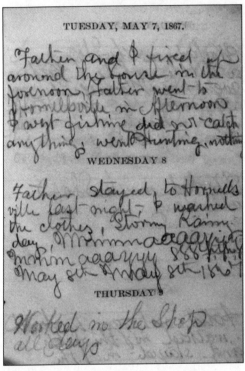

Constricted diary space limited Armstrong's entries during 1867. His unusual entry on May 8 suggests something special happened. (Armstrong's journals)

Note: As I previously mentioned, when I found John Armstrong's (Charles's father) modest headstone in the Arkport Cemetery over two years ago, I discovered that he had served in the Civil War. Engraved beneath his name was: "C 161 Regt. N. Y. Vols." Upon my return from Arkport, I requested a copy of John Armstrong's file from the National Archives and Records Administration in Washington, D.C. As the months passed, I thought less about my request. After a year passed, I figured I would not hear from them. I was mildly disappointed because I felt there might be something of interest in his files that just might be worth a sentence or two in the book.

Then, eighteen months after I had finished this chapter, an unexpected package arrived at my door. It contained copies of 124 pages of material from the National Archives regarding Johnathan Armstrong's Civil War record, his requests for a pension, and more.

Fascinating details quickly emerged. On April 8, 1864, at the Battle of Sabine Cross Roads in Louisiana, a "ball" entered "Private Johnathan

Armstrong's right leg," just above the knee. He "was treated in camp by Dr. Darling," the "Regimental Surgeon." On June 2, 1865, in Mobile, Alabama, "debris" from an "explosion of a Rebel Magazine" came crashing down on Armstrong, who was "on duty" at the wrong place and at the wrong time, "waiting for transportation." The impact of the debris caused an "injury to his back." After the explosion in Mobile, Armstrong's physical condition deteriorated to the point where he could no longer "do his duty." He received an honorable discharge from the Army on November 12, 1865.

Even more fascinating details followed. Requests for Civil War pensions necessitated the sworn testimony of "respectable witnesses." Thus, on November 3, 1868, M. D. Dimick, whom Charles Armstrong called "Dr. Dimick" in his 1867 journal, served as a witness for Johnathan Armstrong's pension petition. Dimick wrote that after Armstrong returned from the Army, he frequently "found him confined to his bed, unable to get out or in without assistance." Further, Armstrong complained of "pain and soreness in his back and right side, [and had] great difficulty in passing his urine." Lastly, Dimick testified: "[Armstrong] is barely able to move without a cane. He is at this time barely able to do half a days work in a day, which will hardly support himself, his *invalid* [author's emphasis] wife, and children." So not only was

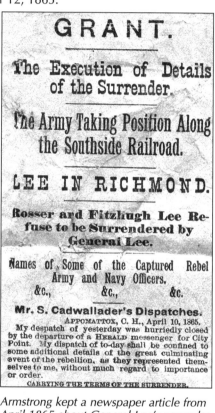

GRANT.

The Execution of Details of the Surrender.

The Army Taking Position Along the Southside Railroad.

LEE IN RICHMOND.

Rosser and Fitzhugh Lee Refuse to be Surrendered by General Lee.

Names of Some of the Captured Rebel Army and Navy Officers.
&c., &c., &c.

Mr. S. Cadwallader's Dispatches.
APPOMATTOX, C. H., April 10, 1865.
My despatch of yesterday was hurriedly closed by the departure of a HERALD messenger for City Point. My dispatch of to-day shall be confined to some additional details of the great culminating event of the rebellion, as they represented themselves to me, without much regard to importance or order.
CARRYING THE TERMS OF THE SURRENDER.

Armstrong kept a newspaper article from April 1865 about General Lee's surrender at Appomattox wedged in his first diary. (Armstrong's journals)

Charles's father severely disabled, his mother was, in fact, an invalid. Regarding this, I wondered how Roxie Armstrong became an invalid. As for Johnathan Armstrong, the Pension Office awarded him "one-half of a full pension," which came to $8.00 per month.

Johnathan Armstrong passed away on August 5, 1890. On February 23, 1891, William Hurlbut, who gave young Charles his first journal in 1866, served as a witness for a request to increase the amount of pension for John Armstrong's widow, Roxie. He wrote: "She [Mrs. Roxie Armstrong] has been nearly blind for over twenty years and that she has no means of support except what is furnished by her daughter." My suspicions about a mother with problems were confirmed.

Although this sheds considerable light on Armstrong's early family years, it does not explain everything, especially his deep estrangement from his invalid and partially blind mother. Indeed, one might expect to find a close emotional bond between a young, healthy son and a mother who needed his assistance. Now we know that his father also needed his help. So what did Charles do? As you will read in the next chapter, at the age of thirty he distanced himself from his entire family, saddling his younger sister, Roxie, with all the problems. In fairness to Charles, the cry of "Go West Young Man" motivated thousands upon thousands of young men to leave their families, many of whom needed them. It also appears that Armstrong's father was able to work more than the stated "half day," at least for several years after the war. And surely such a home and work environment would have been mightily dull and emotionally draining for any young person. Maybe Charles genuinely believed he could earn more money away from home, as he wrote in his 1877 diary (as you will also read in the next chapter) during his stint in the city of Leavenworth. That he repeatedly promised himself to bring his entire family to Kansas speaks well for his intentions, too. But none of that came to pass. For now, thanks to the arrival of an unexpected package from the National Archives and Records Administration, you can read Charles's first journal with a better understanding of his family's predicament, then draw your own conclusions regarding his behavior later in life.

Tuesday, January 1, 1867.

Rise before the sun. Happy New Year. I went fishing in the forenoon on the Marsh Ditch with the boys, caught 14. Worked the Shop in the afternoon. We had roast Turkey.

Wednesday 2

I worked in the Shop all day for Father on sleighs. Cold day but pleasant.

Thursday 3

I went to School all day. Worked in the Shop in night This has been a fine day.

Friday, January 4, 1867

I went to School all day. Went to Lyceum. took the office of Sec & Treasurer. no salary.

Saturday 5

Cut wood in fore noon went skating in Afternoon. No School to day. Father went to Town. I went to Surveying School in the evening

Sunday 6

I went to Meeting and Sunday School. stayed in the house the rest of the day   Chas Mcluskey was up here this evening. did not go to evening meeting.

Monday, January 7, 1867.

I went to School all day. Went to Singing school in evening. full house.

Tuesday 8

I went to school to day all day. fine warm day. nothing special.

Wednesday 9

I went to School all day. Fine day. nothing special.

Thursday, January 10, 1867

I went to School all day. School goes [?] of bully. no whipping to amount to much, all good natured.

Friday 11

Stayed out of School and helped Father in the Shop all day. help iron Mr. Lovelands sleighs. Went to Lyceum in evening I am Sec & Treasurer. the question was that Poligamy in Utah ought to be put down by gov't

Saturday 12

Worked all day in the Shop with Father puting irons on the sleighs

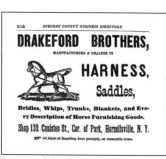

Some of the horses outfitted by Drakeford Brothers in nearby Hornellsville probably pulled some of the sleighs that Charles and his father "put irons on." (Steuben County Gazetteer and Business Directory, 1868 - 1869)

there was no School to day Went to Singing School in evening. big crowd out

Sunday, January 13, 1867.

I did not go to Meeting. Roxy went. Sime Crits and Jeff and Jim Armstrong was in to day. Kent Mathews was in to. John Riley and Chas Thc. was in this evening. talked about the War & the South in gen

Monday 14

I went to School all day. Father went to Hornellsville I stayed home in the evening. Father went up to the corners in the evening. pleasant day. but cloudy looks like storm of some kind

Tuesday 15

I went to School all day Nothing of any note occurred

Wednesday, January 16, 1867.

I went to School all day Nice winter weather

Thursday 17

I went to School all day that is all that I have to write. My life is so smothe and monotenous that there is not any thing much to write

Friday 18

I went to School all day

Saturday, January 19, 1867.

I went to Hornellsville to day. I had a good chance to ride down. I got my hair cut and bought some little trifles. Rode back with Elias Ayers. went to Lyceum in even.

Sunday 20

I did not go to meeting to day. I read a novel that I bought yesterday. I went to Meeting in the evening. Snowing weather is moderating.

Monday 21

I went to School all day- Snowed considerable last night good sleighing. I went to Singing School in the even. Quite a crowd out the Weather is geting warmer

Tuesday, January 22, 1867.

I went to School all day. Cold windy day Snowed some

Wednesday 23

To School all day Snowy and cold. hasn't thawed in 6 weeks. the snow has drifted high: first rate sleighing.

Thursday 24

I went to School all day cold day Went to Singing School in the evening Roxy and I. quite a house full.

Friday, January 25, 1867.

I went to School all day. There has been a missunderstanding with the Teacher and one of the Scholars by the name of Delphia Jones. So she wrote some Poetry to him and he read it to her and she went home. left school.

Saturday 26

I helped Father in the Shop in the morning. He went to Hornellsville. I washed the clothes up to day. Father and I went to Lyceum in the even. very good one.

Sunday 27

None of us went to meeting to day. Very cold stormy day so we all stayed round the fire. Jim was down here and set a while. Jerry Rym the blacksmith was out all last *[continued]*...

Monday, January 28, 1867.

...*[continued]* night. got drunk and layed down, and when found was stiff. but he is all rite now. only he has both feet and hands froze, so he wont get out before spring. I helped Father in the Shop to day. cold day. Singing School.

Tuesday 29

I helped Father in the Shop all day to day. I stayed out of School to get my boots fixed but I did not get them fixed. Wrote for Jim in the evening

Wednesday 30

I went to School all day to day. quite a warm day. got a letter from Shep Woolever. he is prospering   all well the folks are.

Thursday, January 31, 1867.

I went to School all day to day. Warm day. has thawed all day, and the roads are quite wet. We went to Singing School in the evening. there was a big crowd out.

Friday, February 1

I went to School all day

Saturday 2

I worked in the Shop all day

Sunday, February 3, 1867.

I stayed home all day

Monday 4

I went to School all day

Tuesday 5

I went to School all day

Wednesday, February 6, 1867.

I went to School all day

Thursday 7

Went to School all day

Friday 8
   I went to School all day

Saturday, February 9, 1867.
   Help Father in the Shop all day

Sunday 10
   I stayed in the house most of the day. I went up to Uncle Riles in the afternoon. Jim was over to day

Monday 11
   I did not go to School to day. had the head ache and a sore nose got a boil in the nostrell. quite Warm day I went to Singing School in even.

Tuesday, February 12, 1867.
   I went to School Skating in the fore noon   went gunning in the afternoon. did not kill any thing. no school to day. Town meeting to day.

Wednesday 13
   I went to School all day. nose has got well. The weather is very warm and the snow has all thawed off pretty much.

Thursday 14
   I went to School all day. Warm day. I went to School Singing in the evening.
   1868. I am in School to day, nice day. *[inserted a year later.]*

Friday, February 15, 1867.
   I went to School all day.

Saturday 16
   I did not go to School to day. I took my gun and Peat *[Pete]*   I went up the marsh, did not kill anything

Sunday 17
   Stayed home most of the day. Went up to Uncle Riles a little while went to meeting in evening

Monday, February 18, 1867.
   I went to School this morning. but the School Teacher dismissed school and there is not going to be any more school. this evening went to Singing School

Tuesday 19
   I washed the clothes to day got through about 3'oclock. I have been up to the corners, saw Gair and Grove Beckwith yesterday and to day. Father went to Hornellsville to day.
   pleasent.

Wednesday 20
   I worked in the Shop with Father all day

Thursday, February 21, 1867.

I worked in the Shop with Father at welding axels for Platform Spring Waggons *["A low four-wheeled wagon without sides."]*. Went to Singing School in even

Friday 22

I worked in the Shop all day with Father.

Saturday 23

I work in the Shop with Father. Went to Lyceum in the evening. My turn of Office runs out to Night. Jim was elected in my place

Sunday, February 24, 1867.

I did not go out to meeting to day. read the Papers   Eat Dinner with Uncle Riles folk. I went to Meeting in the evening

Monday 25

I helped Father in the Shop today. in the afternoon I went up on Windam. With Alamanson Thomas. after Word for us got it of Maynard. Went to Singing School in Even

Tuesday 26

I worked in the Shop with Father all day

Wednesday, February 27, 1867.

Father went to Hornellsville. I cut Wood and stayed round the House

Thursday 28

I help Father in the Shop all day Went to Singing School in the Evening. Not much of a crowd out

Friday, March 1

I help Father in the Shop all day

Saturday, March 2, 1867.

I help Father in the Shop all day. Went to Lyceum in the Evening. big crowd out not much Sport.

Sunday 3

I set in the House in the fore noon and read. Went up to Uncle Riles in the Afternoon. Went to Meeting in the Even

Monday 4

I worked in the Shop with Father . Went to Singing School in the evening. Jeff started for Mich. to day. he is going to fire in a saw mill for Ally & Co.

Tuesday, March 5, 1867.

I worked in the Shop with Father all day did not do much. Father was not well, so was up to the Tavern in the evening. pleasent day

Wednesday 6

Father went to Hornellsville. I worked in the Shop with cuting bolts for Demacrat Waggons *["A light four-wheeled cart with several* seats behind the other, and usually drawn by two horses. Originally called democratic wagon."]. Weather moderate. Wind South

Thursday 7

I worked in the Shop with Father on waggon irons. Went to Singing School in the evening. I had a good time. Weather moderate. Wind. S.W

Friday, March 8, 1867.

I washed the clothes to day. Father went to Hornellsville

Saturday 9

Worked in the Shop all day with Father. Went to Lyceum in the Evening. not many there

Sunday 10

I went up to Uncle Riles in the Afternoon. Sime Crits came over to day. I went to meeting in the Evening. Very mudy under foot

Monday, March 11, 1867.

I helped Father in the Shop all day. No Singing School to Night.

Tuesday 12

I helped Father in the Shop. Wrote for Jim in the Evening.

Wednesday 13

Worked in the Shop. Wrote for Jim in the Evening.

Thursday, March 14, 1867.

Worked in the Shop with Father   Went to Singing School in the Evening.

Friday 15

Worked in the Shop. Went to Lyceum in the Evening. Myron Hurlbut lectured on the Turkish Empire   First Rate

Saturday 16

Father went to Hornellsville. I did not do any thing much. Went to Singing School in the evening. Teacher was not there so Sam Pitts took charge

Sunday, March 17, 1867.

I stayed to Home all day. Stormy in the Afternoon so that I did not go to Evening meeting.

Monday 18

I worked in Shop with Father all day. Went to Singing School in the evening

Tuesday 19

Worked in the Shop all day

Wednesday, March 20, 1867.

I washed the clothes in the fore noon. Worked in the Shop with Father. Went to Singing School in the evening. last night

Thursday 21
Worked with Father in the Shop on Platform Waggon

Friday 22
Worked in the Shop all day

Saturday, March 23, 1867.
Father went to Hornellsville. I worked in the Shop bolting Carriage Wheels. Went to Lyceum in Evening   Saw Gair Beckwith

Sunday 24
I did not go to meeting   was up to Uncle Riles   eat dinner there. John Eaten and Jim was down   Lse [?] in After noon

Monday 25
I worked in the shop all day. Went to a maple sugar party to Smithes   took Sisman had good time. got Home 1 oclock

Tuesday, March 26, 1867.
I worked in the Shop all day. Felt sleepy and used up. Nice warm day. Wind in the West. was up to the Tavern in the Even

Wednesday 27
Worked in the Shop with Father

Thursday 28
Worked in the Shop with Father

Friday, March 29, 1867.
Worked in the Shop all day

Saturday 30
Father went to Hornellsville   I worked a little in the Shop. Went to Carniers & Henrys Theater in H,ville. Sime paid the bill. Had first rate time. got home

Sunday 31
We got home about 4 oclock this morning. got up 7 oclock. did not go to meeting or Sunday School. fine nice day. went to evening meeting

Monday, April 1, 1867.
I worked in the Shop with Father. I did not get fooled once to day. fine nice day

Tuesday 2
I worked in the Shop all day with Father. Tim Woolever and Lige Jordon are over to Bath tryin of their Law suit in regard to their fight

Wednesday 3
Worked in the Shop all day. Jim & Lige have got back. Lige got judgement against Jim for 200. hundred dollars it will cost Jim $4.40 in all

Thursday, April 4, 1867.

Worked in the Shop part the day. washed the clothes in the fore noon

Friday 5

Worked in the Shop with Father

Saturday 6

Father went to Hornellsville. I went fishing in the afternoon. did not catch any thing watters to high. went to Lyceum in evening

Sunday, April 7, 1867.

I did not go to Meeting or Sunday School. was up to Uncle Riles. he is sick again. I went to meeting in the evening

Monday 8

I worked in the Shop all day with Father

Tuesday 9

Father went to H,ville in the Afternoon. I went fishing caught 8 suckers. water to high to catch fish.

Wednesday, April 10, 1867.

cleaned house to day we   are going to move in to Myron Hurlbuts house where Beebee used to live

Thursday 11

I worked in the Shop all day

Friday 12

I washed to day, worked in the shop in afternoon

Saturday, April 13, 1867.

Went fishing. caught one Trout, the water is to high to catch fish

Sunday, April 14, 1867

I stayed in the house all the day. Gair Beckwith and chas MC was here a short time. Clear pleasent day. Sun shining warm

Monday 15

I worked in the Shop

Tuesday, April 16, 1867.

Worked in the shop

Wednesday 17

Worked in the Shop   went to Singing School in the evening. Mr. Sam Pitts lead the School

Thursday 18

Worked in the Shop   Grace Holzman was to our house this evening. She is a dasher *["A spirited person," or "A 'fast' young lady."]*

Friday, April 19, 1867.

I worked in the Shop. Mary Jane Eaten was here this evening. She is going up to Uncle Riles to Stay

Saturday 20

I worked in the Shop. We had the first Thunder Storm of the season. it was a heavy one to. Rained hard

Sunday 21

Stayed in the house most of the day. Jim and I took a walk in Targarts woods. and fields   Wheat looks fine. we saw some Pidgeons

Monday, April 22, 1867.

I washed the clothes up in the fore noon. in the Afternoon worked in the Shop. Rained most all day. weather warm

Tuesday 23

Father and I partly built a Shanty to day on the House that we are going to live in. the one across the creek. warm day.

Wednesday 24

I worked in the Shop to day with Father. Made a main spring for my gun. Father forged it and I filed and filed it

Thursday, April 25, 1867.

Worked in the shop with Father all day

Friday 26

Worked in the Shop

Saturday 27

Father went to Hornellsville. I sharpened 30 drag teeth for Geo Sylvester at Oak Hill which come to $1.80 Singing School this even.

Sunday, April 28, 1867.

Stayed in the House most of the day. saw Alamanson Thomas. He was in here. Tho,s learning a trade in H,ville cabinet maker.

Monday 29

Worked in the Shop most of the day. in Afternoon fixed the Shanty up some.

Tuesday 30

Worked in the Shop most of the day. went gunning about 2 'oclock. Did not Kill anything

Wednesday, May 1, 1867.

Worked in the Shop all day very warm. last night. about 2 oclock in night heavy thunder shower came up and has lasted all day.

Thursday 2

Worked in the Shop

Friday 3

Worked in the Shop Nice warm day

Saturday, May 4, 1867.

We moved to day in the house on the bank of the creek *[Lime Kiln Creek]* It belongs to Myron Hurlbut, had Bill Mathewses oxen and man

Sunday 5

Jim and I walked arround some. Sime Crites was here this evening. we went to Meeting. I went home with Grace Holzman

Monday 6

Worked in the Shop all day. I got me a new pair of cowhide boots yesterday of Prior cost 5 dollars

Tuesday, May 7, 1867.

Father and I fixed up arround the house in the forenoon, Father went to Hornellsville in Afternoon. I went fishing did not catch anything went hunting, nothing.

Wednesday 8

Father stayed to Hornellsville last night. I washed the clothes. Stormy Rainy day.

Mmmmaaaay mmmaaayyy 888th May 8th May 8th 1867

Thursday 9

Worked in the Shop all day

Friday, May 10, 1867.

Worked in the Shop a little while. Father went to Hornellsville. I fixed the door to the Shanty

Armstrong's rendition of the house near Lime Kiln Creek that his father rented from Myron Hurlbut. (Armstrong's journals)

Saturday 11

Worked in the Shop all day

Sunday 12

I did not go to church. walked in the fields and stay in the House.

Monday, May 13, 1867.

I worked in the Shop all day. Mary Jane Eaten was here to day. She lives below Hornellsville   concert in the Church this evening by Mr. Rorckwell of Hornellsville. Blind man

Thursday [July] 4 [1867]

I stayed at home today I went fishing a short time but did not get anything. Father and I set a set of new tyse [tires] this morning before 9 oclock. Rained

Sunday, July 21, 1867.

I have not wrote in my diary for a long time. went to meeting in the fore noon good congregation out. I wrote a letter to Jeff. Rained some in evening

Monday 22

I worked in the hay field for Myron Hurlbut. I have worked for him for the week past at 10 schillings a day. father is to work in the Shop. Warm nice day

Tuesday 23

Worked for Myron Hurlbut all day in the hay field

Wednesday, July 24, 1867.

helped Myron in hay field

Thursday July 25

helped Mryon on hay field

Friday 26

I helped Myron in hay field Jake Holzman, Shoemaker and I went to Hornellsville this evening with Myrons horse. we did not go to the Show, good for nothing

Saturday, July 27, 1867.

Helped Myron in hay field all day. he has payed me up. I went up to Henry Colgroves to a Raising Barn   Got back 11 oclock night

Sunday 28

I did not go to meeting in the fore noon. I went to meeting in the evening

Monday 29

I helped Myron in hay nice warm day

Tuesday, July 30, 1867.

I helped Myron in hay Jake quit to day he is going to Wisconsin with his folks to live. myron payed me up to day.

Wednesday 31

I helped myron in the hay field He has hired a new hand by the month from Hornellsville. name George Phillips. Nyson

Thursday, August 1

I helped Myron in the fore noon in the afternoon it Rained. So I helped Father in the Shop set waggon tire for Bill Mathews

Friday, August 2, 1867.

I helped Myron all the fore noon in hay field and half the afternoon so he owes me for two days and half. I took my gun and went down on flats. Killed nothing

Saturday 3

Rained in the fore noon so I did not work in the afternoon   I helped draw in hay. some wet, but he wants it drawed in

Sunday 4

I went in swimming in the morning Stayed round the house all day went in swimming in the afternoon Stayd home in evening. warm day

Monday, August 5, 1867.

I helped Myron in the Harvest field. bind grain. Steve Snyder cradels and George rakes. very warm day Themonitor 94° 91° Shower 5. pm

Tuesday 6

Bound grain all day very warm day. but we had a shower about 6 oclock in afternoon.

we finished the field of wheat   Father went to Dansville.

Wednesday 7

Bound grain in forenoon   in afternoon worked in hay field.

Thursday, August 8, 1867.

Worked in hay field all day for Myron

Friday 9

Helped father in Shop Set tire in afternoon got done after dark.

Saturday 10

Helped Father in Shop all day or the bigest part of day He went to H,ville. I took Seib Sismen and Roxy to the Circus in even, Snts [?]

Sunday, August 11, 1867.

I did not go to meeting   Tom Eaten and Jim was down here. I went to meeting in evening

Monday 12

I helped Myron all day in the wheat field draw in wheat got it all in in good order

Tuesday 13

I helped Myron in hay field. very warm day to day looks Rain

Thursday [September] 5 [1867]

I went to Forepaughs great Circus and Menadgerie. 50 cts. admitance. Went in the side Show saw the double girl & fat-Boy and the 7 foot whiskers

Saturday, September 7, 1867.

I worked in the Shop in the fore noon in the afternoon played ball with the Boys. our side beat one inings.

Sunday 8

I stayed arround the house all day. did not go to Meeting

Monday 9

I worked in the Shop all day with Father.

Tuesday, September 10, 1867.

I helped Colgroves thrash their grain to day

Wednesday 11

Helped Colgroves thrash all day got through about sun down They pay me 1.25 cts a day

Thursday 12

Helped Myron Hurlbut   Helped Loveland thrash in the forenoon. in the afternoon cut corn 1.25 cts for this days work

Friday, September 13, 1867.

Help Henry Hurlbut cut up corn all day. Rained some in afternoon. he payed me one dollar

Illustrated ads for "Forepaugh's Mammoth Menagerie And Gigantic Circus" appeared in local newspaper weeks prior to its grand arrival and parade. Young Charles seemed most impressed with the "double girl & fat Boy and the 7 foot whiskers." (Hornellsville Weekly Tribune, August 12, 1867)

Saturday 14

I Helped Myron all day drawed manure in forenoon. cut corn in afternoon. he payed me 2.00 dollars but he must pay me the 25 cents

Sunday 15

Gair Beckwith and Chas MCluskey was here this forenoon. Gair and I went to meeting. I went to meeting in the evening.

Monday, September 16, 1867.

I worked for Henry Hurlbut all day building fence. Henry Robinson helped. Peter treed 2 Partrige but I had no gun with me. L looks favorable.

Tuesday 17

Rained hard last night thundered and lightning good and strong. Rained tell 10 oclock this morning   I went hunting the rest of the day 4 Pidgeons & 1 Partridge & woodchuck

Wednesday 18

clear nice day. I helped Henry Hurlbut all day. drawed manure george helped me. very warm day. I have sweat as much as any day this summer   I dont progress much

Thursday, September 19, 1867.

Worked for Henry all day drawing manure 13 loads. cloudy fogy in the forenoon. clear in the afternoon. Father went to H.ville. L not progressing

Friday 20

I helped Henry all day draw manure. Rained a little in the afternoon. warm day. sweat some He saw her thats all.

Saturday 21

Worked for Henry all day drawed manure & dug Potatoes Pleasent day Father went in Town. I have worked for Henry every day this week but One   He is good natured

Sunday, September 22, 1867.

I did not go to Meeting in the fore noon. mother was worse & I did not get away till to late. went up to Uncle Riles. J. Eaten up there I went to Meeting in evening

Monday 23

I helped Henry all day draw manure. Warm nice day. I was up to the corners in evening. not much going on. L favorable. but dont progress

Tuesday 24

I helped Henry all day cut corn. he payed me the 2 dollars he borrowed of me yesterday. Father went to H,ville got me some ammunition. Nice fine day

Wednesday, September 25, 1867.

I helped Henry all day cut corn fodder. cold windy day Rained about half an hour this fore noon   Ranse Beckwith cut buck wheat for Henry

Thursday 26

I helped Henry all day cut corn foder. cold fogy working but warm day

Friday 27

Helped Henry all day George and I raked Buckwheat in fore noon picked cider apples in afternoon. cold fogy warm day. Father went to Town. Father bought me 2 pr of overhalls and 2 hickory shirts for every day wear and 2 cotton & wollen shirts for winter. all cost about 4 dollars.

Saturday, September 28, 1867.

Helped Henry all day. picked apples in forenoon. Raked Buckwheat in afternoon. cold clear morning. warm day. had an invite to apple bee last night to Lovelands. did not go. He not any progress

Sunday 29

I went to meeting   Mr Westfall preached. not a very large congrigation. stayed in the house the rest of the day & evening. Warm pleasent in fore noon but cold cloudy in afternoon. L was here this afternoon hot. me no good

Monday 30

Helped Henry all day. picked apples and dug potatoes in fore noon. in the afternoon I cleared away old fence preparitory to build a new one. Father went to Town

Tuesday, October 1, 1867.

Helped Henry all day. built fence in the forenoon in the afternoon picked apples and cut corn. there was a heavy freeze last night forse ice and used up everything

Wednesday 2

I help Henry all day drawed in corn foder in fore noon. drawed in Buckwheat in afternoon Warm day. saw L , but I did not speak

Thursday 3

I helped Henry all day built fence & split fence posts, cool cloudy day. looks like Rain. drilled two wagon tire in the evening   L not-see.

Friday 4

Helped Henry all day built fence the most of the day drawed in corn the rest of the day warm nice day. I helped Father in the Shop in even

Saturday 5

Rained the most of the night. I went gunning killed one Pidgeon. rainy day. Father went to Town to day. stayed at home in even.

Sunday 6

I stayed at home the most of the day. read the Agriculturist. went up to Uncle Riles   John Eaten came down to day. Warm nice day. stayed at home in even

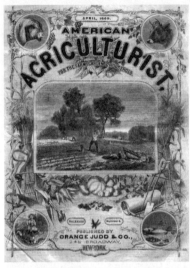

In 1867 Armstrong mentioned reading this popular nineteenth-century magazine. (Author's collection)

Monday, October 7, 1867.

I helped Harm Tomas dig potatoes all day. look pretty good. Busters Hellen Baldwin had a little girl last night. cold chilley day. sun shone

Tuesday 8

I helped Harm all day digging potatoes there was a hard frost last night. warm day to day. I went up to School meeting in even

Wednesday 9

I got up about 6 oclock. and went up to Harms. he had just got up. dug potatoes all day warm day. eat supper to W<u>m</u> Smithes. was to Tavern in even. L not see this week

Thursday, October 10, 1867.

I helped Harm till about 4 oclock in the afternoon. when it began to rain we quite work. I helped Father in the shop in the evening.

Friday 11

I helped Father in the Shop in the fore noon went gunning in the afternoon killed one pidgeon am going to a dance tonight

Saturday 12

had a glorious time up to the dance last night. danced in the farm had supper & oisters, got home about 4 oclock in morn   I took Grace & Sime took Leib. went up with John Patten rain

Sunday, October 13, 1867.

I did not go to meeting to day. set round the house the most of the day Jim and I went up the hills after chestnuts   I did not get but few. went to meeting in evening.

Monday 14

I helped Harm all day dig potatoes. his wife & Bills wife & family picked up. this has been a very nice warm day. I helped Father in Shop in even

Tuesday 15

I helped Harm all day dig potatoes. we dug all but about 20

bushels. Harm dont want me any more, warm nice day. I was up to the corners in even.

Wednesday, October 16, 1867.

I went after chestnuts to day got about 4 qts. Shot one Partrige Peter flushed him. very warm day Father went to Town.

Thursday 17

I helped Sam Pitts dig potatoes. hard work the ground is very hard and stony. Jack Ayers helped dig. warm day. I stay here all night

Friday 18

Helped Sam all day warm day. Jack and I dug about 30 Bushels we all pared apples all the evening. had a good time. warm day.

Saturday, October 19, 1867.

I helped Sam all day dig potatoes. He went to Town. Jack and I dug about 23 Bushells & had to work hard at that. I came home this evening. warm

Sunday 20

I did not go to meeting. went up to Uncle Riles a little while. Jim and I went to meeting in evening. This has been a very nice warm day.

Monday 21

I helped Sam Pitts dig potatoes. potatoes dont turn out at all here. it is very hard diging. this is a nice warm day. I came home this even.

Tuesday, October 22, 1867.

I dug potatoes all day for Sam. we finished this patch to day. nice warm day. Henry Morris went home this even. he worked yesterday

Wednesday 23

I stayed here last night   dug potatoes all day. Chas Thomas helped to day. Sam & Jack dug all day with us. This patch turns out first rate. warm day.

Thursday 24

We dug half a day & finished up the potatoes. Mr Pitts and I settled up. he owed me 12 doll for work & I owed Mrs. Pitts for the making of 2 fine shirts at 1 doll each. he payed me 10 doll

Friday, October 25, 1867.

I worked a little in the Shop in fore noon. I made a spring to shot flask. helped Steward Ayers in the afternoon dig potatoes   both of us dug 14 Bushels

Saturday 26

I helped Steward all day dig potatoes. we dug till dark and then we berried them, took till 8 oclock at night.

Sunday 27

I did not go to meeting or sunday school   I was up to Uncle Riles part of the day went to evening meeting in the Church, a stranger spoke

Monday, October 28, 1867.

I worked in the Shop in fore noon. helped S. Pitts in afternoon survey off S. Haights farm. I helped carry chain. rained so that we quit. mr Bull from Bath. Sur.

Tuesday 29

I stayed all night at Mr. Pitts. Rained so that I went home in fore noon. in afternoon we survied his farm, but it rained so that we did not finish it

Wednesday 30

We finished the Survey this fore noon. Jim Crites and I went hunting in afternoon. I took my gun over in the woods where I was to work at Henrys fence. I shot 1 Black squirell & one Partridge gave the Partridge to Henry.

Thursday, October 31, 1867.

I helped Father in the Shop all day. I read the Ledgers. I borrowed them of Mrs Pitts. we received a letter from downeast, all well. Mary White wrote it

Friday, November 1

Father went to Town. I went to hunting   shot the feathers out of a Partridge, but did not get him. I set my trap for muskrat this evening

Saturday 2

I worked in the Shop all day. set Doc Dimicks Sulkey tire and a set of buggy tire for Smith. was over to Steves in even. Boys playing.

Sunday, November 3, 1867.

caught a musk Rat this morning. skined him and stretched the hide. I did not go to meeting at all   was up to uncle Riles a little while all the music commenced. I wrote a letter down east

Monday 4

I worked in the Shop all day   drilled. Sulkey tire John Robinson drawed a load of potatoes for us A 1/2 Bush. chilies. I was up to corners in even. all politics

Tuesday 5

went to Town in fore noon stayed all day. election day. all quiet. I bought a suit of clothes, cost 17 doll Uncle Riel started for Mich in the 3 oclock train

Wednesday, November 6, 1867.

I helped Myron Hurlbut all day. Thrashing run out - 71 1/2 Bush. Spring wheat & 37 Bush. Hungarian grass end. I carried away grain. saw Rev. J. E. Baker

Thursday 7

Trashed till 3 oclock   run out 30 Bush Hungarian & 29 Bush of Winter wheat   went hunting Muskrat did not see any. was up to corners in evening.

Shown here in the early 1900s, "The Corners" probably looked about the same in Armstrong's time. It still carries the same moniker. (Author's collection)

Friday 8

I worked in Shop in fore noon. Thrashed in afternoon for John Hurlbut & for Samy Pitts.

Saturday, November 9, 1867.

Thrashed all day for Sam Pitts finished about 4 oclock. I went to Town to Theater. Played Uncle Toms Cabin. first rate cost 35 cts admission

Sunday 10

Got home 2 oclock this morning. came up on the train 15 cts did not go to meeting went in evening nice warm day

Monday 11

I helped John Hurlbut all day. chunk up Fallow, cold and snowey. got wet through by the snow. got my pay $6.oo.

Tuesday, November 12, 1867.

Worked in the Shop all day   very cold day snowed most all day Wind in the West

Wednesday 13

Worked in the shop all day at Dr. Dimicks Sulkey. this has been a very cold windy day. The Snow is 3 inches deep

Thursday 14

Worked all day in the Shop. finished the Sulkey. some warmer to day the snow is going off as fast as possible Wind West.

Friday, November 15, 1867.

Worked in the Shop all day. colder today. Snowing some worked in the Shop in the evening

Saturday 16

Father went to Hornellsville today. I went hunting a little in the after noon   saw some Partridge did not kill any thing

Sunday 17

I did not go to Meeting at all to day cold day. read the Ledgers all day

Monday, November 18, 1867.

Father went to Hville. I cleaned my gun and went hunting in the afternoon did not kill any thing

Tuesday 19

Worked in the Shop all day with Father   warmer to day. Sime and I went over to Rogersville to the last day of School. got back 4 oclock

Wednesday 20

I did not get up till 10 clock this morning I did not do much of any thing to day. up to the corners in the evening. warm day

Thursday, November 21, 1867.

I drilled tire in the fore noon, and fixed up the house. some. I went down to the Pond with the Boys. I bought 2 traps of Geo Nusam for 1.20 cts. warm day

Friday 22

Father went to Hornellsville. I fixed the house up a little   pulled the Turnips & put them in the seller. went hunting down the creek did not see any thing. set traps, went to Singing School in the evening Wind West. very nice warm day. smoky

Saturday 23

I caught 1 muskrat. I went hunting up the creek in afternoon. did not see a thing but some Quails shot at them, did not kill any nice warm day

Sunday, November 24, 1867.

I went to meeting. quite a congaragation out. this is a very nice warm day smokey. I set in the house most of the day. went to meeting in the evening.

Monday 25

I did not catch any thing in any traps. I made me a butchers knife for to skin muskrat. I fixed the house up some. very nice warm day. wind South

Tuesday 26

I caught a musk Rat this morning. Father went to Town. I got 2.25 of Sam Pitts. we are square now. I read the Ledgers all the day warm

Wednesday, November, 27, 1867.

I caught another Rat this morning. Uncle Jabe Lamphere was burried this fore noon. went to the funeral. He is one of the Pioneers of this place. age 72 years.

Thursday 28

I did not do much in fore noon. went gunning in afternoon. saw some Partriges but did not kill any   Pete treed 1 nice as you please

Friday, November 29, 1867

I chored arround the house in fore noon. Father went to Town. In the afternoon went up to Mr. Wiant,s to see about a hog came back over the hill

Saturday, November 30, 1867.

Went to Town. walked down.. got 3 dollars of Henry H, he promiced me more to get a suit of clothes but he could not so I came home with out them. very cold

Sunday, December 1

I went to Meeting in fore noon and evening. This is a very cold day. read the Ledgers most of the day.

Monday 2

I worked in the Shop all day very cold ground my ax. worked in the evening

Tuesday, December 3, 1867.

Worked in the Shop all day. Oatly the Singing Teacher is going to work for Smith making Demacrats. Dan Thomas has began keeping house in front part Steves. Singing School this even

Wednesday 4

I cut wood on Mr. Tagarts fallow. he gives it to us for the chipping. it is fine wood. but will do for the Shop. went to Singing School this evening. payed 1.00.

Thursday 5

cut wood for the house in the fore noon. in after noon cut wood on the Fallow. cold Snowey day wind west. Father is not very well, hasent worked any

Friday, December 6, 1867.

I cut wood all day on the follow. quite warm the snow is all melted off. I picked up some pineknots. Father is better.

Saturday 7

Father went to H,ville. I went hunting in the afternoon killed one Partrige   Pete treed 3 but I did not get but 1

Sunday 8

Cold and snowy. I did not go to meeting in fore noon. went up to Uncle Riles a little while   went to meeting in the evening.

Monday, December 9, 1867.

I did not do much to day. went up to Mr. McNortons to see about some money   took my gun along but I did not kill any thing.

Tuesday 10

Father went to Town. I cut wood in fore noon in afternoon went hunting but did not kill any thing. Father got my clothes to go to School in

Wednesday 11

I worked in the house fixing my clothes in fore noon. I helped Father in after noon in Shop cold day. Went to Singing School in evening

Thursday, December 12, 1867.

This is very cold day the Murcury is down to Zero. I sent up on Henrys hill to cut wood but it was so cold that I backed out. helped Father in Shop in afternoon

Friday 13

I helped Father in the Shop all day. This a very cold day, the murcury was 7 degrees below Zero this morning. The Sleighing is good. I wrote to Jeff

Saturday 14

I worked in the Shop all day at work on old leutter[?]. The murcury was 12 degrees below Zero. I went to Singing School in the evening. They have concluded to keep Books

Sunday, December 15, 1867.

I went to meeting in the fore noon. the Almond Parson preached. I think it was a good sermon. Sam Beckwith was over to day. stayed at home in evening.

Monday 16

I went to School to day. there was a good lot of Scholars. that Teacher is a good one, and clever but he teaches the School himself

Tuesday 17

I went to School all day. the weather is cold and blustry

Wednesday, December 18, 1867.

I went to School all day. Went to Singing School in evening

Thursday 19

I went to School all day Helped Father in Shop in the Evening

Friday 20

Went to School all day helped Father in evening in Shop

Saturday, December 21, 1867.

Went to School all day. Gair Beckwith is over here. he eat Supper here And we went to Singing School in the evening

Sunday 22

I went up to Uncle Riles in the fore noon read the papers   went to Meeting in evening

Monday 23

I went to School all day   warm days I went up to Tavern in evening

Tuesday, December 24, 1867.

No School to day I helped Father in the Shop all day. Festival to the Church this even. I helped in 2 Dialogues had a good time

Wednesday, December 25, 1867

Merry Christmas. Warm day rainy I helped Father in Shop in forenoon. Bill Smith and I killed 2 Sheep for Father.

Armstrong sketched this image, possibly a self-portrait, in his 1867 pocket diary. The significance of the date "May 8" will probably never be known. (Armstrong's journals)

Thursday 26

I worked in the Shop in the fore noon. in the afternoon I cut wood on Henry Hurlbut hill. rained all night and most of day

Friday, December 27, 1867.

I worked in the Shop most of the day Father went to town Rained all night and most of the day

Saturday 28

I cut wood in the fore noon. Jim helped me. in the afternoon I cut wood on H. H. hill. warm pleasant day

Sunday, 29

I did no go to Meeting in fore noon. went up to Jims, Sime was there I went to Meeting in evening

Monday, December 30, 1867.

went to School all day. the weather is geting colder and snow began to fall. went up to the Tavern in evening. Jerry [Rym] drunk wanted to fight Mr. Hathaway.

Tuesday 31

went to School all day up to Tavern in even. Jerry drunk wanted to fight Hathaway. snowing.

[Inscribed on inside back cover]

From Wm Hurlbut
to Chas Armstrong.
Christmas, Dec 25/66
Arkport NY
Steuben Co NY

CHAPTER 2

BACK TO ARKPORT AND LEAVENWORTH, THEN ON TO THE ROARING FORKS

1877-1889

HISTORICAL SETTING AND THE MAN

C harles S. Armstrong allowed ten years to lapse before his next journal entry in 1877. Although he had not changed much, the world around him had. Russia conquered key areas in the Balkans, the Suez Canal opened, Canada purchased vast territories from the Hudson's Bay Company, the Franco-Prussian War unified Germany, and Queen Victoria became Empress of India. In the United States, reconstruction ended with the last Federal troops pulling out of the South, George Armstrong Custer lay dead, newly conceived telegraph wire and barbed wire strung out across America, the phonograph had been invented, and gleaming railroad tracks now stretched from the Atlantic to the Pacific—uniting the nation's consciousness. Technology had suddenly started to make the United States smaller and communication faster. In 1870, Amendment 15 legally guaranteed male citizens of "all races" the right to vote, although few did. Six out of ten Americans still lived in rural areas. And Colorado had already become the 38th State in the Union.

Between 1860 and 1890 thousands of fortune seekers invaded the West and present-day Colorado. Viewed from above, this throng must have looked like an army of starving ants slowly surging into nearly impenetrable terrain. At first, a few small groups of prospectors groped their way along the unexplored contours of the Rocky Mountains. If they struck gold or silver, they stayed where they found it. A trickle of prospectors soon followed. Within months the trickle metamorphosed into a continuous line of fortune seekers and adventurers. Soon each discovery site became a thickly populated pocket of frenetic mining and mining-support activity. Once every inch of ground, or so it seemed, had been claimed, and once the mining camp started to mature into a town, restless souls seeking new discoveries headed over the next mountain range. So it was with the first prospectors, including Charles S. Armstrong, who made the arduous journey from the famous boom town of Leadville, Colorado, into the distant valley of the "Roaring Forks" and present-day Aspen.

During the 1880s, Leadville and Aspen became two of the leading silver producers in the world. Relevant to Aspen and the entire silver-mining industry, political combatants began to heat up the debate over America's arcane silver-backed monetary system. No one in the Aspen or Leadville vicinity would feel the effects of this seemingly uninteresting fiscal-system debate for several years. Besides, with the coming of the railroads in 1887,

Aspen's great silver mines remained on an incredible trajectory of success that arched over adversity like a spectacular silver rainbow.

Centuries before Aspen blossomed as a silver queen, another people came to fish and hunt in what is now known as the Roaring Fork Valley. They too valued its breathtaking scenery and natural bounty. In the last half of the nineteenth century, however, it took yet another land-grab by mineral-crazed people to wrest the valley from its rightful landlords, the Ute Indians. So too, for centuries an estimated 60,000,000 buffalo thrived within the geographic boundaries of present-day United States, including Colorado. Then came the white man, and the slaughter began. By the early 1870s professional hunters and "Eastern and European Sportsmen" killed over 1,000,000 annually. By the late 1880s this magnificent mammal could no longer be found in Colorado, nor could the Plains Indians who depended on them for food, clothing, and shelter. So goes the history of America.

The world once again looked different by the time Armstrong penned his last entry of 1889. Chile claimed rich mineral lands from Bolivia and Peru after winning the War of the Pacific, Tahiti had become a French colony, the Canadian Pacific Railway spanned Canada, terrorists assassinated Alexander II of Russia, and Great Britain occupied Egypt. Wilhelm Roentgen of Germany discovered x-rays and Guglielmo Marconi of Italy invented a practical wireless telegraph system. America, now boasting over 61,000,000 citizens, accepted France's gift of the Statue of Liberty. The Interstate Commerce Act became the first federal law to regulate railroads, the recently constructed Brooklyn Bridge claimed the longest span in the world, and the *New York Tribune* used the first commercial Linotype machine. Grover Cleveland, whom Armstrong would see in 1893 in a New York parade, ended his first term as President.

As for Aspen, by the late 1880s the "Crystal City" had become a bustling, full-blown silver-mining community with a population pushing 10,000. Besides the crucial Colorado Midland and the Denver and Rio Grande Railroads, it boasted five smelters, a hydroelectric power plant, several churches, a full range of municipal buildings and services, a centerpiece courthouse, and several elegant brick homes. Of course, Aspen was not without its saloons and red light district, although from the very beginning it gained the reputation of being one of the most family-oriented and cultured camps in Colorado. Meanwhile, the fortunes of the nearby, and once-promising camps of Highland, Ashcroft, and Independence, faded fast.

Yet back in 1877, after a two-to-three year undistinguished stint in the city of Leavenworth, Kansas, a frustrated Charles Armstrong found himself once again in the backwaters of sleepy Arkport, New York. There he lingered for well over a year. Finally, with little money and no prospects for profitable employment, Charles got up enough gumption in the fall of 1878 to return to Leavenworth, Kansas—a major jumping-off-place to the far

West. There an indecisive Armstrong lingered for almost two more years, finding employment as a night clerk in the Continental Hotel. On November 30, 1877, he wrote wistfully, "I dont suppose that there will be much of interest happen to me but still there may."

Now we know that something of interest did happen to Charles. In the spring of 1880, after watching so many fortune seekers go before him and neglecting his diaries for almost a year, he *finally* took the initiative and continued his journey west. It was a pilgrimage that thousands of young men and women took during this era of unprecedented westward expansion. What made Armstrong's journey extraordinary is that he kept a written record along the way. What made it even more extraordinary is that his written record survives.

He stopped in Denver to obtain a surveyor's license, then boarded another train to Buena Vista, Colorado, at that time the end of the line. He took the stage to Leadville, the boom town of boom towns, on May 9, 1880. Billy Schlagg, a friend of his from Leavenworth, came back from the Roaring Forks with encouraging words for Armstrong. Schlagg told him that there was money to be made surveying and prospecting in this new camp. Thus, after less than a week in Leadville, Charles struck out with Schlagg and three other adventurers for the valley of the "Roaring Forks." His descriptions of his formidable trek over the Continental Divide into the valley of the "Roaring Forks" comprise—to date—a unique personal account of an early prospector in Colorado, and perhaps the entire West.

Day after arduous day Armstrong somehow found the time and energy to write in his journal while *in his tent.* While camping above Twin Lakes he described a brief bout of altitude sickness, then unnamed but undoubtedly recognized. He made a bed of "pine boughs." He paid a "jack bridge" toll in bacon, suggesting that food was of more value than money in this remote region. He commented about the unusual wildlife and grand scenery. Finally, after over nine days and seventy miles of brutal travel, a pristine valley spread out before a spellbound Armstrong. On May 25, 1880, he passed through the "City of Aspen" (first called "Ute City") and the "City of Roaring Forks," observing that there was "not a house in either town," although there had to be plenty of tents. That there were no houses is no surprise, since it had been less than a year since the first prospecting party set foot in the valley. (In October 1879, the first prospectors fled back to Leadville because of an "outbreak" among the Utes.)

Charles and his partner Billy Schlagg turned south, then struggled up Castle Creek about six miles to the newly founded mining camp of Highland. At first they stayed in a "camp" that Schlagg apparently put up above Highland a few weeks earlier. Armstrong and Schlagg attended "miners meetings" in Highland camp (located close to the confluence of Castle Creek and Condundrum Creek) and were paid $100 to "lay out" (survey) the town.

During the rest of the summer and fall of 1880 Charles and Billy remained in this general vicinity, staking claims and building a rudimentary log cabin. Like most of the other prospectors in the Roaring Forks region, they headed back to civilization in Leadville during the harsh high-country winter.

Today, reading the foregoing description of Armstrong's journey from Leavenworth, Kansas to Highland, Colorado does not inspire awe, let alone admiration. It should. The problem is that we are spoiled travelers. We cannot even imagine what it must have been like to cross an uncharted mountain range in the early 1880s. We sit in our enclosed, temperature-controlled cars barrelling effortlessly across the plains and over the mountains on seemingly endless ribbons of cement. There is no sense of isolation. Our major concern is the distance to the next fast-foot restaurant or a motel with comfortable beds, remote-control televisions, VCR's, Internet outlets, and a heated swimming pool. As if all this is not convenient enough, we talk on the cell phones to people almost any place in the world. There is no chance of getting lost. For fun we locate our exact position on our route with the most recent global positioning device. Miles above us, passengers in jet aircraft streak across the sky at over 500 miles per hour. They barely give a thought to the terrain below unless it's a clear day, or the pilot draws their attention to some town or notable geological feature. Traveling west across America is like traveling anywhere else in America. It is all old hat. It is also mostly impersonal and mostly non-threatening. All westward paths are now meticulously detailed, over crowded, over publicized, and over rated.

We should also remind ourselves that when Armstrong struck out for Denver, there was not much else in the way of "civilization" in Colorado, except a few mining boom towns high in the mountains. Charles's three-day train trip to Denver must have been comfortable enough, as was his day's train ride to Buena Vista. But once his small group left Leadville and started over the Sawatch Range to the Roaring Forks, it was basically on its own—with few sources of food or shelter. All their camping supplies, prospecting supplies, and most of their food had to be carried or packed on mules. Their very lives depended on primitive, heavy equipment and clothing that any modern mountain backpacker would consider wholly inadequate and downright dangerous. One unfortunate slip by mule or man also meant trouble, big trouble. If a prospector didn't plummet to his death off some narrow rock-strewn trail, a sprained ankle, or worse yet a major broken bone, meant certain agony and possibly death. They simply could not afford to become ill. Further, nothing in Arkport or Leavenworth could have prepared Armstrong for the sheer scale of the West. Armstrong's first look at the majestic Rockies must have taken him aback. For there before his unbelieving eyes loomed the most powerful and forbidding geological phenomenon he had ever seen. Once he crossed the Continental Divide at the summit of the Sawatch Range and started to make his way down into the Roaring Fork Valley, he might as well have been on another planet. It was that remote and threatening to anyone but the most adventuresome.

Educated and observant, Charles remained unassuming about his remarkable personal odyssey. He seemed more impressed with Colorado's crisp bright-blue skies and mountain scenery than the isolation and ubiquitous danger. I do get the sense that Charles knew he was on the cusp of a unique moment in United States history, and that was part of the reason he continued to keep his journals under such difficult circumstances. As much as I treasure his descriptions of his first trip into the Aspen region, I yearn for more information about his winter-long stay (1880 - 1881) in Leadville. As you will see, he says very little about this first winter in Leadville. Nor does he have much to say about the particulars of his life for the next four years. Because of space considerations, I have reluctantly left out month after month of largely repetitious and brief comments about the weather from 1883 to 1884. Then in September of 1885, as though he never missed a beat, he suddenly started elaborating in his journals. So I will remain thankful for what Charles wrote, rather than lament about what he might have written.

Earlier I stated that historians necessarily focus on generalities. I also noted what I like most about Charles's journals is the singular human face he put on history. The details do it. For example, I loved it when he mentioned Ed Hurlbut busting a "poker" over the head of a noisy young man at a "Revival Meeting" in Arkport. Or during his stay in Leavenworth when he wrote about the price of a train ticket to travel to the inauguration of Governor "Saint John's," a friend "hunting" (buffalo?) above Ft. Steele on the Platte River, the "British Blonds," a good "crop of ice," and Indian "trouble." In Colorado he told us what he thought of Denver, his train ride to Leadville, the Aspen militia, the price of food in an early mining camp, stage drivers, trapping methods, fellow prospectors, fishing, mining bonanzas, and his friend Abe Lee—whose discovery of gold in California Gulch had ultimately led to the founding of Leadville itself. All these details, considered in the context of the historical setting, allow us a personal and special view of one of the most intriguing eras in the American West.

As for Armstrong the man, between 1877 and 1889 he created more inkblots for us to interpret, although these are not as ambiguous as the first. While his behavioral and emotional patterns remained largely the same, his self-criticism mounted over time. At the age of twenty-nine, he detested being stuck again in Arkport. Repeatedly he castigated himself for his inability to accumulate money. As for his father's war wounds or his mother's infirmaries, he never mentioned them. Prior to leaving for Leavenworth, Kansas, in 1877, he was also depressed. His resultant listlessness permeated his entries. For the first time he shared short philosophical statements about life in general. Once he returned to Leavenworth,

Kansas, he felt better about himself. He even seemed content to resume his night clerk's job at the Continental Hotel, although he could not refrain from making a sarcastic remark about his "huge salary" of twenty dollars a month. While "night clerking" in Leavenworth, Armstrong started to drink too much. Early on he became a master at making hollow promises about maintaining his sobriety. His post-bender vows contained all the classic signs of a person who simply could not handle booze. Thus began Charles's long struggle to overcome alcohol, his best friend and worst enemy.

By now his journals also took on different functions. Charles's 1867 pocket diary contained, with a few notable exceptions, mostly matter-of-fact daily entries. The journal he started in 1877 became more of a companion and confidant. Months, sometimes years, later he re-read key entries to remind himself that he must not make the same mistakes twice. He struggled for self-improvement. Short, self-motivational articles were carefully glued in the front and back inside covers. He also copied self-help advice verbatim. There were fleeting moments when I thought Armstrong might have been too hard on himself, but ultimately I could not dispute any of his self-recriminations.

Although he never said so, he remained unenthusiastic about what marriage and family life presented. Not once did he pine for a wife or child. So too, his pattern of taking care of himself indicated he had not received much nurturing at home and now, thanks to information found in the National Archives, we know this to be true. Yet on a few occasions, as previously mentioned, he vowed to bring his father, mother, and sister to Leavenworth, and locate them on a farm farther west. When I first read this I wondered if Charles might have been closer emotionally to his family than his first journal indicated. Upon reflection, I changed my mind. His resolutions to bring his family west seemed more a matter of contemporary mores—the eldest son's responsibility—than familial love. In fact, it was about the only time he mentioned them, other than when he received a letter indicating "all is well" back home. One can easily predict that his resolution to relocate his family would go the way of his sobriety vows, which it did.

Suddenly, and without writing a word in his journals (if only he had) for almost a year, Charles took the big step. In the spring of 1880, at the age of thirty-three, he threw caution to the wind. He headed west. He boarded a train in Leavenworth, rode the rails to Denver, then continued on to Buena Vista, Leadville, and ultimately Aspen. To this point in his journals it is hard to envision Armstrong as an adventurer, let alone a risk-taker. Thus, it is not surprising that upon closer examination, selected journal entries revealed that Charles followed in the footsteps of his Leavenworth friend, Billy Schlagg. Surely Schlagg corresponded with Armstrong in Leavenworth prior to Armstrong's departure. Note that Armstrong wrote about Schlagg *returning* to Leadville from the Roaring Forks. Only then did Charles head over the Continental Divide to Aspen City and Highland where Schlagg had already put up a "camp." Charles must have arranged to meet Schlagg, his surveying partner, in Leadville. Recall, too, that he saw several other people from Leavenworth on the streets of Leadville. Taken together, these pieces of information suggest Charles followed a leader, Billy Schlagg. He soon grew sick of Schlagg's gambling and drinking, but there is no doubt in my mind that Schlagg led the way.

This in no way detracts from Charles's venture. He took a big risk when he boarded that train in Leavenworth. With little money and even less hope of employment he set out for destinations unknown. At least he was not beholden to anyone, other than his perceived obligation to bring his family west. So what was the attraction? Why did Charles finally head west? The answer is simple. It was the lure of instant wealth spiced with adventure. The proverbial pot of gold at the end of the rainbow. Thousands upon thousands of fortune seekers chased it back then. A fabulous strike of precious mineral is what the prospectors went after. Gamblers all.

The truth is that very few fortune seekers ever struck it rich in Colorado, or anywhere else in the West. Abysmal odds never seem to faze the glassy-eyed hordes of money-hungry people. So it was with Armstrong and his partner Schlagg. Worse, even if Armstrong and Schlagg had discovered a rich mineral deposit in the early 1880s, it would not have made them rich. Having the Midas touch was not enough. It took thousands of dollars in labor and capital to extract precious mineral from the ore in which it was embedded. Before a prospector saw a dime, unless someone came along and bought the claim, his ore had to be mined, transported to a smelter (a daunting, expensive task in mountainous terrain), crushed, refined, melted into bullion, and sent off to buyers hundreds, sometimes thousands, of miles away. Shipping bulk bullion out of Aspen was impossible until the smelters fired up in the mid-1880s and the railroads arrived in late 1887 and early 1888. Yet this clearly did not deter Armstrong and thousands of other newly arrived Coloradans.

Two things still puzzle me about Armstrong's quixotic quest for mineral wealth in uncharted regions. First, what did he know of geology that made him think he could spot precious ore in the first place? There is no hint in his journals of Charles acquiring geological or mining expertise. An expert surveyor? Yes. An expert geologist with an eye for precious minerals? I don't think so. Perhaps experience taught him quickly. Perhaps he learned from books. Or someone in the Continental Hotel? Did Schlagg teach him? Or maybe other prospectors educated them both on the spot? Second, during Armstrong's initial journey over the Continental Divide between Leadville and Aspen he almost certainly passed through the booming gold camp of Sparkell (also called Independence). Surely he would have mentioned *something* about this camp, if not spent the night there? I don't see how he could have missed it? Perhaps he took some other mountain pass, but it doesn't seem logical since the beaten path snaked through Sparkell.

Once again it's the details that bring a mesmerizing quality to the journals. How often does one read firsthand about the construction of a prospector's log cabin? Or of stage coaches whisking by on runners? Or of the first train engine chugging into town? How about Charles's personal contacts with early Aspen movers and shakers like Henry B. Gillespie, B. Clark Wheeler, and D. R. C. Brown? And consider the odds of Armstrong *befriending* Abe Lee, a Colorado legend who first discovered gold in California Gulch near present-day Leadville. So too, Charles usually gave us reports about what he did and where he went, allowing us to follow him as he tromped through foothills and along the creeks—hunting, fishing, and prospecting along the way. His detailed shopping lists, surveys, and occasional sketches also reveal much about the times. Plus, he built his cabin within a stone's throw of the tri-weekly stage route from Aspen, to Ashcroft, then over rugged Taylor Pass to Taylor Park. This cabin location gave Charles access to current news and tidbits of gossip—which he freely shared with us—for the entire mining region south of Aspen.

Seasonal rhythms in the high country dictated Charles's life even more than when he was in Arkport. Each winter he had to basically "hole up" in his small cabin. (A few times during past winters I have driven by Charles's second cabin site about seven miles south of Aspen. His cabin stood at about 8,500 feet. By mid-winter, deep snow makes it nearly impossible to walk the short distance from the paved highway to his cabin site. If it happens to be snowing and blowing, which it often is, I don't even attempt it.) Each spring he planted his garden and welcomed the "first robin of spring." In summer he picked up his prospecting and surveying activities. By fall the high country was largely clear of snow so he took frequent side trips into the adjacent hills and valleys. And as you will read, his favorite fall activities were fishing, hunting, and searching for new mining prospects on either side of Taylor Pass.

Charles did not need much money to get by. Based on several of his "expense lists," I calculated that he lived on about $200 a year. Some years his surveying skills brought in more, others less. He saved money by eating the fish he caught, game he trapped or shot, and vegetables and potatoes he grew. (Local historian Larry Fredrick thinks that Armstrong may have made the first mention of fly-fishing in the Aspen region.) By the end of 1889 Charles had carved himself a nice little niche along Castle Creek south of Aspen. Unquestionably, he enjoyed his independent lifestyle and the freedom it afforded him. The stage that rumbled by his cabin three times a week brought him all necessary supplies and occasional paying boarders. When city life called, he went down to Aspen.

After observing Charles's comfortable seasonal activities and routines during his first decade in Colorado, I began to wonder if Charles unconsciously really wanted to strike it rich—with all the attendant hoopla and headaches. At times, he did not act like it.

[*Inside cover:* No man can raise to honor. Who is cursed with a stiff back bone. (Russian Proverb)]

Arkport. May 24th 1877

I am still laying arround home doing nothing but reading and studying.. This has been an allmighty dull winter to me. I arrived home last of November with 6 dollars in money.. Father used that and I have not spent a dollar this winter.. I have not been to a spree [*"A lively or boisterous frolic."*] this winter.. have been to a few little parties, nothing more. And it has been about all that we could do to live. I dont believe that it has cost the whole family over 4 dollars a week to live. and there are 4 of us.. and while I was in Leavenworth it cost me 26 dollars a month for board for myself.. beside beer &c cost me as much more. I tell you I dont propose to spend my money so freely hereafter. I dont stop at a first class Hotel and pay first class prices when I can live for half the money and about as good. But above all I dont purpose to spend so much on beer &c.. I am going to quit playing cards and spending so much time loafing.. I have spent enough time in the last 5 years to have made me a first class draftsman & Bookkeeper beside keeping myself well posted in the news of the day.. and had more real fun than I have had and that is considerable. I believe in having fun and all that, but a person wants to get all the fun possible with the least money.. and with as little loss of valuable time as possible.. A little reading every day will amount to something in the course of a year.. If I had kept posted I could have taught School last winter and this spring would have been a hundred or so ahead.. beside having a chance to have studied as I have done here at home.. And have much more fun for I would have been near Leavenworth..

But now I am busted and here in Arkport where there is no chance for work or fun or anything..

Experience is a hard teacher but, I think he has taught me a lesson and I mean to profit by it. When I get flush again, reading these few lines I hope will put me on the right track.. and keep me thinking of the hard times that may come then.. as they have the last winter and as they are now.. Learn by the past how to plan for the future. Read.. If everybody feels as bad and so weak in the Back bone as I do when they are out of money and employment they are to be pilled [*"Stripped of skin; exoriated."*].. For I feel completely used up.. dont want to see anybody or go anywhere.

Folks may talk that money is not necessary to happiness here on earth.. {and of course it is not in the next world}. But it is a very handy thing to have in the house.. and I find it very necessary to my peace of mind especialy when I am out of employment. A man with cash in his trousers is much more of a man than the poverty stricken cuss loafing arround looking for something to do to keep starvation at a distance. These Damd fools that talk of the folly of riches never were busted.. Of course health is preferable to wealth but the two together make a man happy..

Yours Trs et May 3 1877.

[This entry was inserted here over a year later, although he does not mention it in his entry of November 1, 1878, on page 70: Friday Nov 1st 1878: I am at the Continental Hotel, Leavenworth am night clerk on the huge salary of 20 dollars a month. But I propose to keep the job till something better shows itself.. And I propose to profit by the perusal of the foregoing entry in my diary of May 1877.]

Thursday Nov 29th 1877

This is a day appointed by the president of these U. S. as a day of thanksgiving and prayer for the many blessings that we enjoy &c &c.. I am just Thirty years old to day. I have been home a little over a year now. It does not seem as though I had been here that long.. The time flies. Spring will soon be here.. likewise Old Age..

The weather is somewhat cool but rather pleasant for all. We had a good Old fashioned dinner and I feel very comfortable Attended Divine service this evening and came home very much edified.

Tuesday Nov 30th 1877

I think I will have to keep this diary going for this year at least. I believe it will be good exercise and by keeping a diary of every days events will help a fellow to form habits of regularity and method.. I dont suppose that there will be much of interest happen to me but still there may..

Weather Cold and a very cold wind blowing from the North West.. Cloudy and a little snow falling.

We have all enjoyed good health and have had plenty to eat, and have enjoyed all the necissaries of life and some of the luxuries...for the past year and I dont see why we should complain.. But it seems to be necissary to a man's well being to find fault

The last day November 1877

December 1st 1877 Saturday

This has been rather a cold day.. and about 3 oclock the snow commenced falling and for about half an hour came down pretty thick.. I cut some wood over in Ed Hurlbuts grove this fore noon, enough to last over Sunday. After dinner I went out with my gun towards Sharpes after partridges.. Saw quite a number and fired at 13 of them.. but.. did not fetch them.

I attended a lecture at the School House under the auspices of the Arkport Grange.. last evening. The subject was "Fruit culture."

"Brother" Stone of Dansville was the lecturer. He is a nursery man and of course it was an advertisement.. But it was well worth listening to and everybody was well pleased with it.

Although Armstrong found the Arkport lifestyle to be uninspiring, he carried fond childhood memories of "Jimmie Hurlbuts sugar camp." (Armstrong's journals)

1877 Sunday December 2nd

It was most nine oclock this morning when I got down to breakfast.. I put in the day reading the papers. In the evening went to church. The subject under consideration was Foreign Missions.. In my opinion civilization has been the greatest curse that ever befell the "Poor Benighted Heathen.." But maybe I look at it in wrong light. But if a person can change from a state of health and contentment to directly the opposite, and bennefit his condition by so doing.

Surely it is allright. But I would not do it.. This has been a fine day.

Monday December 3rd 1877.

This has been a splendid day. quite warm. with the wind in the South.. Sun shone all day-

Saturday Dec 8th

Have neglected my diary as a matter of course. But will try and do better hereafter.. But there has nothing happened worthy of note.. Last evening I went to Singing School over to the Rev. Mr. Todds house, had a fine time We have been having splendid weather this past week. But the snow is falling pretty smart at present..

January 1st 1878

This the first day of the year and a good time to "Turn over a new leaf &c".. Therefore I will begin by writing in my Diary. The Weather

is quite pleasant for the time of year. The sun has shone out on us a few moments at a time.. but the prospects are good for a storm of some kind. snow or rain.

We have been having a little excitement in this place.. lately.. Christmas we had a sort of a festival at the church which went off in good style.. Then a few days ago the School Teacher had a fuss with one of the Scholars which culminated in a row yesterday, and the scholars rather got the best of him and of course that is the theme of discussion all over the town. I guess it will not amount to anything. Last evening Roxie and I were up to Smiths.. Kate and Will Hathaway and Viollie Tiffany were there. We had a very pleasant time, spent most of the evening discussing the School battle. I received a letter from Frank Jones a few days ago he is 16 miles above Fort Steele on the Platt River.. hunting.. says he is about making expenses.. There is no news from any Surveying any where in the West. The news papers are full of the unprecedented warm weather and wonder what is the cause &c &c.. The cherry trees are in bloom in many places and the blue birds have come back from the South..

January 2nd 1878.

Our warm weather has left us.. and we are having winter, plenty of it. The snow has been falling more or less all day. There has about 2 inches fallen.. but is dry and drifts to much to make sleighing.. The wind has been in the North West most of the day.. Calm and frosty this evening. It keeps one of us busy fireing up.. to keep the Old House comfortable. The School trouble has been settled.. Jim Woolever the Trustee.. visited the school to day and told the scholars that they must obey or leave the school.. Good for Jim.. he did his duty..

February 1st 1878

Snow commenced falling yesterday about 10 oclock and this morning the snow was about 24 inches deep.. The R.R. are about blockaded. only the passenger trains are running..

We have been having a series of Revival Meetings here at the church for the past 4 weeks. And have got about 25 converts.. The religious people from Almond and H,ville have been up to help the thing along.. Every thing has gone off science only. One knockdown.. Edmond Hurlbut broke a poker over the head of young fellow that was somewhat noisy in meeting.. and they have gone to law about it.. But I dont think it will amount to much..

Monday February 4th

This has been a fine day the sun has shone bright, but it has not thawed but a little in the middle of the day.. Yesterday morning the Thermometor showed 16° below Zero.. Sleighing is getting to be good.. Our Revival Meetings have played out.

February 26 1878..

We have had very good weather this month..some cold nights. The sleighing has been good till within the last week. They snow about left us.. The ice is all out of the streams.. There has nothing happened of any note but a donation at Sam Pittses last week for the benefit of Mr. Cress from Hornellsville..the leader of the rivals *[revivals]* here. I was to meeting down to Mr. Zeliffs last evening.. Emma requested it.. she is very low with the consumption and will drop away before long. She is a very smart girl intelectualy.. The smartest one of the family.. But that will not save her..

The war between the Turks and Russians is ended and the Turks are badly whipped.. There is a good chance for a war between England and Russia now.. Our School ended this week. Such is life, all things must have an end. That is a very consoling reflection when a person starts in on a dissagreeable job.

During the nineteenth century the Russian Empire and the Ottoman Empire (present-day Turkey) waged a series of monstrously bloody wars. Even residents of isolated Arkport kept a leery eye on these conflicts. (Frank Leslie's Illustrated Newspaper, October 27, 1877)

May 11th 1878..

This is a very cold windy day.. Wind from the N.E. and frequently squals of sleet and hail.

This has been a remarkable warm spring The apple tress are mostly out of bloom. The wheat is over two foot high and about ready to head out.. corn and potatoes are up.. and all kinds of vegitation is about a month earlier than usual. By the press reports, we will have the most bountiful crops this year that the country every produced.. The West Especialy.. There is a great deal more planted than ever before and the prospects are that the yield will be greater to the acre than ever. If England and Russia will only go to war so as to give us a good market, we ought to be happy.. They are preparing for war and talking peace, and it is hard to imagine what the outcome will be. The Worlds Fair opened in Paris the 1st of this month.

The day before Armstrong left for Kansas, he vowed to move his poverty-stricken family to Kansas as soon as he could afford it. (Armstrong's journals)

Things run along in the old grooves here in Arkport.. I think I will start for the West sometime this month. I will go to work in the harvest fields if I can not find anymore congeniel employment after that I will hunt up a school for the winter.

Sunday October 6th 1878..

I have my trunk all packed.. and have 45 dollars in cash. I calculate to start for the west tomorrow.. I have been going west every since I have been home.. But have spent almost two years here.. And have hardly earned my board.. but now the time has come to go. I would like to put it off.. But that will not do laying arround here will ruin any man.. I am troubled to much with laziness now.. it will not do I must strike out and do something.. Husking corn is just as easy business in Kansas as it is here and there is a chance for a fellow to make some headway here and get above day work..

I shall get a school to teach for the winter if possible.. If I can get one.. Then I will hunt arround a little for a better job.. If I dont get a school I will hunt up a job of something else. I am bound to get a foot hold if I have my health. And in the Spring if Providence is willing the whole family must emmigrate to Kansas. **Shure as shooting !!**

We are growing poorer and poorer here every day. And if there is a possible chance to get away.. It must be done.. I propose to devote all my energies to the accomplishment of that one object.

Monday October 7th 1878

We got up early this morning as I am going away. Very cold and fogy with a heavy frost. Ice 1/4 inch thick. Martin Sharpe takes me down to H,ville. Mother and Roxie hate to have me go and I hate to go but it has got to be done first or last. It will not do to simply vegitate arround here..

On October 7, 1877, Charles S. Armstrong boarded a train at the magnificent Erie Railway Depot in Hornellsville, just three miles south of Arkport. From there he traveled west, and into Western history. Not much remains of Hornellsville's once-proud depot (right). (All from author's collection)

Well I got off on the 8.10 oclock fare to Buffalo 2.50.. arrived in Buffalo a little before 12 got dinner 25 cts.. After dinner hunted up Gair Beckwith. His place of business is with Geo. B. Starbird 208 & 210 Terrace Street Buffalo N.Y. He is foreman gets 2.75 a day. The business is iron fence and cresting for "roofs." After visiting Gair a short time I called on Myron Hulburts brother in law Stewart...who keeps a grocerie store on South Division Street. They have quite a store and seem to be doing a good bis..

I took supper with Gair his wife was not at home but her sister was keeping house for him.. We had a splendid visit. After supper we went up town and to the Varieties. Gair doing the honors. I stopped with him all night and to breakfast.. Buffalo is a much nicer place than I supposed it to be. Gair lives about two miles from his work and the streets and buildings along the route are very pleasant.. He took me through the Court House which has just been finished. It is the finest building I ever was in The stair cases are all marble and the wainscoting also, every thing is splendidly finished. And the boilers that furnish steam to heat with are immence. The material that the buildings are built of is Ohio Granite.. I took in the docks and saw how business is conducted there.. Well we talked over old times and renewed our youth.. I left for Chicago on the noon train fare 24 dollars to Kansas City, making 26.50 from home.. arrived in Detroit in the dusk of the evening stopped there but a few minutes... We arrived in Chicago about 10 in the morning got breakfast 25 cts.. After that I hunted Arthur up, found him.. He is nicely situated with one of the most prominant firms in the country Wirt Dexter & co.. We had a splendid visit Arthur showed me all the sights of the city.. We went to the Water Works which are well worth going to see Arthur sayes that the big engine is very near as large as the Corless engine of the Centennial.. Some thing on this plan

Fascinated by technology and its potential, Armstrong sketched this "big engine" at the Chicago Water Works in 1878. (Armstrong's journals)

In the evening we went to the Industrial Exibition. Which is a big thing.. The biggest shows that I ever saw. There was almost everything there.. A good band and thousands of gas burners. I tell you it was splendid The Jocky Club have their races there to day not at the exibition but at their race course. The City is full of sporting men beside others that have come to see the fair. Well we had a splendid time. One that I will long remember. We went to see the Palmer House supposed to be the finest hotel in the world. Chicago is a splendid City and I would like to live there. But it is over run with people out of employment. I left Chicago Thursday 10 oclock A.M. on the C. B&Q.R.R. *[Chicago, Burlington, and Quincy]*, arrived in Quincy in the night. The cars were crowded all the way with people going to Kansas and the west to settle.. All after farms.. We arrived in Kansas City Friday morning about 10 oclock Kansas City is growing very fast and is destined to make a large City. I visited Joe Mitchell he has been getting married, has a nice woman and he is well fixed has a good position on the LL & G *[Leavenworth, Lawrence, and Galveston]* and Ft. Scott & Gulf R.R. as Road Masters clerk 40 dollars a month pay..

In 1878 Chicago and its fabulous Palmer House (left) impressed Armstrong. (Frank Leslie's Illustrated Newspaper, November 22, 1879)

He says he will try to get me into a job on the R.R.. I stopped at Pat MacFrancis Hotel Friday night.. Saturday morning saw Diefendorf he is on the survey of the Missouri River says he will try to get me a job on it.. Pay 35 dolls a month and board for common hands.. Dief gets 90 he runs a compass..

We came up together on the train, got into Leavenworth 11 oclock. I eat dinner at the Continental Hotel. Found every body glad to see me apparently. after dinner I paid my bill and went up to the Washington House.. Can get board there for 1 doll a day, have to pay 2 at the Continental

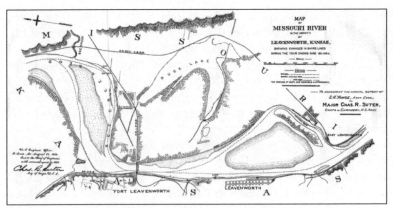

While in Leavenworth, Kansas, Armstrong wanted to be part of the work crew that first surveyed portions of the Missouri River and vicinity. (Author's collection)

Sunday Oct 14 1878

I visited arround to day saw all the old acquaintances. went to Church in the evening after church they told me that some body was after me from the Continental.. So I went down there and they have me the job of night clerk 20 dolls a month and board.. So I am off of expense

A stereocard shows the Continental Hotel in Leavenworth, Kansas, about the time Armstrong worked there as a night clerk "on the huge salary of $20 a month." Is Charles one of the men standing in front of the hotel? (Courtesy of David Phillips; The Leavenworth Daily Times, *May 1, 1877)*

Monday Oct. 15

Have put in the day pretty industriously seeing the folks. Took a ride with Billy Slagg up to the fort and above where the engineers are turning the river   We are trying to get a job there. The engineers name is Church a young chap from NY state.. Troy engineering School..he seems to be a nice fellow.. but had very little encouragement to give us.. I go on duty this evening.. Business is very lively here now as it is court week besides the Republicans hold a convention here. every bed in the house is full..

Tuesday Oct 16th 1878

I came off duty this morning about 7 oclock had breakfast and went to bed   slept till 1 oclock Got up and had dinner.. I find the duties here not very hard..

Saturday 20th 1878

Came off duty at 7 this morning.. Weather cold some frost last night. I generaly go to bed about 10 in the morning and get up about 5 in the afternoon. I dont see but what I feel as well as though I slept at night..

Monday Oct 21st

Came off duty 7 this morning The weather is very lowry [*"Of the sky: dull, gloomy, threatening."*], looks like snow.. Windy in the North.. Nothing has turned up out of the regular order of things.. I am going to bed now and sleep till 2 or 3 oclock when I want to go over to Col Denmans residence to see if he is at home..

Thursday 24th 1878

Just came in from my after breakfast walk. This is a very fine morning.. a little windy and dusty but otherwise very pleasant.. I got a letter from home day before yesterday. The folks are all well. Father has been chopping wood upon Ed Hurlbuts hill.. But I guess he does not make much at it.. Well I must try to get the family moved out into this country. and see if I am not man enough to get them a home to spend their old age in, where they will not be in a continual fret. Father has always wanted to go west and get a farm and if such a thing is possible I propose to get them out here the coming summer..

Monday Oct 28 1878

About 4 oclock in the afternoon I have just got out of bed retired at 9 oclock this morning. This has been a fine day, but somewhat chilly wind in the South. Yesterday morning we had quite a snow storm, came from the north and covered the ground, so it looked quite like winter but it is all gone now.. I put in time during my watch at night reading and writing.. The bar keeps open till 12 oclock and that keeps me from being lonesome through the early part of the evening. I read or write and now and then take a nap for an hour or two.

Tuesday Nov 1st 1878

Have just crawled out of bed 3 oclock.. And concluded to write a little in my diary.. I wrote a letter home to the folks yesterday. I would like to be able to move them out here to Kansas this fall and put them onto a little farm of their own.. I must get into a job though that will pay better than a night clerk at 20 dollars a month if I am to do that.. If it is possible they must come out to this part of the country next spring. We must devote all our energies to the accomplishment of that object.. There is no use of our staying in Arkport unless we want to end up in the poor house.. It is a nice place to live in if a person is well fixed, or has a home of their own so that they are not dependent on working for somebody else   Well I will close for this time

Saturday Nov 2nd 1878.

Have just got up 4 oclock.. nothing of interest has transpired. The Working Men held an open air meeting in front of the Mansion House last evening.. that I could not go as I was on duty..

Monday Nov 4th 1878

I am on duty this evening The time is 12 oclock.. at night I have just eaten my lunch.. The streets were very livly this evening.. The Republicans and Democrats held meetings had two brass band out. Beside the Wizard Oil men held a fine entertainment across the street from the Hotel. They are splendid singers. They board here.. Tomorrow night they have another entertainment when they will sell their infaliable Oil to the assembled multitude.. Tomorrow is election day. and I suppose it will be very warm. There was one fight to day down to the Post Office but it did not amount to anything. a little blood was spilt that was all..

Wednesday Nov 12 1878

I have just got out of bed.. Have had a good sleep.. The weather is splendid, sun shining bright. . I Saw Bob Palmer last evening he has been out with the soldiers after the Cheyeines.. that commited so many murders in Safy and Beaver Creeks up in the West part of the State.. he says that they had a hard time of it.. chasing them through the Sand Hills where there was neither wood nor water He was hired as tracker but did not have anything to do. Bob owes me 12 dollars which he sayes he will pay I hope he will for I need it.

Saturday Nov 16th 1878

I have just got up 4 oclock.. I might get 2 or 3 hours sleep during the night if there were not some of the boarders coming in and out at all hours.. There are five Wizzard Oil men stopping here.. have been here for two weeks now and they hardly ever go to bed to 3 or 4 in the morning.. but they are nice fellows... and the two surveyors Frank Howard and W<u>m</u> Hunt are splendid.

Hanlie the proprietor is here and the two salesmen who do the talking. Dr. Watkins and Dr. McLorky.. Howard and Hunt assisted by Prof Kaufmann a fine violinist and several other musical men of the town gave a concert at the Opera House last evening and every body says that it was tip-top.. It was the largest house what has been out in years. Hunt and Howard used to travel with Cal Wagners Minstrels. H. B. Denman called here at the hotel yesterday afternoon to see me. but I had not got up yet.. and I see by todays paper that he has gone to Kansas City. It beats all that I cant get a sight of him.

Tuesday Nov 19th 1878.

This has been a splendid day but I did not get much benefit from it as I did not get up till about 4 oclock.. H. B. Denman was here at the hotel again to day. but I was in bed. Now tomorrow morning I am going out to his house and see him sure.. I received a letter from home last Sunday. . The folks are all well and everything is lovely. They are having plenty of rain down there but have not had much cold weather yet I must write to them this evening..

Thursday Nov.. 28 1878#

Thanksgiving Day

I got up at 1 oclock this afternoon to get dinner. . We had Oysters stew.. Roast Turkey with Cranberry sauce, Roast Pig.. and other things to numerous to mention.. After dinner I took a strool arround town for an hour or so. and then went to bed and slept till half past 6 oclock. Then I got up and had a supper and went on duty. Have been reading over my diary and thinking of old times. . And thinking what I will do in the future. I have always had very good luck when I have applied myself. and have tried to do anything.. The great trouble with me is I am inclined to be lazy. I must breake up my foolish habit of waiting for something to turn up.

Friday Nov 29 1878

I am 31 years old to day and I have not much too big on in the way of money nor much in knowledge. Still I have done some better than lots of my old school mates. for I have seen a great deal of the world and had a considerable amount of fun.. But that is not as well as I should have done. But it cant be helped now. I am in good health and have as good a chance as any of the young men in the country that have no money or friends to back them.

Saturday Nov 30 1878

This has been a stormy day. It commenced snowing last night a little and it has kept it up pretty much all day. There is as much as 2 inches of snow on the ground this evening. But the weather is so warm that the snow will not lay long.

Sunday December 1st 1878

I went to bed this morning about 8 oclock, but could not sleep so I got up and did not go to bed till after dinner, when I slept sound till 6 in the evening. This has been a very fine day over head, but the streets are very sloppy..

There was a stabing affray last night about 12 oclock up town at a gambling house. A man was stabed and in shooting at his assailant he hit an innocent man. the man that was cut will die

Armstrong probably learned about the "stabing affray" when he read this front-page headline in The Leavenworth Times *on Monday morning, December 1, 1878. (Author's collection)*

Monday Dec 2 1878

I received a letter from home this morning.. The folks are all well, and feeling comfortable. Father feels very thankfull that I have a job for the winter.. He keeps at work in the shop and supports the family in good shape. Old Mr. Colgrove died of Pneunomia just one week ago to day and was buried the day that Roxie wrote me the letter.. That was last Wednesday. He was sick just a week.. Well I suppose that some are glad of it, that is the relatives for he was the worst old Whoremaster in the country and was spending the property very fast. There will be a splendid opportunity for the lawyers to make something for there is a large family and they are all quarrelsome.. and each will want the lion's share.. Wm Hurlbut and Rork have had their lawsuit about the slandering of Rork by Wm, and Wm came out ahead to most everybodys satisfaction. But Rork will not allow it rest there. he is going to appeal it.. The thing will foot up 4 or 500 dollars cost now and it will take a pretty penny if he gets beat there..

Well Arkport is running along in the old grooves as it has run and will run for years to come. I have had company all the evening till about 3 this morning (the 3rd) Dr. Robinson a boarder here has been telling me some of his experience in the practice of Medicine. &c..

Saturday Dec 14th 1878

We have had a heavy snow storm   the heviest that there has been in years in this part of the country (according to the Old Settlers.) It commenced snowing night before last about 9 oclock and continued till last evening.. about 12 inches fell.. All the R.R. are blockaded and biz. is suspended generaly. I have been about down sick for the past week.. I caught a severe cold last Sunday morning and it settled in my bones and head and about used me up.. But I am about over it now.

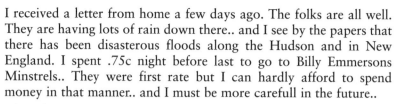

I received a letter from home a few days ago. The folks are all well. They are having lots of rain down there.. and I see by the papers that there has been disasterous floods along the Hudson and in New England. I spent .75c night before last to go to Billy Emmersons Minstrels.. They were first rate but I can hardly afford to spend money in that manner.. and I must be more carefull in the future..

Thursday Dec 19th

This has been a cold day.. The Missouri closed up to day.. A week ago to night it commenced snowing   snowed all day Friday, about 13 inches fell.. Night before last the Thermometor registered 6 below Zero.. This is one of the heaviest snows that they ever had in this countrey. The prospects for a good crop of ice are firstrate..

Thursday Dec 26th 1878

There has nothing of note happened to me since I wrote last. Our cold weather stayes with us and the sleighing holds good.. Snowed some today.

Yesterday was a quiet Christmas to me. I went to bed about 10 oclock in the morning and did not get up till 6 in the evening..

I wrote home last Sunday and sent the folks a two dollar bill to buy a Christmas dinner with, but I am afraid that they will not get it in time.. for I see by the papers that the Rail Roads are all blocked down east with snow. The snow was 3 feet deep in Buffalo and still snowing a week ago..

Jan 1st 1879

The countrey resumed specie payment., We have had solid old winter since the first snow fell.. for the past 3 nights the murcury has ranged to 12° below Zero. The sleighing is and has been fine.. I received a letter from home yesterday.. The folks are all well and enjoying the cold weather..

I wrote them just before Christmas and sent them a two dollar bill to buy a Christmas dinner with.. and that way they had a good one.. I did not get up to get dinner on that day. But New Years day I got up and eat so much dinner that it made me sick, wither that or the "Egg Nog".. But I am getting along finely here not much to do and plenty to eat and a good fire to set by and a warm bed to sleep in.. I am not making much money but how many poor cusses are busted and out of a job this cold weather. I tell you I feel gratefull that I am so well fixed.

Thursday Jan 9th 1879

We have had a little let up on the weather for a few days past.. but this morning the murcury has dropped again to 8 below zero.. I wrote a letter home this morning.

We have some excitement and a rush of business. . "The British Blonds" a sort of leg show were here Sunday Monday & part of

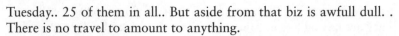

Tuesday.. 25 of them in all.. But aside from that biz is awfull dull. . There is no travel to amount to anything.

Friday Jan 10th 1879

Nothing new to day.. The weather is fine.. but cold.. Ice men are reaping a great harvest this year.. Przybylowicz *[co-owner of Continental Hotel]* and Delf are putting up 500 tons for their own use.. ice is about 14 inches thick and still growing thicker..

Saturday Jan 11th 1879

4 oclock in the morning.. I have put in most of the evening reading my Diary over.. and thinking. . The weather has moderated. Wind in the south.. No news..

Monday Jan 13 79

Nothing of any note has happened since I wrote last.. The weather holds about the same. Yesterday was inauguration day for the Govenor "Saint John" Excursion tickets from here to Topeka were $2.00 round trip. I slept 7 hours to day.. got up shortly after five.. took a walk arround town for exercise and felt much better on account of it.. I get along very well here, only Fritchie *[co-owner of Continental Hotel]*... gives me hell now and then when he feels ugly but I will grin and bear it till something better turns up.. I cant afford to get up on my dignity when I havent any money and in the dead of winter..

Thursday Jan 16th 1879

I haven't much to write only that I am in good health and am able to take my regular meals..

Governor John R. St. John (above) took office on January 13, 1878, in Topeka, Kansas, during the State's first public inauguration. (Harper's Weekly, February 8, 1878)

The weather has moderated a considerable.. Yesterday morning we had about 2 inches more snow.. with some rain which froze as it fell, making the going very slippery. But it has patched up the sleighing so it is first rate again.. Business in the Hotel line is picking up again and we have a full house most every night..

Thursday Jan 30th 1879

I am still in good health and spirits.. Received a letter from home day before yesterday.. The folks are all well.. They have had hard work to keep warm this cold weather and they are anxious to come out West. The Methodists are having a revival of religion down there. The meetings are being held in Rork's Hall.. They can hold a revival every winter in Arkport and still there will be lots of unregenerated Cusses to hunt up..

Wednesday Feby 19th

Since last I wrote in my diary we have had some change in the weather.. along the first of this month it came off warm.. and the snow left us and the ice in the river broke and went out. And the roads have been in firstrate conditions till three days ago about 3 inches of snow fell.. making the roads very bad again Nothing out of the usual run of events has happened to me. Business is very lively now and we have plenty to do.

Sunday March 30th 79

I went to bed about 8 oclock this morning. slept till 12 and concluded to get up.. for after I wake up and lay half an hour or so thinking.. I might as well get up and dress for there is no more sleep for me. I have not written in my diary for sometime. Nothing out of the common run happens. I have been hoping that something would turn up, that I could make some money at.. but it dont seem to show itself..

I have thought some of going out to Leadville.. but I hear such hard stories about destitution and want of work out there that I am afraid to try it.. But the great draw back is my want of money. I could not raise enough to much more than take there and I would not have enough to keep me for a week till I could look arround.. One of my friends here is going out there this week and I will be able to hear through him what the chances are for me. . I hear from home quite often. Roxie has the Arkport School engaged for the coming summer at $4.50 a week and board at home for 4 months. She will clear 72 dollars   I am afraid that is more than I will clear.. But I must try and get enough ahead to get the folks out here sometime during the season and get settled for the winter. By George I wish a survey would turn up this summer.. if I could ever get three or four hundred dollars together again I would feel somewhat better But I see no way to do it yet. There is a great emigration pouring into the state this spring. And I ought to have a few hundred dollars to invest out west in some of the growing towns that are opening up.

Saturday April 5th 1879

This is fine weather that we are having.. But we need rain very badly. The Hotel is full of "Pinafore People." I have not struck anything yet that I can make more money at.. and I dont see any prospects ahead where there would be a chance for anything

Monday May 12th 1879..

I am still at the Hotel night clerking.. Have been hoping that a survey of some kind would turn up so that I could get a job and make some money this summer.. but it dont seem to show it self.. I got a letter from home a few days ago.. Father has been sick but is getting better.. I sent them 10 dollars to help them along.. I must make a strike soon so as to get the folks into good shape. They are getting old and soon will not be able to do anything.. I must rush arround and get them a home. I must live more economical.. I spend to many 5 cts for beer.. I get 20 dollars a month and I draw 10 of that and turn the other 10 on what I owe the hotel.. We are having very fine weather now warm and pleasant.. We have had plenty of rain and crops look fine The trees and grass are green and everything looks fine..

[Now, almost a year later, Armstrong starts writing again, and he is on his way West.]

Thursday May 6th 1880

I am in Denver setting under the porch of the Alvord House. I left Leavenworth Tuesday morning on the 7:50 train. Arrived in Denver last night about 6 oclock. Have been looking the town over to day called on the Surveyor General Mr. Albert Johnson. He gave me a list

In May 1880 Armstrong boarded a train at Leavenworth's Union Depot (right) and rode the rails across the plains to Denver, Colorado. (Leavenworth Collection, Kansas Collection, Spencer Research Library, University of Kansas; Scribner's Monthly, August 1876)

of questions to answer which I answered to his satisfaction and now all I have to do is to get somebody to sign my bond for Ten Thousand dollars which will not be difficult. I think as is more a matter of form than anything else Denver is a fine town lots of business But it looks all torn up.. I have heard a great deal of the beauties of the place but I cant see as it is such a magnificent town as everybody seems to think it is.

Armstrong stopped in Denver (above) to obtain his surveyor's license. He stayed in the Alvord House Hotel (below) on the corner of 18th and Larimer Streets. (Crofutt, 1881; Denver Public Library, Western History Department)

Saturday May 8th 1880

Am in Buena Vista stopping at the Park Hotel. I left Denver yesterday at 10 oclock arrived here at 9 in the evening. Had a fine trip over The ride up Platt Canyon is magnificent. And the sight of Kenosha Hill is worth a trip to the mountains. The grade is over 200 feet to the mile. They run up on one side of the Canyon and cross the head of it on a bridge then down on the other or <u>rather up</u>.. and over the summit The summit is over 10, 000 feet above sea level Thursday night we had a snow storm in Denver but two hours sun run it all off. This morning the ground is covered with snow..

Nothing in western New York could have prepared Armstrong for the stunning mountain scenery he encountered during his train ride over Kenosha Pass (above) to Buena Vista, Colorado. (Reprinted from South Park railroad booklet)

Monday May 10th 1880

Am writing this in the Clarendon Hotel. I have been walking arround so much that my feet are very tired.. and so I am in here to take a rest this is a very fine day and if I had about $100 in my pocket I would feel very good.. I have talked with several men from Roaring Forks and they say that I can get all the work I can do.. but the trouble is that the snow is so deep on the range that there can be nothing done.. But I think that I can worry it through.. I have engaged a room with a man that I met on the train coming out here. We have to pay 6 dollars a week which will make it 3 for each. Then I have 21 meal tickets which cost me 8 dollars and I can make them do me for 1 1/2 weeks. I think I wrote home yesterday..

Tuesday May 11th 1880

I am looking arround town yet.. have moved into own room. I see quite a number of Leavenworth people in town Saw Frank Neubauer last night he is tending bar down at Malta about 4 miles below here.. This is a very fine day I hope it will stay like this for six months at least..

Wednesday May 12th

Last night Schlag got in from Roaring Forks.. He thinks that the prospects are fine for us to make money.. We expect to start for there next Saturday We have been walking arround town to day looking at the mines &c.. This has been a splendid day..

Sunday May 16th 1880

Left Leadville yesterday about noon for "Roaring Forks" Schlag..

John Davenport. George Gladden & Geo.. Hopkins compose the party with myself.. Schlag and I are in partnership We came to this place.. "Twin Lakes" by wagon.. here Schlag had 2 good jacks and the rest of the party have 5 when they get them all together but 1 is missing.. and we have been laying here in the camp till noon and it has not turned up.. Twin Lakes are 2 fine lakes. This upper I should think contained about a mile square. and the lower very near twice as large There are a few houses and a store & Post Office here.. I wrote

In the early 1880s Leadville (top) still swarmed with fortune seekers, including Armstrong. Charles was lucky to secure a room at the Clarendon Hotel (bottom), Leadville's finest. (Leslie's Illustrated Newspaper, April 12, 1879; Denver Public Library, Western History Department)

a letter home to day. We are having very fine weather and I dont like to be laying arround.. but have to wait on the others..

Tuesday May 18th

I am in camp at Seatons Ranch *[later a regular stage stop between Leadville and Aspen]* about 10 miles from Twin Lakes and about 5 from the top of the Range where we have to cross I am waiting here till the boys come back They have gone on to the foot of the range about 4 miles with half the stuff and are coming back for the remainder. The road is bad and they have to double back. We left Twin Lakes yesterday about 10 oclock and came to this place and

Incredibly, in May 1880 Armstrong continued to write in a journal during his arduous trek over the Continental Divide to nascent Aspen City in the valley of the Roaring Forks. (All from Crofutt, 1881)

camped for the night I did not feel very well yesterday night. And I was very much afraid that I was going to be sick. but I feel pretty good this morning. There are lots of people going by this morning bound for Roaring Forks. There is lots of snow all arround here I am setting within 10 feet of a big snowbank..

Wednesday May 19th 1880

I am in camp waiting for the boys to get back   they have gone over the summit with part of the stuff. We have to double back till we get over the Range It is about 2 miles to the summit by the trail, and about a mile straight over. The snow is 8 & 10 feet deep in places

Thursday May 20th 1880

We camped on the summit of the range above timberline Had a very rough time of it the snow on the summit is from 3 to 12 feet deep where the trail is shoveled out. We had a snow storm of about 1/2 hours duration.. I slept very cold and did not rest worth a cent last night. This morning I saw a couple of mountain quail. shot at one but did not kill him.. They are white as snow.. and about as large as a partridge. We have had a hard time to day getting down off the range. We had to carry everything down the mountain the jacks could not carry their loads on account of the steepness of the mountain and also the snow.. The snow is about 5 feet deep here in the woods. Some good pine timber here   trees 18 inches through.

Saturday May 22 1880

Nooning on the North Fork of Roaring Fork River. Yesterday we left our camp at the foot of the Range and doubled to "Seadans Ranch." where we left some of our stuff.. was delayed there for a couple of hours by a snow storm. camped at night about 1 1/2 miles below Sedans had a nice camp. cut pine boughs and made a fine bed. There is much more snow on this side of the Range than on the other. Camped to night near the North Fork of Roaring Fork in the timber. Had a hard afternoon   Trail very muddy & bad.

Sunday May 23rd 1880

We left camp early this morning and had about 400 yds to go to North Fork where we had to cross on a Jack Bridge   Three trees felled across the river and pine bows put on and covered with dirt We had to unpack our jacks and carry our things across. Had dinner. then we had to carry our stuff about 1/2 mile through the snow. I saw some kind of a wild animal to day. did not know if it was a young bear or a wolverine

Well we finaly got a very good trail and got to the Forks of Roaring Forks.. where we had to cross again. carried our stuff over on foot log and drove the jacks through. camped on the banks of the river. The river is about 4 rods wide below the forks and very swift..

Shown above are two pages of the journal that Armstrong carried with him as he approached Aspen City for the first time in late May 1880. (Armstrong's journals)

Monday May 24th 1880

Left camp before breakfast and traveled about 2 miles over a very bad trail muddy and lots of fallen timber. found some grass for the jacks and stopped for breakfast..

Afternoon we had a good trail traveled about 4 miles and are camped on the level with fine grass. There are some small lakes here origanly beaver dams. The mountains are very high and rocky here. The scenery along Roaring Forks is grand..

Tuesday May 25th 1880

We pulled out from camp early this morning Had a good trail all day. We crossed Roaring Forks on a jack bridge, paid our toll in bacon 5 lbs at 30c pr pound. 25c a jack. The bridge is a big pine with two smaller on each side. We passed through the City of Aspen crossed Castle Creek and passed through the City of Roaring Forks not a house in either town. They have a fine location.. a fine level bottom and no timber. We camped for the night on Castle Creek about 4 miles from Highland a mining Town. where we are going to locate. Snowing this evening..

Wednesday May 26th 1880

Moved out of camp earley. Passed through Highland the future great city. There are quite a number of log cabins going up. It is a very good location. We passed through the place and came up to Schlags camp.. Had a fearful hill to climb. I thought we never would get up it but like everything else we got to the end of it. and finely got into camp. We have had a very fine day to day..

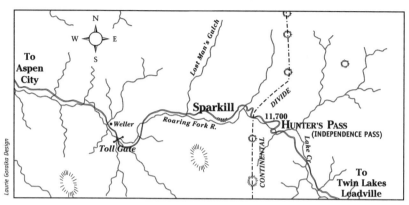

A reproduction of a portion of an 1884 Pitkin County map shows Armstrong's probable route over the Continental Divide. Hunter's Pass (Independence Pass), Sparkill (Independence), and a "Toll Gate" are shown along the trail. Armstrong wrote about paying a toll in bacon, but he did not mention Hunter's Pass or Sparkill. (Courtesy of Larry Fredrick)

Thursday May 27th 1880

To day Schlag and I went down to Highland to attend a miners meeting and also to see about getting the job of laying out the town.. We got the job of laying out 2 streets. Main and Highland Av.. We got $100. for the job which will pay us pretty well. We can do it in 4 days easy..

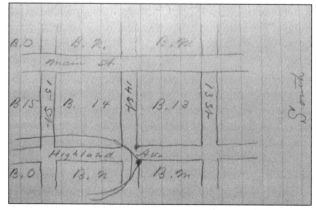

On May 27, 1880, participants in a "miners' meeting" at the newly established Highland hired Armstrong and his partner Schlag to "lay out the town." Armstrong's rough sketch of their work is shown above. (Armstrong's journals)

Friday May 28th 1880

Moved down to town with 4 days grub.. Took Besser along to help.. We put in the afternoon getting out stakes found a good pine log that we can soon get them cut off

Saturday May 29th

Commenced our work on Main St. Fine day..

Throughout Armstrong's surveying career, he ordered equipment from W. & L. E. Gurley in Troy, New York. A Gurley's transit is shown above. (Gurley's Manual, 1908)

Sunday May 30th

Worked till about 6 oclock in the evening when it got so cold that we quit.. did not finish Main St. Wrote a letter to Gurley for a Transit Chain & Tape. Rec'd a letter from Bob Ramsay and Katie Miller everything lovely.. &c..

Monday May 31st

2 inches of snow this morning.. snowing. now 1 oclock. Laying in camp doing nothing. Did nothing all day but set arround the fire

Tuesday June 1st 1880

Put in a good days work.. Snow all gone by noon. Had a fine day

Wednesday June 2nd 1880

Finished our job this afternoon Had a fine day to work.. not a sign of a cloud..

Thursday June 3rd 1880

Fine morning I am setting in the shade of a tree waiting for Schlag who has gone to see about the pay for our work.. We saw 2 deer on the side of the mountain across the creek this morning.

Friday June 4th

We left Highland City and came up to our old camp on the hill stayed all night And this morning we packed our stuff on the jacks and moved over to Old Highland.. We had a rough trip got into camp about noon got dinner and.. set to work to build some sort of a shelter we put up some logs about 3 feet high and spread some blankets and some old canvas over for a roof..

Saturday June 5th 1880

Snowed on us last night about an inch fell. But to day has been a fine day. Schlag went down to Highland to attend a miners meeting.. I stayed in camp and fixed up the claim and fixed arround.. camp some.. Went out to see some of the claims on copper hill just back of camp. They show up well..

Sunday June 6th 1880

Fine day.. Schlag and I slept till late this morning.. spent part of the day looking over the hills at the claims

Monday June 7th 1880

I was the first up this morning was out before sun up.. Schlag spent the most of the day making a windlass for one of his claims up on the hill.. I made a plat of our work down at Highland and started a letter home.. Fine day..

Tuesday June 8th

I finished the plat and finished the letter home and also wrote one to Katie Miller.. Schlag and a man that he has hired have been at work on the claim putting in a windlass   I was up there this evening This has been a fine day..

Thursday July 8th

Setting in our cabin.. just had dinner. Since I wrote last/ just a month to day.. Schlag and I have moved off the hill down to the town of Highland.. and have built a house. Schlag left here 3 weeks ago to day and went to Leadville after provisions. but he has failed to get back. I have been expecting him every day. I have not done anything in the surveying line.. When we came down here the town was lively and full of people but now there is but a very few in town and there is nothing doing.. Have been up on the hill twice since Schlag left.. but I have not got any work to do. The 4th I spent here doing nothing managed to get pretty full of rotgut which made me very sick.. the next morning I threw up about a pint of gall which did me lots of good.. I have felt much better ever since.. There is considerable excitement down at Aspen City there has been some good strikes down there.. One mine the Smuggler was sold a short time ago for 165,000 dollars.

Monday Sept .6th 1880

Camped on Taylor River.. bound for Spring Creek Mining Camp.. We left Highland day before yesterday about 2 oclock P.M. Camped that night at Ashcroft Town   We are using Woods jacks to pack our stuff.. Schlag & I bought a mule of Harris paid $50 for him.. he is a good riding animal. We had a heavy frost this morning.. froze ice about 1/2 inch thick in the bucket.. We are at Red Mountain Ranch snow..

Wednesday Oct 14th 1880

Camped at Highland on the hill.. We left Spring Creek a week ago to day. got in here Friday.. went into camp and covered up our claims and fixed them for winter. except the Bear Lode.. which we put a windlass on and cleaned out.. We would have been done. but the weather has been very bad.. we have about a foot of snow and it has been stormy for a week.. besides we have spent 3 days hunting our jack Jerry.. found him once.. but Tuesday morning he left again with one of Beebee's mules.. A bear stampeded them. But Tuesday morning.. Some miners working in the Eva. Belle Mine caught and killed Mr. Bear.. They built a log trap and baited it with fresh meat.. mr. Bear went in and did not come out alive.. I have killed two deer 1 fine buck and a doe/ and a rabbit and grouse in the past week so are having plenty of meat.. Schlag has gone to Aspen to day to look after Jerrie and also to get some things..

Friday Nov. 26th 1880

Am in the City of Leadville once more. We arrived in town two weeks ago to day.. We were the last ones to leave Highland. We sunk the Bear 16 feet and the Leavenworth about 17 feet.. We moved down onto Castle Creek and camped in Harrises cabin 4 days.. I put in the time hunting but did not kill anything. We brought out with us the carceses of 2 fine deer that I killed. We have rented a house here. have gone to keeping house. Besser, Schlag and myself..

[Written in the back cover the journal.]

It is wonderful what a hold habit has on a man. Some get in the habit of spending every cent they can raise and spree arround while some get in the as bad habit. of never going in company. never spreeing and spend very little money anyway But are lazy and thriftless. They have few wants and instead of cultivating economical habits and energy they are either spend thrifts or sluggards. We find the successful man has habits of industry and economy and I hold it is a mans power to form any habit that he wishes to.. If he will pursist in anything even what is most distasteful he will eventualy get to like it and it will get to be almost a second nature.. The great trouble is to break off old habits, it is easy enough to form new ones. Just break up the old ones. Life, Thoughts everything is habit.. It not only controls our bodies but also our minds.. A person gets in the habit of dreaming and planing things that he never tries to accomplish and it gets to be almost impossible for him to come down to the practicle he is always in the clouds Let him break up that habit and work out one of his plans and make to go to work at something anything then plan to accomplish it.. Break off your old habits those that you know to be bad.. and good ones will come in their place and in a short time you will find that you have no desire for what once you thought you could not live with out

[Now comes the five-year gap of "weather reports and surveys" that I mentioned I would reluctantly omit. Then, thankfully,Charles resumes writing.]

As witnessed by one of Armstrong's early journals, he considered himself a resident of tiny Highland. Like most miners in the region, he did the majority of his shopping in Aspen. Armstrong kept meticulous expense lists (above and right) in the back of his journals. (All from Armstrong's journals)

Friday September 4th 1885

Got out at 5.20 this morning, cooked breakfast for 4 beside Schlag & myself. clear fine morning. wrote home yesterday. 6 for dinner.

Saturday September 5th 1885

Got out 5.30 this morning. 2 for breakfast. fine morning. little cool and looks some like rain.

Sunday Sept 6

Stormy day.. Pete & Bill P were down to day. they are in 162 feet in the tunnel & have not struck it yet. got dinner for 7.

Monday Sept 7

About an inch of snow this morning. cold stormy day

Tuesday Sept 8th 1885

Got out 5 1/2 this morning heavy frost. promises a fine clear day

Thursday Sept 10th

I went to town on Croppie to day on business.

Friday Sept 11th
Stopped in town all night and all day today. rainey this evening

Saturday Sept 12th 1885
Snowing this morning when I got up. snowed all day snow fell about 6 inches.

Sunday Sept 13th
Came home to day.. with Jim Kinney

Monday Sept 14th
[no entry]

Wednesday Sept 15th 1885
Got out 1/2 past 5 this morning.. 5 for breakfast.. fine day

Saturday Sept 19th
Got out at 5 1/2 this morning 6 for breakfast.. Fine clear morning.. Schlag went to Aspen last Tuesday with 55 dolls cash and has not got back yet.. I suppose he has blowed it all in and all that he could collect beside... Pete & Bill went on the hill to work on the tunnel again Bill has been to town since last Sunday on a drunk.

Sunday Sept 20th
Got out 5 1/2 this morning.. 4 for breakfast.. Fine clear day.. I hear this morning that the Union Pacific R.R. have contracted to freight

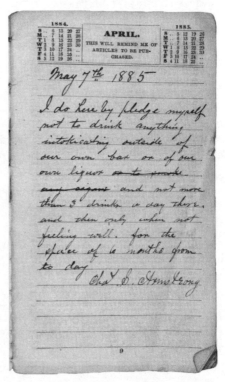

Armstrong's vows to stop drinking were a flimsy as the Pierce's Memorandum pamphlet in which he wrote this one. (Armstrong's journals)

15000 tons of ore to St. Elmo.. which will all go by here.. insuring a good road and trade for us all winter. Also that they are going to build big reduction works at Aspen which is a good thing for this countrey.. As the smelter here

[Inserted later: Never did it June 24/ 87] has everything their own way now.. I just hope it is all true.. The stage was filled with passengers this morn A big 40 horse power boiler & machinery went down this morning for the Enterprise Tunnel

Thursday Sept. 24th

Have not had any lodgers for the last two nights.. I have been alone.. Got up this morning 6 1/2 fine clear day.. I was up at midnight last night to see the eclipse of the moon about 3/4 ths of the moon was obscured. Travel is light by here now..

Friday Oct 2nd 1885

Got out at 5.45 this morning 5 here for S & B. Schlag got home last night Monday after spending 75 dollars.. He went to town again last night after a team took $10 with him.. He is getting more no account every year   he is lazier than any body..

Saturday Oct 3rd 1885

Got out 5.30 this morning   2 for breakfast fine day.. put in most of the morning hunting jacks found 2.. been digging potatoes to day

Sunday Oct 4th

Pete & Bill were down to day. the tunnel is in 202 feet.. and no change of rock..

Monday Oct 5th 1885

Got out 6.45 This morning.. Had a sick man here last night he is better this morning.. Fine day.

Tuesday Nov 3rd

Election day I went to town to the Election   Schlag went down yesterday.. I stopped in town all night did not go to bed at all. Won $2000 at faro [*"A gambling game at cards, in which the players bet on the order in which certain cards will appear when taken singly from the top of the deck.]..* Came home on the stage Wednesday morn.

Thursday Nov 5th 1885

Commenced snowing last evening about 4 inches fell.. Snowing now quite hard "(noon)" Pete gone out hunting this morning

Saturday March 13th 1885

Fine day.. It has been very stormy weather for the past week.. I went to Aspen Sunday evening after provision.. Stayed till Thursday morning.. Pete was down Sunday.. They are in 315 feet in the tunnel.. Schlag has been up there for 2 weeks helping there

[Now comes an inexplicable year-and-seven-month gap.]

Sunday November 28th 1886

I got back from Aspen yesterday. Went down last Tuesday after provisions and stayed till Saturday did no good but run in debt.. Tomorrow is my birth day am 39 years old   it will be a good time to turn over a new leaf for the better.. I am getting to be a little to recklass for my own good. Cap. Carey has quit work on the Grand Union Tunnel for the winter   a snow slide came down the mountain and took the black Smith Shop down the dump but did not hurt any one as it was at 5 in the morning.

Dangerous, dark, dank, and dirty "mine tunnels" seldom amounted to more than that. Only a very few prospectors struck it rich. Of course this did not deter thousands like Armstrong from trying. (Courtesy of Lake County Public Library)

Monday November 29th 1886

I am 39 years old to day.. Which will be a good time to turn over a new leaf for the year.. Pete Olsen came up from Aspen this evening.. This has been a splendid warm sunshiny day..

Tuesday Nov 30th 1886

Fine sunshiny day.. Pete was up to Robinson Gulch looking at one of our prospects and to take the Jacks &c onto good grass. Abe Lee *[a Colorado legend who discovered gold in 1860 in California Gulch near Leadville]* was here to dinner.. Also after us to do some assessment work on the Placers.

Wednesday Dec 1st 1886

Pete and myself commenced work to day.. I am building a log cabin about 1 1/2 miles up Conundrum Gulch.. for assessment on the Erie Placer claim.. I am to get 16 dollars for it.. Fine day.

Sunday Dec 5th 1886

I finished the cabin yesterday have had splendid warm clear weather and I made good time built cabin 12 + 14 inside 8 feet high and split and put roof laging on the roof and cut a door in..

Armstrong took this photograph of his cabin by Castle Creek in the late 1890s with his new Kodak camera. On the back he wrote: "Charles Torrey in front of my cabin with our horses and dog." Armstrong lived in a small "house" near Highland from 1880 to 1892. On October 21, 1892, he moved into this new and improved cabin near his Little Jessie claim (soon renamed the Industrial Lode) about two miles south of Highland. A portion of the Little Jessie's tailings pile can still be seen across the road from Armstrong's second cabin site. In the late 1930s the highway department used most of the Little Jessie's tailings as ballast for the new road between Aspen and Ashcroft. (Armstrong's journals)

Was up there this afternoon after the remainder of any tools.. Fine day.. But looks threatening this evening.. Cloudy but warm. Rec'd 20 dollars last evening from Adams of Bowman for potatoes..

Monday Dec 6th 1886

Splendid fine sunshiny day I went to Aspen this morn walked down with McCabe.. I have a boarder here for a few days. He is doing assessment work on the Maggie Bell.. I paid my dues to the Lodge and paid some debts. Paid 3.75 to Freeman & Root interest for Schlag Found Crop & Petes poney in town   the poney was in Blakes Stable charges $3<u>00</u>.. We rode them home got home 4 1/2 oclock..

Tuesday Dec 7th 1886

Got up at peep of day.. Sent 216 lbs potatoes to the dinner stations in Taylor park by the stage bill 3.25 Fine warm morning

Sunday Dec 12th 1886

Fine morning but cold.. Have had stormy weather for the past 3 days about 4 inches of snow fell.. I went to Aspen Thursday eve to Masonic Election for year 87. Stopped all night.. Spent most of Friday looking over town after Crop. found him and got home arround 4 oclock P.M. Bot 70# beef sent it up by stage 70c charges pd.. Ed Higenbothom kept house while I was gone.. We bet each other a big supper that neither of us would take a drink of intoxicating beverage for one year from the 10<u>th</u> of Dec /86. Schlag came down from Conundrum basin and went to town the morning of the 10<u>th</u>

Aspen is very dull. All the topic is the great "Apex trial" at Denver..

Monday Dec 13th 1886

Cloudy morning looks very much like snow.. I had intended to go onto the hill and go to work fixing up the cabin on the Phoenix.. But thought it was going to storm but in the afternoon the sun came out bright and warm put in the day fixing things arround the house.. Will go on the hill tomorrow.. Schlag came from town and went up Conundrum yesterday.

Wednesday Dec 22nd 1886

Went to Aspen this morning walked down.. Snowed a little all day.. Collected 12 dollars due me from "Bush, Bonnell & Blyly" Rode home with Morris the Tenderfoot.. I put in 2 days last week fixing cabin on the Phoenix.. Stopped one night with Besser & Sam Selden. The snow is about 2 feet deep in the park and soft. I went up day before yesterday and did some work and stopped with McCabe the next day was so stormy that I came down home..

Saturday January 1st 1887

New Years morning opened up clear and pleasant.. I went up to the Milk Ranch and relocated the Peru a claim that we did not do the assessment on last year.. I went on the hill last

Tuesday afternoon stopped in Bessers Cabin worked on our cabin Wednesday & Thursday about finished it except daubing.. Came down in the evening snowed quite hard all day.. Found the house full of bums. Pete and Tom Ogburn are packing grub up Conundrum. They are going to work up there all winter.

It is blowing & storming very hard this evening.. I am alone with the dogs & cat. Schlag has gone back to town.. He is no good. he is dead gone on Faro Bank.. Blows in every cent he can get of his own and mine too..

Saturday January 8th 1887

This has been a very cold stormy day. I packed the jacks on the hill Thursday. With stove window door &c for the Cabin got them to Bessers cabin.. Will have to carry them across the Park.. Yesterday morn the new snow was about a foot deep.. And it has been snowing some ever since I must get the Jacks & pony down the river they are liable to be snowed in any time now.. I relocated two claims this year up near the "Milk Ranch" I hear that Robinsons have struck a good thing in the Dick Tunnell if true it will help us as we are on the same contact South of them.. Things are looking up brighter in this section than they have for some time..

Wednesday Jan 26th 87

This has been a clear nice day Very cold morning. I was down town a week ago yesterday.. Schlag came up with me we were calculating to go on the hill but have been put off on account of the stormy weather..

Tom Ogburn and Pete came down from Cary s camp yesterday. They have been up there since the first.. The stage has been blocked most of the time for the last 2 weeks.. The snow is about 3 feet deep here on the level.. Got a letter from home last week all well.

Wednesday Feby 9th 1887

I was taken sick with the Erecyfelas a week ago last Monday and very sick I was for 3 or 4 day.. But am over it now and am feelling very well the hide has been peeling off my face and I have been very carefull about going out much for fear of catching cold. Since Monday we have had fine warm weather.. But it is cloudy and looks favorable for more snow this evening.. Schlag went to Aspen Monday and is still there. Pete came down from the gulch Monday and has been here till this morning he went to town.. Times are extreemly quiet and money very scarce..

Saturday Feby 19th 1887

Clear cold day.. Pete Schlag and myself went on the hill a week ago yesterday to work on the Baer Lode   had very good weather for this time of the year.. We finished and came down last Thursday.. got through just in time as it commenced to storm very hard.. Pete & Schlag went to town yesterday.. I see by the papers that this has been the worst storm of the season east of the Range Last night was very cold..

Wednesday Feby 23rd

Moved up to the Milk Ranch. Stormy cold day

Wednesday Mrch 2nd 1887

I have been for the past week up the gulch about 2 miles working on two claims that we have there Pete & Schlag were with me.. We surveyed them to day We have had fine weather since last Friday which was very stormy & cold.. But since then it has been clear and warm and has taken the snow off very fast. We gave 1/8 of a interest in the 2 claims to Al Werpely for 75 dollars worth of grub leaving Schlag and myself 5/16 apiece and Pete 1/4..

Sunday March 13th 1887

Pete & myself came down from the Milk Ranch Cabin to day.. We have been at work on our claims right along but have not struck miniral yet. We are having splendid weather and the snow is going very fast.. The ground is showing up on all the South hill sides.. And it looks as though spring had come to stay Schlag went to Aspen yesterday.. Times are very quiet in Camp..

Monday April 18th 1887

I have been at work on the claim right along.. Pete quit last Tuesday the 12<u>th</u> and has gone to work for Cap Carey on the Grand Union.. Schlag quite Friday noon sick.. I worked till Saturday night and came down here Sunday.. have been washing &c.. We are having very stormy weather and the roads are very muddy.. We struck Black Lime in the Tunnel last Friday noon   we expect to have 40 or 50 feet more to go to the lead

Tuesday Apr 19th

I went to Aspen to day after the jacks

Monday May 9th 1887

I came down from the claims Saturday evening Schlag & myself are working.. Pete layed off on the Grand Union two weeks ago on account of snow.. And worked 5 days with me.. We had very stormy weather in April but are having splendid weather now. Schlag went to town this morning

Saturday May 14th 1887

Schlag came back from town Wednesday noon.. Thursday I came down home to put in garden &c Schlag is going to continue in the tunnel.. I have been tinkering arround the house the past two days.. Fine weather cold night..

Thursday May 19th 87

I packed 4 Jacks up to the Grand Union Tunnel yesterday loaded with grub.. The trail is pretty good most of the snow is the remains of last winters slides and it bears the jacks up so I had very little trouble.. I took dinner at Cap Careys and examined the tunnel Cap has 4 men at work in it.. Coming back it rained very hard accompanied with lightning and thunder. I got an old coat at the placar cabin or I would have been wet through.. I got some fine specimens at the tunnel. The snow is going very fast.

Sunday June 5th 1887

I finished planting potatoes a week ago last Saturday (28th of May) and finished putting in 1 1/4 acres of oats and Timothy *["herds-grass," introduced via Europe]* last Friday.. Set out cabbage plants this evening

Schlag commenced packing for Cap Carey two weeks ago last Friday and has been at it ever since for Cap.. And other parties.. We have been having splendid clear warm weather and I would like to see it rain now.. I bought me a pair of boots last week paid $6.50 for them

Friday June 10th 1887

Our clear dry weather continues we need rain badly. I have about finished farming as far a putting in seed is concerned.. Schlag is still packing for Cap Carey.. I am irrigating the garden have peas lettuce radishes & beets up.. I was out a little while this evening fishing saw some but they would not bite creek is a little to high yet.

Saturday June 11th /87

I went to Aspen to day rode down on Foggs *[stage driver]* Stage & rode back for $1.00 purchased some things that I needed.. Town rather quiet

Sunday June 12th /87

Schlag was down from the gulch.. Packed some potatoes &c to the Wilton Belle..took dinner here and packed a load of potatoes up to Cap Carey's in afternoon.. This had been a very warm day. We need rain badly..

Friday June 17th 1887

Very warm dry weather I was fishing a couple of hours this fore noon caught 6 trout which made me a good meal at dinner.. I am feeling rather lonesome this evening and kind of disgusted with this place.. Have been here the most of 7 long years and have not made anything yet..

St Johns day..

Friday June 24th 1887

I ought to be in town today the lodge turns out and marches in procession and winds up with a supper & Ball this evening.. But I dont feel able to spare the necessary Five Dollars.. Schlag went to town Monday staid till Thursday took $65<u>00</u> with him which he spent I suppose. Started to work on the claim to day.. Feeling mean as usual.. I have been washing to day.. Weather very warm & dry..

Monday June 27th 1887

I was up to the Jersey Lily this fore noon to see how she looked since Schlag did last years assessment Rainy day which I am glad to see.. Baked bread to day..

Tuesday June 28th 1887

I went to town to day by the Stage Spent #15.40 only 90cts for cigars.. Got back at 3 oclock

Monday July 4th 1887

I went to Aspen to day to see the celebration.. It did not amount to much.. The firemen had a parade and races by the different hose companies for prizes. That was all. I road Crop   Schlag rode Peters pony.. Pete came back with me one splendid moonlight evening..

Thursday July 7th 1887

Yesterday I packed a lot of goods up Conundrum for Hamaker. He took his wife up there and is going to keep house this summer Today I packed 7 jack loads up for Cap Carey..

Sunday July 10th 1887

I went to Aspen yesterday.. Finished packing for Cap Carey Friday evening.. I fixed up the deeds on the Hornellsville Lode for Pete & myself yesterday

Thursday July 14th

Rained quite hard most of the day. Bob Weaver has been here bumming his chuck. Since last Saturday (5 days) today he went on the

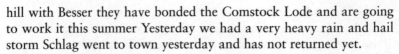

hill with Besser they have bonded the Comstock Lode and are going to work it this summer Yesterday we had a very heavy rain and hail storm Schlag went to town yesterday and has not returned yet.

Saturday July 16th 1887

Very rainy day. rained hard most of yesterday and all night last night. I was up to the tunnel yesterday still in blue lime.. Schlag is making little or no headway   he dont seem to be doing anything.

Sunday July 24th /87

Last Sunday night Schlag came back from town and went up to the tunnel.. Monday & Tuesday I packed timber & mining timbers for John Boland on the Marion Mine.. Wednesday I was at home went fishing for a short time caught 3 nice ones. Thursday packed a lot of stuff for Capt. Carey up to big camp.. Friday I went up to Conundrum basin with Abe Lee to hunt mountain sheep.. stayed till this morning.. did not see a sheep.. But had a couple of splendid baths in the hot springs. We have been having splendid weather for the last 4 or 5 days

Wednesday July 27th 1887

Monday I packed some stuff for Cap Carey in the Afternoon packed timbers up to the A.J.P. mine for him made 2 trips Tuesday packed timbers all day. got along very well with the exception of Crop.. he got to bulling and rolled down the mountain about 100 feet this morning I came home. We are having splendid weather I dug a mess of new potatoes this evening. they are small yet..

Saturday July 30th 87

Was on the hill to day and surveyed a claim for Besser & Bob Wever.. for 5 dollars. rained some. I have a boarder that has been with me since Thursday noon. Mr. Wm Chambers from Texas a friend of Major Pickrell & Cap Carey..

Thursday August 4 1887

I went to Aspen yesterday morning   walked down and stayed in town till 6 oclock walked home in the cool of the evening. fine and pleasant.. Paid our taxes and bought some groceries &c sent for the N. Y. Sun & a waterbury Watch $3.50 The town is very quiet and will be till the R.R. gets in here.

Mrs. Carey Caps wife came up from Aspen last Friday and went up the gulch to stay a while with the Cap..

Tuesday August 23rd 1887

Schlag quit work on the tunnel the 8th and went to Aspen. came back the 20th and went up Conundrum to work on the Jersey Lily &c. Ed Higenbothom is with him.. Ed stopped with me here week before last.. we had a fine time picking berries and Ed killed 5 nice grouse and I caught plenty of trout so we lived high.. I was up and measured the tunnel Sunday it is 164 feet. showed a little galena through the lime.. I was up on the hill yesterday and examined the Rip. *[Rip VanWinkle Mine]* the water is below the drift.. will have to fix it up some as it has caved some. W<u>m</u> Oliphant is boarding with me has been here a week.. he is sick and laying up and doctoring. The Utes have got up a war scare over at Meeker and the state is sending the militia over there the Aspen company went over there last week. and Sherfiff Hooper with 45 men volunteered and have gone to fight the Utes too.. I got a letter from home last week the folks are all well.. I have put up a nice lot of redrasberry jelly & jam the past week.

Thursday August 25th 1887

I went to Aspen yesterday after a few things calculated to come home in the evening but one of the severest rain & wind storms came up that I have seen in Colorado so I

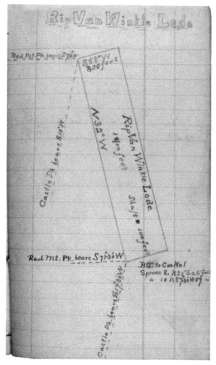

One of Armstrong's journals in the late 1880s contained several of his claim surveys (see map on page vii). His sketch of the Rip VanWinkle Lode is shown above. Of the hundreds of claims surveyed in the Aspen and Ashcroft region, only a few were patented. (Armstrong's journals)

stayed in town all night and came up this morning.. The mountains are white with snow this morn.. There was a bear in sight of the house this morning.. Oliphant saw him.. when I got home he and I went after Mr. Bear. but he had skipped so I did not see him..

Sunday Aug 28th 1887

A cold rainy day. I stayed in the house most of the day went fishing a while in the Afternoon caught 10 trout.. Judge Max Miller & wife and sister and brother in law were here a while to day they were outriding and stopped on account of the rain.. The news from the Ute war is a battle fought on Thursday 3 whiles killed & 7 wounded one of the dead is from Aspen Leitinant of the Aspen militia Folsome by name also one of the wounded is from Aspen.. 3 Utes killed & some hurt.. I went after redrasberries Friday got 5 qts.. they are about gone and I don't expect to get any more this year.. Ed Higenbothom &

Schlag went to Aspen Friday Quite a thunder storm this evening with rain & hail..

This assembly of men called themselves the Aspen Volunteers. In 1887, according to Armstrong, one of them died during a skirmish with a group of Utes who had "fled the reservation" in Utah Territory. During this era, no love was lost for Utes or anyone sympathetic to their cause. (Aspen Historical Society; Colorado Historical Society, Stephen Hart Library)

September 1st 1887

Fine fall day.. Cap Carey and all the hands went to Aspen this morning.. pay day.. Night before last I saw a Lunar Rainbow the first I ever saw It was raining down the gulch and the moon was shining in the east and made a clear distinct rainbow in the North West. I saw a bear day before yesterday at noon on the hill side opposite the house I & W<u>m</u> Oliphant went after him but he saw us and skipped out and we could not find him again

Saturday Sept 17th 1887

Clear nice morning. had a nice shower of rain in the night and the mountains above timber are white with snow. I got up at 5.30 this morning   W<u>m</u> Oliphant left this morning has gone to work on the Little Annie at running the hoister. For the last two days I have been picking & making jelly of Oregon Grapes they are very plenty the hill side opposite the house is blue with them.. Schlag is with Abe Lee up in Conundrum Basin.. I commenced cutting the oats to day they were nicely headed out and will make fine feed if I can cure them good.. Cap Carey s wife came down the gulch to day bound for her house in Texas..

Saturday Sept 24th 1887

Rainy day I raked up a few of the oats yesterday but it rained on them again all night Mr. E. P. Cowan & Mr. Scudder of St Louis went up to the Grand Union Mine day before yesterday came down this morning with Cap Carey. Pickerel & Tom Ogborn. E. P. Cowan appears to be pleased with the property So I guess he will go ahead with the work.. W<u>m</u> Chambers started for Texas this morning. much improved in health & spirits.. says he will be out again next summer..

Sunday September 25th

Raining hard when I got up this morning.. rained most all day

Monday Sept 26th 1887

Clear & cold this morning quite a hard frost.. The mountains above timber are white with snow Ed Higenbothom stayed with me last night.. Rained very hard in the afternoon. Hamaker & wife Major Pickerel & Tom Ogburn & Mc Cormack were here all the after noon in to supper

Tuesday Sept 27th 1887

Clear & Cold this morning.. had a house full last night of Conundrum folks they got away about 9 oclock this morn Very hard frost. ice 1/4 inch thick in the wash tub

Thursday Sept 29th 1887

Got up 5.30 this morning packed some provisions up to the Marion mine Conundrum Gulch.. Fine clear fall day. The Little Jessie lead is looking fine and Cap Carey is feeling very jubelant over it.. There is about 10 inches of mineral full of Grey Copper.

Sunday Oct 9th 1887

I have been on the hill since monday morning working on the Rip Vanwinkle Lode doing assessment work. Ed Higenbothom is helping me.. The claim is looking fine we put a good ladder in the shaft and a platform & new up rights for the windlass also fixed up the cabin in good shape Yesterday morning we waked up with 13 inches of snow on the ground. Ed and I came down to the house last evening very muddy & wet down here but clear & sunshiny this morning

Wednesday Oct 12th 1887

Finished the work for this year on the Rip & left her in fine shape. Came down this evening..

Thursday Oct 13th

Went to Aspen with Ed Higenbothom we walked down.. I collected $6.25 off of S. L. Inom's for his share of the work on the Rip. paid Ed $6<u>oo</u> I came back alone in the evening after dark when I got home

Friday Oct 14th

I went on the hill to day and put a lock on the cabin and covered up the Rip shaft &c.. after dark when I got home Ed was here and had a fire & light

Saturday Oct 15th /87

Ed stayed with me last night.. we went up the road and got the jacks this forenoon dug some potatoes in the afternoon very stormy & cold this evening & snowing quite hard..

Sunday Oct 16th

About 2 inches of snow this morning.. I packed some supplies up to Cap Carey s camp to day   He paid one 10 dollars for that and 2.00 potatoes.. everybody up there feeling well. I got back home about 6 oclock in the evening had a fine day.. but somewhat cold. Eat dinner up there and a good one it was   Kelly is a good cook

Monday Oct 17th 1887

Fixed up the cellar and dug some potatoes in the afternoon fine day..

Tuesday Oct 18th 1887

Dug potatoes most of the day   sold W<u>m</u> Emery 300 potatoes at 1 1/2c per lb and lost some time helping him & Cap Carey to. had a little packing to do and of course I had to help him some   nice day but cool..

Wednesday Oct 19th 1887

Jim Kinney stopped here for S. & B and went over to Italian Mountain this morning to do some assessment work. I was taken with the dirreah last night about 12 oclock & was up most all night and had a bad time.. This morning was quite cold and it has been very chilley all day   I dug potatoes in the after noon.. Schlag came down from Conundrum & went to Aspen this afternoon

Thursday Oct 20th 1887

Very cold morning Thermometer down to 20p [?] I dug potatoes all the time I could. it is so cold and the ground is frozen so that I can not get to work till late.. I let Ed Higenbothom have $5<u>oo</u> on a/c this afternoon clear cool day & clear & cool to night

Monday Oct 24th 1887

Digging potatoes to day.. Got a letter from Roxie ... The folks are all well and anxious to see me but I do not see how I am to get home this winter.. But there is no use of fretting about it I must keep rustling and times will surely improve with me before long.. The RR will be in Aspen by the last of the week and times must be good in this camp this winter if they ever are good.. We are having fine weather but quite cold for this time of year.

Tuesday Oct 25th 1887

Digging potatoes all day.. Schlag came up from town and went up the Gulch.. says the D & R & G will be in Aspen tomorrow so I think I will go to town to see it come in had a little skift of snow this evening.

Wednesday Oct 26th 1887

I walked down to Aspen this fore noon. Walked down to see the R.R. with Fred Bassager   it is about 2 1/2 miles below town.. had a ride on the construction train about 1/4 of a mile. the first ride and the first train of cars that I have been on since March 1881 They are laying about 3 miles per day. The gauge is narrow but the ties are long enough for another rail which they propose to shortly make Standard gauge. The first engine which will be into Aspen is No 83 *[82?]*. This is fine weather for all kinds of work out of doors.. I had the floor fixed and bought me some goods and sent them home by Mr Morris of the Tenderfoot

To reach Aspen from Leadville the Colorado Midland Railway had to construct a grade over the Continental Divide. Here a Colorado Midland engine cautiously chugs across the great 1,084-foot-long timber trestle above Busk Creek on the Leadville side of Hagerman Pass. Meanwhile, the Denver and Rio Grande Railroad construction workers raced toward Aspen from Glenwood Springs through the more receptive topography of the Roaring Fork Valley. On October 27, 1887, the Denver and Rio Grande Railroad reached Aspen first. (Courtesy of Adeline Zupancis Kirsten; Colorado Historical Society, Stephen Hart Library)

Thursday Oct 27th 1887

I stayed in Aspen last night with Sam Selden, we attended the Variety Show, &c. I came home to day got home about noon. fine Sunshiny day. gathered the cabbage and put them in the cellar The R.R. got into Aspen this evening the town people are going to treat the hands with a Barbacue & grand blow out..

Saturday Oct 29th
I dug potatoes yesterday and to day. W<u>m</u> Oliphant stopped here for supper B & Breakfast and went to Aspen to day. They have shut down work on the Little Annie mine.. We are having splendid weather and I am in luck it is so.. so I can get the potatoes out..

Monday Oct 31th 1887
Finished digging potatoes this forenoon and the rest of the day dug & carried in turnips.. Fine weather. W<u>m</u> Oliphant was here for dinner

Wednesday November 2nd
Gathered turnips most of the day yesterday and in the evening went to Aspen to see the celebration in honor to the D & R. G. R.R. The first R.R. in the Camp. and a grand time it was fire works &c.. Governor Adams and about a thousand excursionists came in on the trains 3 trains of coaches all double header..

The wind up of the jubilee was a Banquet & lots of champagne.. I was up all night and walked up this forenoon.. Schlag was here and packed up to do the assessment of the Jersey Lily..

Thursday Nov 3rd 1887
I packed potatoes &c up to Cap Carey s camp to day.. got back just at dusk Splendid weather we are having now day..

Friday Nov 4th
Packed 600# potatoes & turnips up to the climax.. got an order on Hoops & co. for $12<u>00</u> for them..

Saturday Nov 5th
Hauled in the oats this forenoon Packed 300# potatoes & turnips up to Russells got the cash for them 7<u>00</u>. Morris has been plowing for me over in the park part of yesterday & today.. I paid him $10.50 this evening for it

Sunday Nov 6th 1887
I took the gun and went up on the hills to day and located a claim near the Blue Lime Lode for the propose of joining our claims into a groupe.. did not see any game

Tuesday Nov 8th
Elections of County offices to day I went to town and Voted the Republican Ticket except for District Judge the Democrat candidate Jude Rucker is the best man I think therefore I voted for him.

A train came up for us and also brought us back got home about 5 p.m.

Snowed last evening and some today.. but it is about all gone this evening

Thursday Nov 10th 1887
Yesterday washed up my clothes Today got up at day light to get an early start to pack some goods up to Cap Carey s but some of his

men that had been to town wanted breakfast about 10 oclock and so I did not get started up the gulch till about 12 noon.. packed 4 of our animals & 3 of Cap's got back home 7.30 in the dark and was so chilled that I could barely unsaddle.. Gordon stayed with me last night.. John White was elected Sheriff and Thos. Rucker Judge

Saturday Nov 12th 1887

Yesterday the condemed Anarchists at Chicago were hanged.. 4 hanged and 2 to statesprison for life.. I went to Aspen to day rode Petes poney. Aspen is quite lively now the mines are shipping about 20 carloads of ore per day and the R.R. cannot get cars enough to bring in the Goods that are ordered in town.. It looks as though we are going to have boom this winter

I got home after dark.

Monday Nov 14th 1887

Tinkered arround the house to getting ready to go on the hill to do some work on the Phoenix will go up tomorrow I guess

Sunday Nov 20th 1887

I went on the hill last Tuesday worked some on the Phoenix. Friday afternoon I went over on the Difficult slope to survey 2 claims for Besser stayed over there all night in Kelly's cabin finished the claims and got back to the cabin on the Phoenix about 3 in the Afternoon saturday.. in the evening came down home. today I have been choring arround the house

Monday Nov 21st 1887

I packed some coal and rails up to Cap Carey s today. nice weather we are having I got a late start to day and it was after dark when I got home

Wednesday Nov 22nd

I went to Aspen yesterday afternoon. settled with Cap Carey had to allow him $7.40 on the work on the tunnel. but he says he will never ask us to put up again till he can take the pay and of [?] the mine. Cap goes to Denver on the 9.55 Am train to day. I stayed in town all night went to McHenry Johnson the colored pugilist exibition it was pretty good . after that I was out took in all the sights of town till day light got home to day at noon.. Snowed all last night and to day and is still snowing

Thursday December 1st 1887

I have been getting up wood for the house to day. used Old Jerry to pack it. I went on to the hill a week ago to day to finish assessment work on the Phoenix about a foot of snow fell Thursday & Friday and the weather was very cold

I saw the train on the Mid Land R.R. for the first time Monday. looking from the park on the hill.. I finished work Tuesday afternoon and came down home.. yesterday I hunted up the jacks and packed the bedding &c down off the hill. Very fair sleighing to town. Cap Carey's men quit work and came down the gulch last Friday   that finishes the work on the Grand Union for this year

I was 40 years old last Tuesday Nov 29th I was born Nov 29th 1847.. Growing Old! Growing Old!

Sunday Dec 4th 1887

Clear cold morning in the afternoon for a couple of hours. Pete & I packed wood with the jacks   I went to Aspen yesterday rode down with Morris in a very cold snow storm sent my things up with him.. Walked up in the evening with Pete Olsen.. I borrowed one hundred & fifty dollars of Pete to day & paid H.P. Cowenhoven 150⁰⁰ on our debt to him.. bought some groceries & clothing.. got home about 7 oclock in the evening collected 6²⁵ of Mc Clintock for work done on the Rip.. Friday I packed some wood up to the house with Jerry

Tuesday Dec 6th 1887

clear nice day.. Pete & I have been packing wood with the jacks yesterday & to day..

Wednesday Dec 7th 1887

I have been fixing up things arround the house baking bread &c Pete was up Conundrum to the Ingleside Cabin & packed down the bedding & things that Schlag took up there last summer..

Clear nice day.. I got a letter from home yesterday the folks are all well & prosperous.

Thursday Dec 22nd 1887

Yesterday morning the Thermometer registered 20 below zero..

Pete and I went up to the Blue Lime claim the 8th and did the assessment on that and the Pilot Knob.. got through in 6 days and came down and fixed up the Milk Ranche cabin in good shape and got out 200 foot of track for the tunnel and put it in.. went to town day before yesterday after grub got some of Al Hopely. We stayed in town all night and came up yesterday after noon.. have been fixing up the tools &c today as to go to work tomorrow

Sunday January 15th /88

Came down to the house to day   Pete & I have been at work on the Tunnel since the 23 of Dec.. have got in about 30 feet since we commenced. We have been having very cold weather & quite stormy this morning the Thermometer was 16° below Zero and to day is bright & clear. Schlag went to work on the Puzzler mine last Wednesday for wages

We are in black lime and expect to have from 30 to 50 feet to go yet before we strike the contact

Monday February 6th 1888

I have been confined to the cabin since Saturday morning with a bad cold. Pete and I went to Aspen a week ago yesterday. got a supply of grub to do us about 4 weeks worked half a day   Tuesday & all Wednesday and Thursday Friday Pete could not work sick with a bad cold and I went down to the house and washed my shirts &c.. and caught a bad cold myself   we have been having splendid weather for the past month and the snow is about all gone from the hillside where we are working. Fogg took down the bodies of Culver & Nelson that were killed in a snow slide up Pine Creek above Ashcroft last month the bodies were found last week.. Schlag quit work on the Puzzler about a week ago Sunday

The Midland RR have finished the bridge over Maroon and are running into Aspen.

Sunday February 12th 88

A very fine sunshiny day.. Schlag came up here last Tuesday and has been here ever since.. he got rid of the money he earned on the Puzzler mine and has to come here to eat now.. and be in the way.. We are beginning to get along with the work again .. in good shape..

4th March Sunday 1888

It has been stormy so far this month and according to the old sign .. Come in like a lion go out like a lamb.. March ought to end with fine weather.. Pete & myself have been hard at work on the tunnel and are 260 feet in under cover. since we have been here this time we have drove it 96 feet and no signs of a lead yet.. But we will keep at it till we are satisfied. We had company last night Conroy & Lawrence They are going to work on a claim west of the cabin in the hill for Stewart & Co.. They struck out this morning with a back load apiece to climb the hill.

Monday March 5th 1888

The boys could not make it up the hill yesterday so they stayed with us last night and went to town this morning   Pete and I went to town in the afternoon walked down..

Tuesday March 6th

Stayed in town all night did not go to bed. went to Charlie Boyd's comique. it was a good show.. got to Highland at 3 oclock in the Afternoon walked up.. got to camp at 4.30 stormy weather

Wednesday March 7th 1888

Lay arround the house all day resting up got our grub all right..

Thursday March 8th

Worked to day. the tunnel looks promising the formation stands straight now.. Amos Bourguin was up to see us to day. he is pleased with our prospects and thinks we will strike it sure.. I hope he is right.. Stormy day.

Sunday March 11th

We went down to the house to day got some Potatoes & Flour. Fine sunshiny day.. No mineral in the tunnel yet..

Sunday March 18th 1888

Pete and I were down to the house to day.. after some caps & powder.. Warm nice day.. & very pleasant for a walk.. but this evening it is snowing.. We are still working in the tunnel are 280 feet under cover and no mineral yet..

Friday April 6th 1888

Pete and I are still working in the tunnel. last Saturday we went to town came up Monday.. We are having splendid spring weather and the snow is going very fast.. There is nothing new in camp

Thursday April 12th 1888

Very fine spring weather   We were up to the Puzzler and Tenderfoot mines last Monday. worked in the tunnel Tuesday & yesterday were prospecting up at the Blue Lime claim.. Both the Puzzler & Tenderfoot have shut down.. Went to Aspen to day

Friday Apr 13th /88

We came up from town this afternoon   got here to the cabin about 7 oclock in the evening. brought the jacks up with us.. Saw Cap Carey in town he is making preparations to go to work on the Grand Union once the roads are nearly dry between here & town

Saturday April 14th 1888

Pete & I went up and did some work on the Pilot Knob claim to day   opened up the Blue & Short Lime.. splendid nice day..

Sunday Apr 15th 1888

We worked on the Pilot Knob to day fine weather

Monday Apr 16th 1888

We moved down to Highland this afternoon we have run the tunnel in 140 feet this winter. all shooting ground Pete & I did it all. Schlag has layed arround Aspen all winter doing nothing.. We came up from town with 5 men that are going to work on the Grand Union Tunnel.. Rained quite a shower the first of the season

Tuesday April 17th 1888

The boys went up the gulch this morning. Schlag packed the jacks with some stuff for Cap Carey.. Pete went along he is going to dress tools.. I washed my shirts &c and fixed up arround the house .. splendid nice day   The snow is going very fast..

Wednesday April 18th 1888

Roscoe Conklin of New York died 1.50 oclock morning. Age 50 years

I sorted over the potatoes in the house cellar to day   a lot of them were frozen the past winter while there was no body here to keep the house warm

Thursday Apr 19th

I went on the hill to day to look arround   called on the Russel family.. Was in Fred Bassagers workings on the Esxkamo [Eskimo] claim. He is getting a little galena He thinks he has a mine. but it may be nothing but float the same as Russel found on the Famous.. I took dinner with John Nash at Castle City

McCabe is working for Millner on the lease on the Calavaras.. Mc has planted some potatoes already.. I was up to the Rip VanWinkle.. The snow is about 2 1/2 feet deep on the park and very sotton.. Atkinson and Holbrook are working the Little Anna and are getting plenty of mineral.. west of the Porphyry The same vein as the Rip vein.. I came down by the Eva Belle and down the gulch home

Friday April 20th 1888

Fine weather.. I sowed some lettuce and onion seed to day to make garden.. The onions I left in the ground last fall are showing up green and nice. I wrote a letter home yesterday   There is a little travel on the road by here   all of them prospectors

Saturday April 21st 1888

I went to Aspen to day bought some groceries & garden seeds Stayed arround town all day Came up in the evening got home about 7 oclock.. The town is full of Experts on the Apex & Sideline case.. otherwise there is not much going on

Sunday April 22

I went up to the Blue Lime to day   Got home about 6 in the evening

Monday April 23rd 1888

I got up early this morning and went up to the Jersey Lily claim to see if anybody had interfered with it. found it all there and the snow about gone. Got home at 11-30 Ed Higenbothom was here for dinner in the afternoon. Tom Ogborn and Major Pickrel were here stopped a little while and went on up the Gulch.. Schlag came up from town in time for supper

Tuesday April 24th /88

I worked in the garden most of the day in the afternoon. the weather was cold and rainy drizzeling some this evening Ed Higenbothom was here this afternoon with some fine looking ore from the Little Anna. They are shipping some ore now

Friday April 27th 1888

Stormy day the snow was 2 inches deep this morning when I got up.. Schlag went up to Cap Carey's with the jacks packed. Snowed quite hard this afternoon and is still snowing this evening

Saturday April 28th

About 10 inches of new snow this morning. I had a lodger last night a man that is going to work for Cap Carey. had supper & breakfast for which I got $1<u>00</u> Schlag came down to day and went back as far as Engleside [Ingleside?] with a load this evening.. Maj

Pickrel came down from the gulch and went to town   I got 50 - 38 cal cartridges for him for 75c.. John Nash was here to day.. says the Little Anna way up which is good news for me

Tuesday May 1st 1888

Fine day. I have been making garden.. Sunday I caught 4 trout with the fly   I did not expect they would raise but thought I would try them a whirl Hamaker & another man went up to the Grand Union yesterday to work.

Wednesday May 2nd

This fore noon worked some in the garden but the weather was cold.. This afternoon very cold and stormy snowing this evening

Thursday May 3rd

Cold & stormy this morning   I was up to our old cabin this forenoon   In the afternoon worked in the garden. cleared up in the evening. looks as though the storm was over

Saturday May 5th 1888

I rode crop to Aspen this morning and brought him & Petes pony back in the evening.. Very story bad day snowed most of the afternoon I got home late in the evening.

Monday May 7th 1888

Snowed most of the day yesterday & last night about 6 inches fell here.. Cleared up some to day..

Tuesday May 15th 1888

clear warm weather

We rented our shop to a Mr. Flagg & wife & 2 children   they have some cows and are going to keep a dairy & sell milk in town Flagg is to pay us five dollars a month for the use of the Shop and fix it up himself. I was up on the Sheep pasture Sunday and uncovered the Rip Shaft   there is no more water in it than there was last fall.. was over to the Phoenix Cabin found that allright. Visited the Little Anna Mine. they are on the Rip contact are taking out some heavy iron ore that runs well in lead but nothing in silver.. I was to see McCabes Calavaras mine they are taking out some ore that runs as high as 350 ozs. to the ton.. They have but a small streak of it but it is continuous and dipping to the east.. Hamaker took his wife un Conundrum to day I guess she is going to cook for Carey s outfit as they took up a new stove & put a floor in the Cook house.

Wednesday May 16th 1888

I went to Aspen to day walked down & back Not much going on in town I got back in the evening about 9 oclock

Tuesday May 22nd

Sunday had Morse plow the potato ground   yesterday I finished planting them. Ed Higenbothom stayed with me last night.. To day I worked for Judge J. I. Sampson on the tunnel   he is running about a mile above here on the road commenced this morning

Sunday May 27th 1888

About 6 inches of snow on the ground this morning. I did not get up till very near 8 oclock feeling pretty tired.. have worked hard on the tunnel the past 5 days.. washed some shirts and cleaned up to day. snowing most of the time all day. Schlag went to Aspen last evening

Friday June 8th

I finished work on the tunnel for Judge Sampson last evening making 15 days I have been at work on it at 3.50 day making $52.50.

powder & c   <u>2.50</u>

55.00

Saturday June 9th 1888

I went to Aspen this morning   walked down.. stayed in town all day. nothing going on I drank considerable beer more than I needed but not enough to get off

Sunday June 10th 1888

I stayed in Aspen all night did not go to bed at all. went to the show and it was about 1 oclock when it let out so I set up till day light. took several cocktails in the morning which did me no good.. So I just came to the conclusion to not touch any intoxicating drinks for a year from to day

I walked up home this forenoon got home about noon. very warm day have not felt good all day.. the evil effects of beer and getting no sleep all night.

Monday June 11th 1888

I sowed and harrowed in about an acre of oats to day which about finishes the farming business for this spring..

Tuesday June 12th 1888

I was on the hill all day prospecting arround the Phoenix and looking over the hill to see what people are doing very warm day..

Wednesday June 13th 1888

I was up to the Tenderfoot Ranche and came down over the hill by the Blue Lime prospecting arround saw nothing new..

Thursday June 14th

Washed some of my duds to day was out fishing a short time in the afternoon caught one trout   The creek is to high to do much fishing.. Travel is very dull and there is not much sign of a boom at present.. It seems to be the same song of every summer.. It is might discouraging

Friday June 22nd 1888

Monday morning I went on the hill to survey a claim for Sam Martin. The ground is thickly covered with young Aspen and it was very slow work and it rained most of the day so we could not finish it I stayed all night with them but Tuesday it rained all the forenoon so I came down home altered a stud jack in the afternoon that Schlag bought a few days ago.. He died Thursday morning.. Wednesday I finished surveying for Martin surveyed two claims charged him 12 dollars.. Yesterday I washed some of my duds and puttered arround the house all day.. today I am baking and fussing arround

Thursday July 5th 1888

Have been doing nothing much to day   caught a mess of trout this evening. had them for supper.. I went on the hill a week ago yesterday and have been doing some work on the Phoenix and prospecting arround over the hill.. last Friday I was on Aspen Mountain look the mines over.. The first time I have been there in 4 years.. There has been a great change in that time.. Night before last I came down to the house and went up Conundrum with Cap Carey   yesterday we spent looking the A.J.P. mine over and also the Grand Union Tunnel. The Grand Union Tunnel is in 670 feet they struck a large Cavern filled with water a week ago today.. The water came out of the tunnel with such force that it washed away the dump track water wheel & came near taking the Black Smith shop.. I was in the cave yesterday it is about 10 feet wide & I dont know how long & as high as a person can see.

The Republican Convention at Chicago nominated Ben Harrison of Indiana for president & Levi P. Morton of N.Y. State for Vice President June 25th 88 on the 8th ballot..

I Recd a letter from home dated June 17th   All well..

Friday July 20th 1888

Pete Olsen & I came down from Conundrum basin to day.. we went up last Saturday & stopped with Abe Lee had a good time bathing in the hot springs & hunting   Pete killed a sheep   we saw some deer & mountain sheep

Saturday July 21st

we went to town to day   Rainy

Sunday July 22nd

Have been fixing up preparatory to going down the river on a prospecting trip with Russell & George MaGee on Elk Creek

Monday July 23rd

We did not get off to day Russell was not ready.. So I went fishing in the afternoon   Caught a fine mess   Rained considerable to day

Tuesday July 24th 1888

We go started on our prospecting trip to day. Howard Russell George Magee Pete Olsen & myself   We left Aspen about 2.30 oclock stopped 15 miles down the river for the night very poor feed for the horses

Wednesday July 25th 1888

Got up early this morning   took dinner at the Valley House kept by Dr. White. Russell's step brother. I paid him $1.00 for Pete & myself.. this place is across the Roaring Forks from Carbondale. camped for the night on 3 mile creek   poor feed for the horses

Thursday July 26

Up early and got into Glenwood Springs about 9 oclock A. M Stopped about 2 hours got 9 dollars worth of grub   saw some of our old friends & had a good time. In the afternoon it was very dusty & hot got into New Castle city about 4 oclock. Struck some more friends & had some beer Got into camp about 4 miles up Elk Creek camped in Nelson & Piersons pasture   Nelson came after us and was going to drive us out but when we told him we were prospecting he gave us permission to stop all night

Friday July 27th

Up early & got into camp about 9 oclock where we are going to prospect   I went fishing in the afternoon but did not have very good luck.. Elk Creek

Saturday July 28th 1888

Moved camp up on the mesa to day. fine open country up here splendid grass and parks

Sunday July 29th 1888

We saddled up this morning and road over to prospect the land that we came down to see   It is iron hematite and I dont think it will amount to anything Rainy day

Monday July 30th

Prospecting to day and we have come to the conclusion that there is nothing here

Tuesday July 31st

We road out north of camp 6 or 8 miles to look at the countrey.. saw plenty of signs of Elk & Bear but saw none saw one deer which Pete shot at but missed. I killed several grouse with my revolver..

Wednesday August 1st 1888

We broke camp this morning and moved down on Elk Creek caught a good mess of trout in the evening

Thursday August 2nd

Moved out early this morning got into Glenwood Spring   In the Afternoon stopped a short time and pulled out for Four mile creek for camp   got in late and it came on to rain so I put in a miserable night

Friday August 3rd

Got started in good season this morning   camped this evening on the ridge between Rock & Sopris Creeks

Saturday Aug 4th 1888

Camped on Snow mass creek to night   caught a mess of trout

Sunday Aug 5th 1888

Got home to day and am glad of it..

Wednesday August 15th

Pete and I have been doing assessment work in the Blue Lime & Pilot Knob claims   came down home to day.. rainy weather we are having now..

Thursday Aug 16th

Went to Aspen to the Firemen Tournament. Pete, Schlag, and myself

Friday Aug 17th

Came home this evening from town

Saturday Aug 18th 1888

I had to go to town to day went down in the afternoon

Sunday Aug 19th

I got home from town this morning.. I drank a little to much to feel good so I have come to the conclusion to not touch any liquor for the remainder of the year

Monday Aug 20th 1888

I went after redrasberries to day picked about two gallons and caught a nice mess of trout beside. Got home after dark.

Tuesday Aug 21st

I went on the hill to day. surveyed the Comstock Tunnel for the boys got $4.50 for it. It rained very heavy this afternoon and this evening the mountains are covered with snow. I got home after dark..

Wednesday Aug 22nd

Canned & preserved some berries to day and took time easy arround the house

Thursday Aug 23rd 1888

Packed some grub on the hill for Bill Emery & Chas. Miller. got back about 2 oclock   Schlag went up Conundrum with most of the jacks in the Afternoon packing a lot of women & children up to the hot springs.

Friday Aug 24th

I went after berries to day got about 2 gallons

Saturday August 25th

Canned my berries this forenoon & caught a mess of trout and put in the rest of the day hunting jacks.. Fine nice weather

Thursday Aug 30th 1888

I packed up to the Placar Cabin & commenced work on the Jersey Lily Lode to do the assessment for this year

Sunday September 2nd

I came down last evening from the Jersey.. picked a few berries on the way down   Cap Thatcher and Co Rhett stopped with me all night.. At 12 oclock Sam Selden Loney Nugent & Fred Bassager woke me up and we stayed up till morning playing cards and drinking They staid with me all day to day started for town this evening..

Saturday Sept 8th 1888

I finished the work on the Jersey Lily this forenoon & packed down home this evening   Fine nice weather we are having

Friday Sept 14th 1888

I finished cutting & putting up the timothy *["herds-grass"]* to day there is about 1/2 tons of fine hay. We are having splendid weather now

Saturday Sept 15th

Stopped in town to day

Monday Sept 17th

Left town this morning at 3 AM   Came up home over the hill to take a view of the mines got home about 2 P. M.

Tuesday Sept 18th

I went to town this afternoon   got back home after dark in the evening   rained quite hard to day

Monday Oct 1st 1888

I went to Aspen last Thursday evening and did not get home till yesterday   Have leased the Rip for 2 years 20 percent royalty on all ores sold and a bond for $40,000. They do 1000 dollars worth of work the first year   Are to do 20 shifts of work 3 men each, each month in the year

Thursday Oct 4th 1888

Cold rainy morning   the clouds are hanging very low. the snow is about 4 inches deep on the mountains. Tuesday I commenced to cut the oats but it commenced raining and has rained more or less ever since yesterday. I washed my clothes and set arround the house all day forming good resolutions

Tuesday Oct 5th 1888

Rainy cold morning   in the afternoon I took Bear and the gun and went up on the mountains west of the house saw 2 deer but they were so far a way that I did not hit them after shooting at them twice. . got home at dark.. tired.

Saturday Morning Oct 13th

I came up on the hills day before yesterday to finish the assessment work on the Phoenix claim.. worked at sinking the shaft about 100 feet above the tunnel   Ed Higenbotheom & Hank Stuck are stopping at the cabin with me They are doing some assessment We are having splendid weather

Tuesday Oct 16th 1888

I came down off the hill this morning and went up to the Tenderfoot Ranche and surveyed two claims for Jack Lawson charged him $10<u>00</u> for it.. a stand off..

Wednesday Oct 17th 1888

Pete went up to the Phoenix with me to day..

Tuesday Oct 23rd

Pete & I came down off the hill this afternoon sunk a shaft 16 feet on the claim   are in the foot wall short lime

Thursday Oct 25th

Pete & I went to town yesterday and came up this afternoon Snowed very hard to day

Saturday Oct 27th

Cleared up to day it has been storming most of the week I wrote a letter home to day.. have been fixing to go deer hunting this first of the week down the River

Monday Oct 29th 1888

We started on our hunt this morning & camped on West Sopris Creek this evening about a 23 mile drive

Tuesday Nov 6th 1888

Election day Pete & I are camped on the West fork of Muddy creek We have had no luck so far stormy most of the time so far on the trip

Saturday Nov 24th 1888

We got home this evening about 7 oclock have 7 1/2 deer and good big ones, killed 10 on the trip Eat up the small ones

Tuesday Dec 11th

I have been busy ever since I got back home packing jacks and fixing up arround the house. Pete and I went to town Saturday evening got home yesterday afternoon We are having splendid weather the roads are dusty & the South hill sides are bare of snow

January 1st 1889

Pete. Schlag and myself had a contract to run 40 feet in a tunnel for John Robinson   finished Christmas Eve and Pete & I went to Aspen Christmas day got back Friday.,. spent our money and were drunk of course To day I quite drinking in Aspen any intoxicating drinks for this year any way..

Yesterday I earned $5<u>00</u> surveying To day I have been in the house all day.. alone and it has been somewhat lonesome. The mercury stood 2° above Zero this morning It has been a very clear cold day..

Sunday January 6th 1889

Clear fine day.. I have been at home all day.. Pete went to Beloit Hill this afternoon to work with Chas Miller on the Hesse Tunnel for an 1/8 interest   Last Thursday Pete & I were over to Tourtlotte Park to see the last big strike   it is in the Edison Mine They have sunk 20 feet in good pay and are still finding mineral.. Pete Lonergan is 50 feet deep in the new shaft on the Rip Van Winkle   they find some galena scattered through the black lime..

The 2nd I filed on the N. E. 1/4 of Sec 2 T 11 S R 85 W cost me $3.00. also paid the P.O. Box sent $1.00 for last 1/4

Armstrong surveyed claims in Tourtelotte Park, a small mining settlement on Aspen Mountain. Nothing remains of this small camp, except a ski run with the same name. (Aspen Historical Society)

Wednesday Jan 16th 1889

Eclipse of the moon this evening I am setting up to watch it. We have been having stormy weather for the past week.. but very little snow falls.. I have been at home alone most of the time since Pete went on the hill. No much news only they keep opening up new bodies of good mineral on Tourtlotte Park.. I hope they will get into the Sheep Pasture this winter with good mineral.

Friday January 18th 1889

I went up on the sheep pasture to day to see how they are getting on with the Rip.. they are down 70 feet and the rock is showing considerable galena. I also relocated the Baer Lode We did not do the assessment work on it last year I claimed 500 feet West &^ 1000 feet East the snow is about 3 feet deep on the park.. the water is troubling them some on the Rip.. I eat dinner with McCabe and supper with Con Brennan.. Burt Fuller & Ed Huges are stopping in over Phoenix Cabin..

Monday Jan 28th 1889

We are having splendid weather clear and the sun shines warm and pleasant.. The sleighing is fine.. I am stopping here at the house alone. I was in town Saturday rode down with Fog and walked back. Business seems to be good. They are striking good mineral all over Tourtlottes Park and every claim in that section is working or about to be worked. I got a letter from home last week.. The folks are all well.. I answered it at once.

Armstrong "relocated" his Baer Lode claim (above) on January 18, 1889. Notice that Armstrong listed himself as one of the four "Locators" of this claim, thus his attention to details. On August 30, 1889, he sold his interest to Ike Baer, but wrote that "when I pay him my share of 1/4 of the expense of getting the patent he is to deed 1/4 back to me" [see August 30, 1889]. Armstrong's sketch of the Baer Lode appears with his hand-drawn section map (above) on which he marked the location of his cabin in Section 18. The Baer Lode, however, is located on Richmond Hill (see Map V), about a mile northwest of his second cabin site. (Armstrong's journals)

Sunday Feby 10th 1889

Splendid weather we are having teamsters have to use waggons on the road.. Tom Ogburn came up here the 29th of January and has been here with me till yesterday morning   he went back to town we have been to most of the good claims on the hill. He has never been to the mines on the lime belt and so I was showing him arround.. Pete Olsen quit on the Hesse Tunnel came down last Thursday   went to Aspen Friday has not got back yet. M. R. was here with me saturday evening the 2nd

Monday Feby 11th 1889

Wrote to Cal Denman to day Snowing

Sunday Feby 17th 1889

Very cold Stormy day.. It has been storming most of the week.. Pete & Tom Ogburn have gone to work on the Etcetera Mine for an 8 interest in the base and 2 dollars a day a piece & board.. they went up day before yesterday.. The Thermometer shows 10° above Zero now 2.45 P.M. & a fine snow falling

Friday Febuary 22nd

I went to Aspen yesterday   walked down stopped in the town all night and got up at 7 this morning and came up home with Mr Morris   fine weather we are having now. But for the past week or ten days it has been very cold and stormy..

I got a supply of grub this time

A few nineteenth-century miners had some fun skiing down an incline on a snow-covered wagon road in Independence, far above Aspen. Of course there was no future in such winter frivolity. (Aspen Historical Society)

Saturday Feby 23rd 1889

I went up to the Ectectra Mine to day to see Pete & Tom and take their mail up to them.. The mine is looking fine considerable lead ore they are taking out.. but it is a mean place to work a tunnel and incline and then a drift

Sunday Feby 25th 1889

Mrs. Russel and Miss Tyler stopped here last night   they were on the way home from town and got belated..

Monday Feby 26th 1889

Fine day thawing considerable   Torrey Nugent was here to day, he has been on the hill looking at Bill Emerys claim to see about a contract to sink a shaft 75 feet deep.. Mrs. R. went to town this morning   stopped in to see me..

Tuesday March 5th 1889

Was up on the hill to day and surveyed the Baer Lode. Ed Higenbothom helped me.. we had a tough time at it the snow is deep and soft and very hard to get through   Splendid weather we are having

Saturday March 16th /89

I was in town last Monday came up home Tuesday.. Wednesday set arround the house Thursday went on the hill and helped Fred Bassager put in air pipe on the Escanmo   Friday helped him in the forenoon came home in the afternoon. Today I washed some shirts took a bath and stopped in the house most of the day. Snowing this evening..

Wednesday March 20th 1889

Spring begins today   Warm and bright. snowed about an inch last evening   Pete got him a new rifle yesterday. Colt repeating 22 cal target gun it is a dandy. we were shooting with it all yesterday fore noon. cost him 20 dollars.

Monday April 8th 1889

Splendid weather we are having   the roads are dry and getting dusty. I sowed some lettuce seed to day.. and salted the venison that is left about 110 lbs.. Abe Lee was here for dinner and went up Conundrum Gulch   Tom Ogburn and Major Pickerel were here this afternoon and went up on the gulch to commence work   Day before yesterday I caught 21 trout with a fly.. This has been the finest winter that we have had since I have been in Colorado..

Wednesday April 10th 1889

Got up 6 this morning. Snowing very hard.. Has been a stormy day but warm.. Abe Lee took dinner here.. he did not go above Carey s camp.. he found snow is to soft and it is dangerous up the gulch on account of snow slides.. so he came down again and went to town.. Schlag went to town this afternoon.. he is getting quite a lot of packing to do.. but I dont know what he does with the money.. I dont see any of it..

Thursday April 18th 1889

Started in to snowing yesterday and it still keeps at it it has snowed about 6 inches   Abe Lee came up here day before yesterday and went back to town to day   he intended to stay here several days and prospect up the gulch but the storm stopped him. I have been arround the house. baking pies &c.

Sunday April 21st 1889

Pete & I were up Sandy Gulch to day.. I surveyed a tunnel for Mr. Hadly.. get $5.00 got 1.50 cash and will get the rest the first time he goes to town.. We were in Aspen yesterday.. Today have been working in the garden some. I caught 4 small trout this evening got a letter from home saturday the folks are all well and Roxie is to be postmistress of the City of Arkport..

Sunday August 11th 1889

I have been helping some surveyor on the hill for the past 3 days we surveyed the Baer Lode for a patent.. Pete and I have been working on the claims all the months of May June & July   run the Blue Lime Tunnel in 40 feet and sunk 20 feet in a shaft on the Phoenix and timbered 36 feet   Pete went to work for Major Pickeral the later part of July for wages.. Schlag has been running the jacks all summer packing for different parties. I have picked up a few dollars doing a little surveying.. No of my marlin Rifle 2655

ECONEMY/ IS/ WEALTH

Saturday Aug 24 1889

milk Sugar Flour Beef Potatoes Butter 10lb Sugar Dog Meat See Neuberry see Dave Brown see Floyd *[all crossed out]*

Aug 24

Neuberry promised to exclude the conflict with the Blue Lime & Pilot Knob from his survey in making application for a patent

Sept 6 [inserted later]

P of scissors. Dog Meat Overalls

Location Blanks

coffee tea sugar Butter Salt Pepper Overalls closet paper Beef Pens

Sept 26 [inserted later]

see George Rice see Jim Downing see Floyd

Friday August 30th 1889

I walked to Aspen this fore noon   took down a nice lot of trout for Sam Selden and for Lily. I took supper with Sam and had several drinks with him   I rode "Poor" up home got home about 12 oclock at night. saw Dave Brown about getting our claims patented   he is to let me know in 4 days time.. Made a deed to Ike Baer for my interest in the Baer Lode and when I pay him my share of 1/4 of the expense of getting the patent he is to deed 1/4 back to me. Schlag did the same thing. Ed Higenbothom was a witness.

Sunday September 1st 1889

Toney Nugent and Tom Ogburn took supper and stopped all night and to breakfast here. I went up the creek fishing this afternoon caught 26 nice trout.. I have a fine trout rod cost 4 dollars it has an ash but and lancewood preond [?] second joint and two tifs [?].. C. C. Morgan gave it to me. I lent him my other rod to take over to Taylor River and he busted it up pretty bad. so he go me another one.

Monday Sept. 2nd 1889

Dave Brown and Mr. Mc Farlan came up this morning to look at some of our claims.. I offered him 1/4 interest in them if he would get them patented   he seemed to be very well pleased with them but did not say that he would do it or not but wanted me to call at his office when I came to town.

Wednesday Sept 4th 1889

I went up on the sheep pasture this morning with John Miner to look at the Phoenix   he wanted to take a look at it with a view of leasing it.. I got back home about 4 oclock. The Little Annie is showing some 5700 oz ore. Little Jim MaGee has a lease on it and says he is going to ship mineral at once.. There was a big forest fire on Aspen Mountain yesterday afternoon   came mighty near burning Tourltottes Park out.. But by hard work they go it stopped before much damage was done.

Thursday Sept 5th

I was up to the Blue Lime to day running out a line to see about how to connect the group of claims.

Saturday Sept 7th 1889

I went to Aspen to day rode Croppie.. Got 2.50 of Schlag

Sunday Sept 8th 1889

Stayed with Sam Selden last night and stopped in town most all day spreeing arround   got home about 9 oclock in the evening

Monday Sept 9th

Fine morning I am at home all alone but am feeling pretty good considering as I spent foolishly for drinks &c $7.50 cash money that I needed. It seems though that I never will learn anything. I saw Dave Brown but he wants 3/8st interest in our claims to get them patented and I do not think I will give any such interest. 1/4 is to much..

Tuesday September 10th 1889

John Boland stopped with me last night and to breakfast. I moved some grass and fished a little. This has been a very nice day..

I do not spend any more money this year for bargoods and do not take any intoxicating drinks for the remainder of this year. Sohelpme

Friday Sept 13th 1889

Rained very hard last night and this morning the mountains above timber line were white with snow. Rained more or less all day. Ed Higenbothom has been stopping with me for several days.. sobering up he has been drunk for a month or more. Schlag packed up a load for B. Clark Wheeler to day and brought down a load of ore from the Little Annie mine. I have been arround the house all the week cutting grass and loafing.. Washed my clothes to day..

Saturday Sept 14th 1889

Rained very hard last night and kept it up at intervels all day.. I cut some grass between showers.

Sunday Sept 15th 1889

I got up shortly after day this morning took my rifle and went up Conundrum about 3 miles hunting but did not see any game. "Bear" killed a woodchuck.. In the afternoon I raked and cocked up what hay I had cut. Very fine day but a heavy frost last night froze about 1/4 inch of ice in the water barrel on the poarch..

Monday Sept 16th 1889

Got up earley this morning fussed arround this house all the fore noon in the afternoon cut grass.. had four experts here for dinner They were up Conundrum to look at the Phoenix Mine and went on the hill to look at the Rip Vanwinkle.. Splendid day

Thursday Sept 19th 1889

I went to town to day   walked down and back. Put the location certificate of the Mineral Belt claim on record which took $1.50. Town seems quiet   I got home 9 in the evening.

Friday Sept 20th 1889

I went on the hill to day to see what was going on. Schlag and Jim are packing lumber off of Richmond Hill to the Little Annie Mine for a boarding house   they have the machinery moved down to the west shaft and partly put up . This has been a rainy day..

Saturday Sept 21th 1889

Caught 20 nice trout to day   Rainy fogy day am alone this evening

Sunday Sept 22nd 1889

Arround the house most of the day

Monday Sept 23rd

Snowing quite brisk this morning. I took the rifle and went up back of the Jersy Lilly prospecting and hunting saw the fresh track of a buck and a mountain lion.. I killed two fine grouse all the game that I saw.. Snowed very hard in the afternoon and is still snowing this evening.. Looks very much like winter..

Tuesday Sept 24th 1889

Cold this morning.. I fixed up arround the house and stayed in doors most of the day so it was cold and stormy all day.. The ground is white with snow this evening

Wednesday Sept 25th 1889

Ice 1/2 inch thick in the water barrel this morning. I was out in the forenoon with the gun but did not see any game   Wrote a letter home this evening

Thursday Sept 26th 1889

I went to Aspen this morning walked down   calculated to get back this evening but did not

Friday Sept 27th 1889

I stopped in town last night.   Same Selden Tony Lugent Fred and I were arround town till 3 oclock in the morning   I slept with Sam and took breakfast with him. I stopped in town till evening.. to see Ben Pierce's funeral.. There was a fine turnout.. the firemen Patriotic Sons of A. O. U. W. beside lots of people in carriages. I got home about 8 in the evening.

Saturday Sept 28th

Dug some potatoes and staffed arround the house most of the day

Sunday Sept 29th 1889

Dug the balance of the potatoes and caught a mess of trout this evening

Monday Sept 30th
I went up to the Blue Lime to day and located a claim on the porphyry to connect the two groups of claims making 5 claims in all.. Very fine weather we are having.

Tuesday Oct 1th 1889
Gathered the reutabagas in the garden this forenoon   in the afternoon went up to the falls of Conundrum and fished down caught six nice trout

Wednesday Oct 2nd 1889
I struck out about 9 oclock this morning and went to the summit of the Red Mt Peak opposite the house   got up there about 1 oclock built a monument about 4 feet high.. killed 2 grouse saw lots more beside saw 3 deer.

Thursday Oct 3rd 89
Walked to Aspen to day and back took some trout down to Sam Selden

Friday Oct 4th 1889
Was prospecting up Engleside creek this afternoon washing for gold.. but did not find any   rode Crop and took up some tools

Saturday Oct 5th 1889
Worked on the trail to the Jersey Lily.. am doing assessment Rode Crop and took a lunch along.. located the Old Timer Lode

Sunday Oct 6th
At home all day.. Splendid weather we are having

Monday Oct 7th
Worked on the trail

Tuesday Oct 8th
Worked on the trail.. Bear killed a grouse on our way up..

Wednesday Oct 9th
Worked on trail. Nice day but storming this evening

Wednesday Oct 10th
At home all day rustling arround..

Friday Oct. 11th 1889
I got up 1/2 past 4 this morning   road up to Pearl Pass by 10 oclock. and surveyed claims for Ellithorpe called the Browmide. Snowed some and was very cold. I got home about 8 in the evening got $1000 for the job

Saturday Oct 12th
Went to Aspen this afternoon   calculated to get home but did not.

Sunday Oct 13th
Got home about noon very cold and stormy this afternoon..

Monday Oct 14th

I went up on the hill this afternoon to see if any body was working on the Rip.. Nobody there nor any signs of work   some of the boys have been taking some of the timber. I hunted them up and told them to return them.. The Little Annie is working in good shape and will make a mine with out doubt.. Everybody on the hill is feeling good over the prospects

Tuesday Oct 15th

Republican Primaries to day.. to elect delegates to County Convention.. I was up to the Blue Lime to day killed 2 grouse

Wednesday Oct 16th 1889

I took the gun and went up on the range between here and Maroon.. saw lots of grouse and killed one.. saw some deer sign but no deer.. saw a mountain lion but could not get a shot at him

Thursday Oct 17th

I went to town this afternoon to attend ledge work in the M.M degree. After lodge I got in with Sam Selden and Bush bumming arround town and did not get to Bed all night..

Friday Oct. 18th 1889

Stopped in town all day bumming arround

Saturday Oct 19th

Stopped with Tony Nugent last night at the hotel   Came home with Fogg on the stage.. Schlag and Jim got back from Brush Creek this evening..

Sunday Oct 20th

I was up to the Blue Lime after some stuff to get assayed.. Pete was down town and went back up the gulch to day..

Monday Oct 21st

I started to go up to the Jersey Lily this morning to do some work but it snowed so hard that I came back and did my washing. Received a letter from home this evening.. Aunt Betsy died a short time ago of apoplexy.. Roxie is very anxious that I should come home.. Folks well as usual.

Rained and snowed most of the day.

Tuesday Oct 22nd

Staffed arround the house most of the day. Another Rail Road is being surveyed up the Gulch to Ashcroft. They got as far as our house to day..

Wednesday Oct 23rd

I went up to the Jersey Lily to day and worked on the trail .. Fine day..

Thursday Oct 24th

Snowed and stormed so I did not go to work

Located about four miles above Armstrong's cabin on Castle Creek, Ashcroft (also known as Castle Forks City and Chloride) rivaled Aspen in 1880.

By 1889 Ashcroft's summer population had dropped below seventy-five. Its beautiful high-alpine setting, however, remains one of nature's jewels. (Courtesy of Ralph Kemper; Denver Public Library, Western History Department)

Friday Oct 25th
Went up to the Jersey and did a little work to day

Saturday Oct 26th 1889
I went up to Aspen this afternoon.. Signed an option on the Ranch to Duke Mayham for 6000 dollars for 40 days. Also leased the Phoenix to B. Clark Wheeler for 16 months and a bond for 6000 dollars   Paid Slavens $5.00 a/c

Sunday Oct 27th
stopped in town all night   did not go to bed at all   was in town all day to day

Monday Oct 28th
Came home with Pete to day   got home in the evening

Tuesday Oct 29th
The ground is covered with snow this morning and it is still storming. Pete went on the hill to shown Wheeler the Phoenix.. I wrote to Pete Lonengan to day to notify him that the lease on the Rip Van Winkle was forfeited

Wednesday Oct 30th
I went on the hill to day to see what was going on. B. Clark Wheeler had put some men to work on the Rip. but I think he will have to quit I located a small *[for them ?]* of ground lieing between the Etcetera Alma Baer and the Phoenix Lodes. Snowed very hard this afternoon on the hill and there was about 8 inches of snow on the park

Thursday Oct 31st

Stopped in the house all day. Baked some light bread. Pete went hunting killed a rabbit and that was all   Very cold day for the time of year

Friday November 1st

Clear sunshiny day but a cold wind. Went up Conundrum after some tools that I had using on the Jersey Lily..

Saturday Nov 2nd

Pete & I went to Aspen this morning got back at dark. Election is lively in town. I got $5_00_ from John White. I bought pr boots and some clothing   Has been rather a fine day.

Tuesday Nov 5th

County election. I had to go to Tourtlotte Park to vote   went to Aspen from there   Election is lively

Wednesday Nov 6th

Stopped in town all night and all day to day

Thursday Nov 7th 1889

Stopped in town all day to day waiting to fix up the Bond for a deed on the ground in conflict between the Patti and the Blue Lime claims   fixed it all right

Friday November 8th

I started for home this forenoon about 10-30 oclock.Got home about 12-30 fine day and the roads were rather muddy from melting snow.. The democrats gained the day on the elections with the exception of John White sherriff and the Assessor Tom Cunningham. Election is over now and I propose to rustle arround and get a little money and get out of debt.. I have been fooling arround and taking a little more beer than was absolutely necessary and I am going to do different for the rest of the year

Saturday Nov 9th 1889

Fine sunshiny morning   the weather seems to be settled for some time to come cut wood to day

Sunday Nov 10th 1889

In the house most of the day. Some men are stopping in our cabin that are going to cut mining timber down the creek   moved in to day I wrote to Wood bros Denver about getting the Rip patented   Schlag is packing some stuff over to the head of Taylor river left here at noon. Snowing this evening

Monday Nov 11th 1889

About 6 inches of new snow this morning cold and blustery all day.. Pete went to town to day got back this evening.

Thursday Nov 14th 1889

About five inches of snow here and good sleighing all the way to town.

Clear and cold today. I have been in the house all day.. have a bad cold but it is some better this evening   Abe Lee stopped here last night he has been up the gulch and packed his goods to town for the winter.

Thursday Nov 21st

I went to Aspen Monday and got back last evening. It has been snowing and blowing for the past 2 days and the storm is not over yet I guess.. Got a letter from home yesterday. Folks all well

Friday Nov 22nd

Pete & I took Old Jerry and moved up to the Blue Lime Cabin to do some assessment for Jim Deroning   Fine day

Saturday Nov 23rd 89

Snowed about 8 inches last night. We started to work. I am not feeling well.

Sunday Nov 24

Snow about 10 inches deep this morning.. Snowed all day.. I am pretty sick ache all over hardly able to get out of bed.

Monday Nov 25th

Snowing.. Set in the cabin all day feeling bad.

Tuesday Nov 26

Clear nice day about 2 feet of new snow We broke trail to our work and finished it.

Wednesday Nov 27

Moved down home to day. fine day I am feeling a little better not nice

Thursday Nov 28th 1889

Thanksgiving day and a fine sunshiny day it is   I was in the house all day not feeling very well. Pete went to Aspen this morning.. I put in the day setting by the stove and talking with Joe Cambell and old Mr. Neuffman the people that are stopping in our cabin next door. John Boland came in about 8 in the evening and had supper and stopped with me the night

Friday Nov 29

I am 42 years old to day. A good time for good resolutions which I have made and propose to keep for the coming year. Splendid fine sunshiny day. Sad news to me though to day. L. J. W. Vary one of nature's noble men died this morning about 7 oclock of heart disease. He was elected county Treasurer this fall but did not go into office. He is an old timer in the camp and has rustled with the rest of us but has never been able to catch on till lately he has been able to get out of debt and a little ahead.. I dont see where they will find a man to fill his place among masons here   He was Grand Master here and had been several times before and was the best posted and pleasentist officer I ever saw. He was one of my best friends and it hurts to loose him.. but such is life.. "Gods will be done." Pete and Schlag got home this evening.

Sunday Dec 1st
I went to Aspen today to attend Varys funeral   It was the largest turnout what ever attended a funeral in Aspen   The Masons and Knights Templer were about 200 strong beside about 1/2 a mile of vehickles..

Tuesday Dec 3rd
I got home from Aspen to day   I had some business in town that kept me..

Thursday Dec 5th.
I rode down to town with Fogg.. went down to see about the bond for a deed on the Blue Lime got it and put it in Slaven & McEvoys safe   came back with Fogg

Saturday Dec 6th
Wrote home to day Pete & Schlag. Have been packing supplies up to Chas Miller to day.. Rained some to day   we have having very warm weather for this time of year.

Saturday Dec 7
Raining and snowing all day.. Pete and I packed up preparatory to moving up to the Milk Creek Ranch to do the assessment on the Leavenworth & Hornellsville claims

Sunday Dec 15th 1889
Pete & I came down from the claims.

Monday Dec 16th
We went to Aspen to day

Tuesday Dec 17th
Came home

Wednesday Dec 18
We got a contract of Frank Shepherd to do 40 ft. of work on some of his claims for $250<u>00</u>   We went up to are stopping in the Milk Ranch & Cabin

Thursday Dec 19th 1889
I went on the hill to day to help survey the Rip for a patent

Friday, Dec 20th
Stopped in Mr Warners cabin last night.. Finished surveying got through about 4 oclock The snow is about 2 1/2 feet deep on the park. I got back to our cabin about 6 oclock in the evening

Saturday Dec 21st
Worked on the tunnel to day   I did not feel very good to day

Sunday Dec 22nd
Worked in the tunnel

Monday Dec 23rd 1889

Worked in the tunnel today, came down to Highland this evening to go to Aspen tomorrow after grub   We are having very nice winter weather

Friday Dec 24th

Went to Aspen with Fogg   Got some grub and Pete went home. I stayed in town.   B. Clark Wheeler wants me to go on the hill to show the survey or where the Phoenix corners are as he has to survey and get it patented for us according to the terms of the lease.

Wednesday Dec 25

Stopped in town all day waiting on the surveyor fine day and town is quiet for Christmas

Thursday Dec 26 1889

Went on the hill and showed the surveyors were the corners are on the Phoenix.   B. Clark Wheeler owes me 6 dollars for the time I have spent waiting on him. I got home to Highland at dark.

CHAPTER 3

ALONG CASTLE CREEK,
IN ASPEN, AND A TRIP EAST
1890-1894

Historical Setting and the Man

Historians often argue about which generation of Americans has experienced the greatest amount of change. Some believe it was those of us who lived throughout the latter half of the twentieth century, with the introduction of computers, television, the jet airplane, and thermonuclear weaponry. Others, like historian and author Stephen E. Ambrose, contend that people who lived through the second half of the nineteenth century, like Charles S. Armstrong, experienced the most change. Writes Ambrose: "They saw slavery abolished and electricity put to use, the development of the telephone and the completion of the telegraph, and most of all the railroad. The locomotive was the first great triumph over time and space. After it came and after it crossed the continent of North America, nothing could ever again be the same. It brought the greatest change in the shortest period of time." He could have added that Darwin's theory of evolution also changed what it meant to be human. Still others believe the generation to come, the one that lives through the first half of the twenty-first century, with its Internet, e-mail, space stations, artificial hearts, cloning, genetic engineering, numbing acts of terrorism, and who-knows-what-else, will experience the most change. One thing throughout human history, however, is certain: change itself. And the early 1890s had its share.

In 1893, the gigantic Chicago World's Fair, also known as the Columbian Exposition, celebrated those changes. Besides being the largest international carnival in the world, it stood on the shores of Lake Michigan as a monument to the breathtaking industrial and technological achievements of the latter half of the nineteenth century. One could wander for days, as Charles S. Armstrong did, among grand buildings and halls with names like Manufacturers, Electricity, Mines, Transportation, Machinery, Agricultural, Horticulture, Fisheries, and more. Today such themes evoke yawns. Back then this massive shrine to the promise of technological and human "progress" inspired awe. But not from everyone.

When invited to speak at the Fair, Chief Simon Pokagon, a Potawatomi, declined. Instead, he wrote these words: "On behalf of my people, the American Indians, I hereby declare to you, the pale-faced race that has usurped our lands and homes, that we have no spirit to celebrate with you the great Columbia Fair now being held in the Chicago city, the wonder of the world . . . [No] sooner had the news reached the Old World that a new continent had been found, peopled with another race of men, then locust-like, they swarmed on all our coasts. The cyclone of civilization spread westward; the forests of untold centuries were swept away; streams dried up; lakes fell back from their ancient bounds; and all our fathers once loved to gaze upon was destroyed, defaced, or marred, except the sun, moon, and starry skies above, which the Great Spirit in his wisdom hung beyond their reach" (Pokagon, 1893).

By the mid-1890s, President Benjamin Harrison presided over 63,000,000 Americans (triple the population of when Armstrong was born) living in forty-four states and several territories. American planters on Hawaii had led a revolution to dethrone Queen Liliuokalani. The French had erected the Eiffel Tower and New York City newspaperwoman Nellie Bly had traveled around the world in a record seventy-two days. James Naismith, a physical education instructor, had originated basketball. The Sherman Antitrust Act had passed and the Sherman Silver Purchase Act had been repealed. Diminutive entrepreneur, Lucien Nunn, had flipped the switch for the first commercial use of alternating-current electricity in remote Ames, Colorado, and for the first time in history photographers' flashbulbs blinked throughout the White House. In the White House the Harrison family, fearing shocks, often had the recently installed electric lights and bells turned off. They preferred the old-style gas lights. Armstrong would have preferred electric lights, although he did not have that option along isolated Castle Creek above Aspen, Colorado.

As Aspen's fortunes went, so went the fortunes of hundreds of people, including Charles Armstrong, in the surrounding region. And in the early 1890s Aspen boomed on the backs of fabulously rich silver mines, like the Mollie Gibson and Smuggler. In 1892 Aspen even outshone its big brother, Leadville, by producing over $10,000,000 in silver, one-sixth of the nation's supply. Now the third largest city in Colorado (behind Denver and Leadville), Aspen acted the part. Its citizens had their choice of four news-papers, three banks, two railroads, two opera houses, thirteen physicians, twenty-one attorneys, twenty-seven saloons, eight churches, thirty-five secret and benevolent societies, and two cemeteries. A state-of-the-art hook and ladder company and three fire hose companies stood ready to douse any fire that threatened to reduce Aspen to ashes. Demanding schools pointed young lives in proper directions. A modern, hygienic hospital min-istered to the needs of the injured and sick. An impressive courthouse and sturdy jail served as constant visual reminders that the law would be obeyed. Public, horse-drawn trolleys made travel from one end of the city to the other safe and convenient. Stimulating cultural events edified upper class citizens' minds, while theatrical productions, galas, and costume par-ties filled their social calendars. Avid fans flocked to see crucial baseball games against Leadville and Ashcroft. Boating in the summer and ice skat-ing in the winter could be enjoyed by all on lovely Hallam Lake just north of town. Even the noxious smelter smoke hanging over the city signaled that the town's money machines—the silver mines—thrived.

In downtown Aspen, a two-and-a-half-hour walk from Armstrong's cabin above the city, businesses flourished. Astute brokers sold investors high-quality mining stocks. Drugstores and pharmacies carried their own brands of cures in customized bottles. Bookstores stocked popular novels, weekly magazines, a wide array of office supplies, and leather-bound journals. Clothing stores displayed the latest in fashions. Hardware shelves groaned under the weight of mining and maintenance supplies. Blacksmiths and wagon makers wore out their tools trying to keep up with demands. Photographers competed for the lucrative portrait and landscape trade. Laundries scrambled to keep up with cleaning needs. Booze flowed and stacks of poker chips tilted on gaming tables. "Soiled doves" beckoned. Land prices soared. Small wonder train excursionists left Aspen believing that it would soon become the "Denver west of the Continental Divide."

As you will read, Armstrong took part in Aspen's bustle, but more frequently partook of its booze. Thus, while he did not shun city life, he struggled mightily with its temptations. That, in part, may account for his self-imposed isolation in his small cabin seven miles south of Aspen near the stage route along Castle Creek. He also, as you will discover, enjoyed this quiet, pristine environment where he could plant his garden, hunt, fish, prospect, and socialize with his friends who ran the stage line and those remaining in the vicinity. Ashcroft has long since faded, victim of shallow ore deposits and no railroad. Still, a few families and miners, most of them friends of Armstrong, hung on.

On February 12, 1892, Armstrong sold his "ranch" to B. Clark Wheeler, an early mover and shaker in Aspen, for $6,500. This "ranch" must have been two or three of Armstrong's adjacent mining claims near his place in Highland. He received $2,000 cash and notes for the rest "due in 30 and 60 days at 1 1/2 percent interest." For a man who lived on $200 a year, this equalled 30 years of income! Armstrong's financial ship had finally come in. Charles immediately "stopped at the Clarendon all night." One can easily imagine what he did there. Indeed, he spent so much time at the plush Clarendon Hotel that the 1892 Aspen City Directory listed him as a "miner" residing at the Clarendon. Somehow he managed to hang onto enough money to take an extended trip back east during the spring of 1893. His timing could not have been better.

Maybe Aspen's runaway success kept people in the vicinity from thinking about the financial disaster that loomed so near. On a more basic psychological plane, maybe people could not seriously entertain the possibility of an abrupt halt to such heady prosperity. Yet all the signs were clearly there. Everyone, including Charles Armstrong and B. Clark Wheeler, knew that for years the United States government had been purchasing silver at inflated prices because of the Sherman Silver Purchase Act. Everyone also knew that powerful forces back East wanted this practice stopped. Even the president of the United States wanted gold to back our currency, not silver and gold. Yet for whatever reasons, silver-mining towns in Colorado, including booming Aspen, chose not to take this monetary issue seriously.

By the time Aspen saw the gold standard coming, it was too late. During the early 1890s, Colorado politicians did what they could to defeat the powerful eastern "goldbugs," who wanted the "demonic gold-backed monetary system." However, there was probably nothing Coloradans could have done about it. The general economy of the United States was already in the doldrums, and with the steadily declining price of silver on the world market, several of Britain's silver mints in India closed on June 26, 1893. More nations throughout the world were turning to gold, rather than silver, to back their currency. Even the entire West did not have enough clout in Congress to buoy the bimetallic (silver and gold) monetary system. Suddenly, during that fateful July in 1893, when the United States finally repealed the Sherman Silver Purchase Act, the bottom fell out of the price of silver—dropping it to about sixty cents an ounce, less than one-half its value in 1879. Within weeks most silver mines in the Aspen region closed, crippling the economy of Aspen. The first boom was over. Aspen would have to wait for over a half-century for another one.

The collapse of silver prices in the early 1890s strikes most people as nothing more than a bit of uninteresting historical fiscal policy. But consider the implications. In a matter of days in 1893, a change in the United States government's "uninteresting" monetary policy led to the demise of many great silver mining centers, including Aspen and Leadville—both of which had been the envy of the world. Even today few people understand that our specie (coins) and paper currency are no longer backed by either silver or gold. Rather, our money has value only in that people are willing to accept it for goods and services. Should people suddenly decide not to accept our money, because it cannot be exchanged for either silver or gold, it could become worthless overnight.

Because of the calamitous monetary events, by the end of the summer of 1893, fewer than fifteen percent of Aspen's work force was employed. A trickle of people leaving the Crystal City to seek employment elsewhere increased to a steady stream during the fall of 1893. In 1894, when the price of silver climbed slightly, a few mines reopened. A brief period of optimism resulted. It did not last long.

From the past, Charles Armstrong speaks to us about these events. Historians necessarily speak in generalities, "boom and bust," "fiscal policies," and "crippling unemployment." Armstrong personalizes these generalities. In other words, Armstrong—although at times maddeningly mundane—puts a human face on the West's boom-and-bust decade.

During this period Charles remained physically active and in good health for a man in his late 40s. This is remarkable given his continued battle with booze. He also smoked and maintained a diet that would make modern dieticians cringe. As for having a wife and children, there was still no hint of yearning for a family. There were also moments when he seemed incapable of emotion. He wrote about a suicide, or a man blowing his hand off, in the same tone as he wrote about the number of fish he caught. Of course those were tough and dangerous times, when death and injury were closer companions. Still, Charles seemed to have grieved more for the death of his dog than for the death of his father.

Charles did not excel at saving money. His modest life style and constant self-recriminations bear witness to that. He managed to squander his one financial windfall, from B. Clark Wheeler, within two years. At least he had a trip back East and to the World's Fair to show for it. Charles did not pay his debts quickly, either.

On a more positive note, Armstrong's journals from 1890 through 1894 offer us many personal and historic gems. Who would have thought that a man who lived in one of those tiny log cabins scattered across the Rockies would leave such a record? Where else can one read firsthand about the daily activities and observations of a log-cabin-dwelling miner and surveyor, then accompany him on his journey to New York, Washington, Chicago (The World's Fair), and places in between?

Moreover, *everything* he wrote, no matter how mundane, fascinated me. What he ate, grew, trapped, shot, read, and bought. His interest in local and world news, weather patterns, and benevolent societies. His comments about illnesses, cabin construction, bed bugs, boarders, mining accidents, suicides, surveys, friends and foes—famous and forgotten, dogs, horses, new camps, stagecoach drivers, trips to Aspen, and regional sojourns. The letter that Tom Ogburn wrote to him on October 27, 1891, from Carson City, Nevada, tells us, among other things, that his friends called him "Charlie."

Then there are those tantalizing details that suggest there is more to learn about Colorado's pre-statehood history. For example, conventional historical wisdom holds that the first prospectors entered the Roaring Fork Valley in 1879. Yet on June 7, 1894, Armstrong noted that gulches on the immediate south side of Taylor Pass "were worked [for gold] in the [18]60s." I suspect this date is correct, especially with the likes of his friend, Abe Lee, the man who discovered gold in 1860 in California Gulch near present-day Leadville, telling him about the old days. This earlier date suggests to me that prospectors may well have trekked over Taylor Pass, or Hunter's (Independence) Pass, then continued down into the Roaring Fork Valley, Indian territory or not, in the 1860s. I have always wondered why none, *not one,* of the more than 5,000 gold-hungry placer miners in Oro City, with its surface deposits "panned out" by the mid-1860s, ever chanced to explore the Roaring Fork Valley in search of new goldfields. Now I believe some did.

Larry Fredrick, a local Aspen historian, independently came to this same conclusion. He points out that in 1866 Twin Lakes, then called "Dayton," was the county seat of Lake County. Twin Lakes is almost twenty miles closer to the Continental Divide than Oro City. Fredrick contends, and I agree with him, that some of these Twin Lakes residents must have trekked over the Continental Divide, then made their way down into present-day Aspen well before 1879. He also notes that Warner Root, an early Aspen pioneer, mentioned blazes in the trees along Independence Pass left by the "prospectors of 1860."

Saturday January 26 1890

Pete and I finished our contract day before yesterday and yesterday we moved down to Highland   Pete went to Aspen to day.. We did 40 ft of work for Frank Shepherd & co for $25000 and did $6300 for McMaster & co.. The wind is blowing very hard to day and the weather is mild and the snow melting.. Schlag has Bill Rose here taking care of the Jacks & horses while he stays in Aspen gambling & bumming

Saturday January 27th 90

Rained all night and rained this morning until 8 oclock when the wind changed to the North and it began to snow and it has been snowing a wet heavy snow all day   Bill Rose went to Aspen this afternoon to see Schlag about hay for the stock. I took a bath and baked some light bread cut stove wood & c.. Nobody on the road today

Tuesday Jan 28th 1890

I went to Aspen with Fogg to day Snowed very hard all the morning till noon.. I had paid the Warrack $20.95

Clarendon 9.40

Slaven & Mc Elroy 6.65   40.00

Paid McDonald on the Rip Patent $4000

Got $7500 from the Wood Bros. their share on the Rip Patent..

Got $22.00 of McMasters on work we did for him

Paid Chas Marshall $200 that I borrowed sometime ago Lent to Tyler $200 Paid Pete $500

When Armstrong walked to Aspen, he would enter the bustling mining community from the lower right of this bird's eye view (below). A few years before the silver crash, a stereo-card (right) captured the south side of Aspen at its frenetic best—a jack train readied to depart,

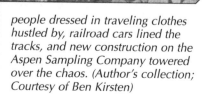

people dressed in traveling clothes hustled by, railroad cars lined the tracks, and new construction on the Aspen Sampling Company towered over the chaos. (Author's collection; Courtesy of Ben Kirsten)

Thursday January 30th 90

Came home to day   walked up with Pete. Schlag and Toney Nugent came up to day   Fine warm day. the roads are very soft..

Monday Feby 3rd 1890

Pete and I walked down to Aspen this morning. Fine warm day. I got $136.40 dollars of Frank Shepherd & Sebree on our contract We went down to Chas Boyds show this evening and had some fun

Tuesday Feby 4th 90

Stopped with Fred Bassager at the Clarendon this morning. Got a bill of grub and sent it up with Fogg   walked up myself.   Tom Ogburn stopped all night   Pete came up this evening

Wednesday Feby 5th

Pete went to town this morning with the jacks to accomidate Schlag. Tom Ogburn went up Conundrum this morning.

Saturday Feby 9th 90

Splendid weather we are having. I wrote a letter home also one to Cap Carey.. Major Pickrels man was here to dinner supper and lodging came down the gulch to bring letters.

Monday Feby 10th 1890

Cloudy this morning   our lodger from Conundrum went up the gulch this morning. Bush Schlag and Tom came up from town here to dinner & supper very stormy this afternoon

Tuesday Feby 11th 1890

Cold and clear to day. I set two traps for martin this evening.. Schlag was up to Climax

Wednesday Feby 12th

Clear and cold this morning   Bush and Schlag went up to the Climax this morning

February 13th

Bush, Pete and I walked to Aspen this afternoon.   Fine day   I went to Lodge this evening paid my dues for 88 & 89 amounting to ten dollars

Friday Feby. 14th /90

In town all day collected $22.25 of McMasters on assessment work gave Pete $20.00

Saturday Feby 15th

Came up with Fogg this afternoon.   Fine day.   Lent Fred Bassager $1.00 Malon Hamaker was killed in the Aspen mine yesterday by falling down a shaft   there was a man killed day before and this morning another one met his fate on Aspen Mountain   accidents seem to go by threes..

Sunday Feby 16th 1890

Stormy windy day. Pete and Schlag came up to day Bill Rose and Toney Nugent were here to dinner.   Went up to the Climax this afternoon

Monday Feby 17th 1890
Cold and windy with a little snow to day.   I sold 14 old deer skins yesterday for $13.32 and ordered two pair of shirts one for Pete and one pair for myself.. deer skins worth 18cts per lb.. ..

Tuesday Feby 18th 1890
Cold and stormy some snow falling   Schlag and Pete are here with me   Set in the house all day reading &c

Wednesday Feby 19
Snowed most of the night about 8 inches of new snow this morning.. Stopped in the house all day. Schlag went to Aspen this afternoon. Snowing this evening

Thursday Feby 20th /90
Warm but snowey.   I put in the day around the house baking light bread and cake

Friday Feby 21st
Snowed most of the day warm and thawing .. snowing hard this evening

Saturday Feby 22
Somewhat colder to day   Bill Rose came down from the Climax and went to town

Sunday Feby 23rd
Cold and stormy   Bill & Schlag went up to the Climax

Tuesday Feby 25th 90
Cold and stormy stopped in the house all day

Wednesday Feby 26th /90
Cold and stormy this morning and this afternoon there is a regular Blizzard blowing.   Still snowing this evening   Schlag went to Aspen this forenoon.

Thursday Feby 27th
The coldest day that we have had this winter I think. The sun shines a little but dont seem to warm the air al all

Friday Feby 28th
Very cold to day and clear.. Pete went up to Russells this morning to work on the Austin for 1/6 interest in the lease and bond.   Schlag packed a lot of grub up there to day..
I set around the house and tried to keep form freezing up. This has been the worst storm that we have had this winter

Saturday March 1st 1890
Clear and cold day last night was very cold.. I rode to Aspen with Fogg got some groceries and came back with him got home 8 oclock.. Times are quite in town but it is not to be wondered as the weather is so cold..

Sunday March 2nd

I did not get out of bed till after 9 this morning.. Got up some wood, and set in the house most of the day. Clear sunny day and the weather has moderated greatly   this evening is much warmer and a south wind is blowing..

Monday March 3rd 1890

Hauled up some wood to day by hand.. Warm pleasant. But cloudy and threatening snow this evening at home alone but not lonesome

Tuesday March 4th 1890

I rode to Aspen with Fogg to day. Collected 3.50 from Hadley

Wednesday March 5th

In town all day borrowed $200 of John Nash Storming all day

Thursday March 6th

Borrowed $1000 of Dave Brown to day   paid 100 fall fax and some small bills I owed

Came home with Fogg.   Chas Miller came up with me and stopped all night with me..

Friday March 7th

Storming very hard all day   Chas Miller went on the hill and I am here alone this evening.   I got a letter from home yesterday Father is in poor health and I must try to get home and see him this year

Saturday March 8th 1890

Snowing and stormy all day.   I stopped in the house most of the day. Carbonata Miller from Ashcroft stopped with me for supper this evening

Sunday March 9th

Snow snow snowing all the time. Weather warm and just right for snow   Have been alone most of the day   Had a few callers   Still snowing this evening

Monday March 10th

Cold and stormy snowing most of the day

Bill Emery here with me this evening   he started for town but it is storming so hard that he concluded to stop here all night

Tuesday March 11th

Storming hard to day

Wednesday March 12th /90

Had the stage here last night Foggs team was played out when he got here so he stopped had two passengers Ben Ellithorpe and Miss Carlisle..

Very cold morning and it was cold all day but clear and the sun shining

Thursday March 13th

Clear and cold   I got some wood this afternoon from one of the old cabins

Friday March 14th
  Clear Cold day. I did not get up till after 9 this morning. Got up some wood this afternoon

Saturday March 15th
  Clear and nice this evening the weather is getting much warmer. Tom and Maj. and his wife came down from Conundrum this morning and caught the stage here and went to town. Mighty glad I was to see them. I had commenced to worry about them.. but they are all right.
  I was up at Russells this afternoon borrowed a lot of magazines and novels.

Sunday March 16th
  Splendid nice day the snow is settling fast under this warm sun. Pete came down this afternoon and went to town this evening. I set in the house most of the day reading

Monday March 17th
  Warm day..

Tuesday March 18
  I road to town with Fogg to day   bought some provisions and came back with him   Warm day and the roads are getting soft so that it is bad for teams to get along

Wednesday March 19th 1890
  Pickrel Tom Ogburn and their man stopped here last night and the morning   went up Conundrum each hauling 50 lbs of grub on a sled. I was awake with the tooth ache most of the night and it is bothering me all day to day.

Thursday March 20th
  John Boland stopped with me last night he has been up looking at the Little Annie Mine. Clear and pleasant this morning Tooth bothering me yet

Saturday March 22nd 90
  Fine warm day snow settling very fast   Bill Rose was here this afternoon and went to Aspen.

Sunday March 23
  Warm and pleasant in the fore part of the day but snowing hard this evening. Pete was here this afternoon   My tooth bothers me some yet

Monday March 24th
  Clear but quite cold this morning   about 4 inches of new snow fell last night

Tuesday March 25th
  Nice day warm. Mr Penel was here for dinner   he started for the Climax but as there was no one there   he went no farther than here.. Cloudy and snowing a little this evening

Wednesday March 26th 90
Clear and nice this morning   I turned out at 6.30 got breakfast and went up Lime Gulch called on Mrs. Russell and also went up to look at the Austin Lode   They have about 2 feet of nice looking mineral.. Came home had Toney Nugent and John and McRobins on here for dinner.. This evening it is snowing hard.

Toney is very much discouraged and says he is going to leave the country. The mineral in the Climax is no good and as he is in the hole bad .. he thinks it would be better for him to seek new fields and I think it would be the best thing he could do for himself   There is a lot of us old timers that dont seem to catch on here and it seems as though it would be best to emigrate.

Thursday March 27th 90
Very cold and stormy about 6 inches of snow fell last night and the high wind drifted it very bad..

Fogg got this far with the stage and had to stop all night with me.. Toney Nugent and his hired man stopped here all night supper & breakfast

Friday March 28th 1890
Cold and clear this morning. Fogg got away about 8 oclock. There has been a lot of people on the road to day   Thomas' jack train went up to the Little Annie with supplies   Bill Rose came up from town and went up to the Climax

Saturday March 29th
Rode to Aspen with Fogg   Was in town about 2 hours came back with Fogg. The town is quite. Fine day. Maj Pickrel here for supper..

Sunday March 30th 1890
Storming this morning when I got up.. Pete Olsen and Tom Ogburn were here for dinner

Storming hard this evening 4 or 5 inches of snow fell to day. 40 jacks loded with ore from the Little Annie went down to day. and the same yesterday

Monday March 31st
Storming most of the day   I stopped in the house all day only going out to get stove wood..

Sunday April 1st
Fine day thawing very fast.. Toney Nugent stopped here to supper lodging and breakfast. Quite a number of people on the road to day. City election in Aspen to day. B. Clark Wheeler is republican for Mayor A. D. Hooper democrat

Saturday April 5th 1890
I rode to Aspen this morning with Fogg   Fine day I stopped in town

Sunday April 6th

Stopped at the Clarendon Hotel last night.. went to the brewery to day with Bush.. Toney Nugent and Fred Bassager have left the Country gone to Denver Toney sold his interest in the Climax. he is badly in debt and I think will stay away from here now. Pete Olsen came down to day

Monday. April 7th

Pete and I stopped at the Clarendon last night.. We walked up home this forenoon. Warm and pleasant

Tuesday Apr 8th.

Storming very hard this morning.. Bill Rose stopped with me last night and went up to the Climax this morning.

Wednesday Apr 9th

Clear and warm to day   I was alone to day wrote to the Land Office at Glenwood about the Ranche to see if I could prove up on it

Thursday April 10th

Went fishing this forenoon but did not get a raise.. Bert Fuller was here to dinner & Supper. Very warm sun

Friday April 11th 1890

Bert Fuller stopped with me last night & to breakfast. I went up to see John & Mc Robinson they are working on the Dick Tunnell.. I took dinner with them Tom Ogburn here to supper

Saturday Apr 12th 1890

Tom Ogburn here last night and to breakfast.. he went up Conundrum this morning I rode to town with Fogg and back with him.. I collected $32.25 for work that Pete and I did last winter.. I paid Dave Brown 10 00 that I borrowed sometime ago. paid John Watkins $6.40 and the Clarendon Hotel 5 00 and bought some groceries &c to amount to $8.35 more. Warm day and the roads are in very bad shape between here and town

Sunday Apr 13th 90

Stormy most of the day I did not stir out much   Got a letter from home yesterday they are all as well as usual

Monday April 14th 1890

Got up a 5 oclock this morning went on the hill to see about posting patent notice on the Rip VanWinkle Lode.. Interviewed the Phoenix the Winnie and the Little Anna mines.. had dinner with McCabe.. he is fixing up his cabin in fine shape putting in a floor and pavillon &c.. Stopped at Russells a while on my way back.. Maj Pickrel & hired man here supper this evening..

Tuesday Apr 15th

Got up about 5 oclock this morning Major & man here to lodging &

breakfast   they pulled out for up the gulch on the crust with about 60 lbs a piece on tobogons   Fine warm day. but snowed in the afternoon

Thursday April 17th 1890

Fine day   I put in the most of the day working on the road throwing out rocks &c.. Fogg upset the stage near the bridge this side of Lime Gulch and I helped him get righted up

Friday April 18th 1890

Fine day but threatening a storm.. I was down to the creek to see if I could catch some fish but it was no go saw but one.. Baked a lot of pumpkin pies this afternoon   Quite a number of people on the road to day..

Saturday Apr 19th

Got up earley this morning and walked to town calculating to get home this evening but failed

Sunday Apr 20th 1890

In town all day drinking beer   was down to the Road House to the Brewery with Bush and Chas Boesch and others fine day

Monday Apr 21st

In town all day doing no good   got letter from Cowen

Tuesday Apr 22nd

In town all day doing no good

Wednesday Apr 23rd

Came home this afternoon feeling bad.. I owe the Clarendon Hotel for board 6.50

Saturday Apr 26th

Got up earley and went up the road to shovel out some snow banks. The road is pretty good now from Town to the Tenderfoot Ranche   the stage is going on wheels now

Sunday April 27th 90

Got up about 9 this morn had the tooth ache last night.. I caught 8 trout to day.. the first of the season.. Fine most of the day but stormy this evening not much travel on the road to day..

Monday Apr 28th 90

Fine warm day. I spaded up some ground and sowed some lettuce & radishes also some cabbage seed I ought to have sowed the cabbage a month ago.. Quite a number of people on the road to day.

Tuesday Apr 29th

Tom Ogburn & man stopped here to Supper Lodging & Breakfast left early for up the gulch

Thursday May 1st 1890

Road to Aspen with Fogg to day.. The road is good to town about all the snow is off and the roads are about dry. I gave an order on

Dow Seebree to Clark & Denman for $2000 which more than settles my grocerie bill.. I missed Fogg and walked up in the evening. Rained quite hard and I got quite wet

Friday May 2nd
Was up to Russells to dinner and also up to the Austin. The boys are feeling rather blue as the claim is not looming up very big.. Raining and snowing most of the day in showers..

Saturday May 3rd
Was up to the Milk Ranche this afternoon Fine weather.. tried the fish but the water is to high

Sunday May 4th 1890
Ten years ago to day I left Leavenworth City for the country expecting to stay a year..

Pete Olsen came down from the Austin last night he thinks of quiting work up there We were out fishing a short time after dinner but did not catch any. Very cold and stormy most of the day..

Monday May 5th
Up in good season this morning. Dave Mitchell stopped here last night.. He Schlag and Pete went to Aspen this morning.. I put in most of the day locating a ditch for the Ranche .. Very windy and cold.. Quite a number of people on the road to day

Tuesday May 6th 90
I went up on Richmond Hill to day took the Eva Belle trail.. Shoveled out the Rip so I could get down the shaft the snow on the park is about 3 feet deep took dinner with the boys on the Phoenix.. they are drifting in the shaft that Pete and I sunk last summer.. I was down to the Little Anna mine they were loading a jack train with ore.. the mine looks first rate.. The snow held me up anywhere on the park.. Pete quit work on the Austin and brought down his blankets to day fine day

Wednesday May 7th
Fine warm day Pete and I were fishing I caught 3 small ones

Thursday May 8th 1890
Road to Aspen with Fogg to day Fine day

Friday May 9th 1890
Stopped in town all night at the Clarendon Hotel owe them 1.50 S. B. & D. walked up this evening.. Stormed last night and most of to day

Wednesday May 12
Cold and stormy to day

Tuesday May 13th
Ground white with snow this morning.. Morse plowed the garden to day finished by noon Tom Ogburn and Tyler here for dinner.. Tyler

is stopping in our cabin while he does some prospecting back of the house.. Pete is down town working for his pony to day

Wednesday May 14th
Schlag got dumped of the mule to day and was pretty badly hurt

May 15th 90
Rode to Aspen with Fogg to day   Pete rode his pony   we stopped in town paid Box rent

Friday May 16th
Pete and I stopped at the Clarendon last night $2.00 and to Breakfast this morn   Came home this evening   Abe Lee and wife here they came up yesterday from town

Sunday May 18th
Worked a little in the garden. Took a walk up Conundrum about 3 miles this afternoon.   Mrs. Russell here to dinner with Abe and wife fine day

Monday May 19th
Abe and wife started up Conundrum this morning with 6 jack loads of stuff   I worked in the garden most of the day went up to the Milk Ranch in the afternoon to show Larson our claims   he is talking of leasing them

Tuesday May 20th 90
Fine day.. had a nice shower of rain this morning Worked in the garden all day. Pete got the water to running in the ditch

Thursday May 22nd
I rode down to Aspen this morning with Fogg.. also came back with him got 1/2 case of eggs 5lbs coffee some lemons &c at Clark and Denmans Pd

Saturday May 24th
Pete went to town this morning.   I went up on the Park to take a look at the Rip and Phoenix   the snow is nearly gone off the park there is nobody working on the Phoenix water in the shaft. The Little Annie is looking fine they are getting ready to move the machinery onto the new shaft.. I got home about 5 oclock in the evening.. Just as Pete returned from town..

Sunday May 25th
Quiet day

Monday May 26th
Finished planting the garden to day

Tuesday May 27th
Pete and I struck out this morning about 9 oclock and walked up Conundrum   took dinner with Mrs. Pickrel and supper with Tom Ogburn.   Tom has his cabin fixed up in fine shape

Wednesday May 28th

We stopped with Tom last night had a pleasant time   was up to the Cummings mine this forenoon   the boys are taking out some fine ore.. We took dinner with Abe Lee and wife and strolled leisurely home in the afternoon   got here about 5 oclock after a very pleasant visit

Thursday May 29th

Got up early this morning.   Morse plowed some potatoe ground for me in the lower field and Pete and I dropped the potatoes and he plowed them in.. Fine weather we are having..

Monday June 2nd 1890

I went to Aspen Saturday and came home to day and went up Conundrum Gulch with George Nyce to help him make a patent survey on a placer claim   Stopped with Tom Ogburn

Tuesday June 3rd

Worked on the line all day. The weather turned very cold in the afternoon and commenced to snow

Wednesday June 4th

Snowing this morning and we did not get to work till late   cold and stormy all day

Thursday June 5th

Nice weather this morning. We finished the survey by 9 oclock packed up and got home by 3 P.M.

Friday June 6th 1890

Worked in the garden and around the house. Fine day but cool

Saturday June 7th

Pete and I went to Aspen to day. I got my pay from Geo Nyce $9 00 also $10 00 for timber on the Rip bought pr trousers 6.00 x for Overalls 70c x pair fine shoes 3.50   we got home about 6 oclock all right

Sunday June 8th

Pete and I went up the gulch to see Tyler this afternoon   Fine day The Little Anna has 11 feet of 80 oz ore and are shipping

Tuesday June 10th 1890

Fine day. Judy & Deane S. I. Wallett & wives and two other ladies were here and took dinner   they were out horseback riding. George Travis a friend of mine shot himself to day in town   got tired of life shot himself through the head and died instantly..

Wednesday June 11th

Pete and I was up to the Blue Lime to day doing some surveying Fine day

Saturday June 14th

Pete and I went to Aspen to day.. I paid for Box Key 50c Got 75 lbs oats for seed 190 and got some provisions we got home at 6 P.M. allright.. Pete bought 2 jacks paid 25 dollars for the two

Sunday June 16th 1890

Fine day.. Tom Ogburn here for dinner.. I wrote a letter to Cap Carey..

Friday June 20th

Pete and I surveyed two claims for Charley Miller back of the house to day   Very hard days work   I am to get 10 dollars for the job. I have been working in the garden the past week irrigating &c. Wednesday I was up on Richmond Hill looking around.. Wheeler has not done any work on the Phoenix for about a month now.. The Little Anna Mine is taking out lots of ore they ship about 10 tons per day. I stopped and visited Russells folks for a while on my way back

Saturday June 21st 1890

I surveyed two claims for Larson & Barber up near the Old Milk Ranche to day   very hot day and the ground was very brushy.. I got a letter from home this week   Father is failing all the time and Roxy sayed I will have to come home before many months if I want to see him again

Sunday June 22nd

Warm day was up the creek to day with Chas Miller located some placar claims & a ditch Ed Higenbothom here for Supper. Tom Ogburn here for dinner.

Monday June 23rd

Barber paid me 10 dollars for surveying. I wrote a letter to day. Warm day

Tuesday June 24th 90

Went to Aspen to day   Collected 69 dollars of Dow Seebree which makes us even on the work done for him last winter. I paid McDonald 50 dollars on the Rip Patent.. paid the Clarendon Hotel $500 got a pair of shoes 1.25 a reel 75 flies 30 stopped in town all night

Wednesday June 25th

In town all day   Rained quite hard this afternoon

Thursday June 26th

Came home with Fogg to day..

Friday June 27th

Chas Hubbard stopped with me last night. he left this morning for Italian Mountain.. I located two claims on the porphyry to connect our other claims up at the Blue Lime. Warm day

Saturday June 28th

Was up the creek and did a little work on the irrigating ditch to day.. Warm day.

Sunday June 20th /90

Went up Conundrum falls after fish but the water is to high for good fishing   caught about 1/2 doz small ones. Very fine day

Monday June 30th

Baked bread to day and worked in the garden   very dry warm weather we are having

Tuesday July 1st

Be temperate in all things!

Thursday July 3rd 1890

Was up to Russells this forenoon after a morter to ground rock in

Friday July 4th 1890

Fine day. I did not go to Aspen to the celebration.. but went fishing caught a doz in the forenoon in the afternoon caught 4 more. Pete returned from his prospecting trip on Taylor River yesterday he did not find anything to locate   He went to town to day

Saturday July 5th 1890

I put in most of the day fishing caught a good mess.. worked on the garden part of the day brushing peas.. Pete came home this evening.. Jim Gordon came up to day he is going to punch for Schlag

Sunday July 6th 1890

Around the house most of the day irrigating the garden &c. Went fishing a while this evening caught 4 trout Very warm day.

Al Napely Chas Marshall and Ed Bethell were here for dinner they are going to the Southern part of the state prospecting in Conejhos County.. I lent Al my six shooter

Monday July 7th 1890

Pete and I surveyed the Brother Jonathon and Ingells claims to day. two claims that we located to connect the Leavenworth and Blue Lime group of claims.. It was hot & hard days work.. got home about 5.30 P.M. Warm dry weather.

Tuesday July 8th 1890

Worked in the garden irrigating most of the day.. Moved up the creek in the afternoon

Wednesday July 9th

In camp up at the Milk Creek Ranche   Pete and I are doing some assessment work on the two claims we surveyed Monday.. We were at work this morning by 1/2 6 oclock   quit at noon   lay around camp in the afternoon. Visited Cap Dwyer in the evening   he stoppes in the Cabin and is running a tunnel on the porphyry just south of our claims

Thursday July 10

Up at 5.30 and finished our two assessments by noon.. Robinson Bros got their machinery on the Little Dick Tunnel to day   An engine and air compressor and drills. They are figuring on running the tunnel at the rate of 8 feet per day

Friday July 11th

We were up to the little Dick this morning to see the machinery &c. they are building a boarding house and fixing up in good shape..

We moved down to Highland.. I put in the day irrigating the garden.. Bush Bixby and Oscar Everhardt passed by here this forenoon going to Taylor River fishing   They were loaded for bear

Saturday July 12th 1890

Pete and I went to Aspen to day   Got home late in the evening

Sunday July 13th

At home most of the day went fishing in the afternoon but had poor luck

Monday July 14th

I went to town to day   Chas Franklin is after me to lease the Rip. I proposed to lease it to him for 1 1/2 years and 60000 dollars bond and to have a job of work on it   did not sign any papers

Tuesday July 15th

Did nothing much to day.. Made a plat of our claims up at the Blue Lime   Rained a little this afternoon

Wednesday July 16th 90

Went fishing up Conundrum to day   caught a mess   Rained quite hard here.. Abe Lee & wife and a young lady here to supper Lodging & Breakfast

Thursday July 17th

I went up on Richmond hill this morning. Got home in the evening Nothing new.. Pete & Schlag went up Conundrum with Abe this morning

Monday July 21st

Went to Aspen to day did nothing much

Tuesday July 22nd

Worked in the garden to day

Wednesday July 23rd

Worked in the garden   got a letter from Robert Armstrong, Leavenworth asking for the $100 that I borrowed 10 years ago. He has had bad luck had both legs broken this spring and has been laid up all summer

Wednesday July 30th 1890

Pete and I started for Taylor river this morning on a fishing trip. Got into camp about 5 oclock in the evening   had a pleasant trip over the range

Thursday July 31st
 I caught 31 trout to day

Friday Aug 1st
 Good fishing

Sunday Aug 3rd
 Good fishing

Monday Aug 4th
 We started from camp this morning about 7.30   Got home at 3 oclock.. I caught 102 trout on the trip   Pete caught 30

Tuesday Aug 5th
 Went to Aspen this morning. Came home in the afternoon and joined a fishing party going to Spring Creek Bixbee.. Bush, Fred Bassager.. John Cole & Jim Kalabeen... We got as far as Ashcroft and camped.. Got a letter from home

Wednesday Aug 6th
 We got up early and crossed the Range before breakfast   got onto Spring Creek about 5.30 P.M

Thursday Aug 7th
 I caught 79 fine trout to day

Friday Aug 8th 1890
 I started out fishing this morning and meet Schlag who had a telegram for me from Roxy telling me that Father died the 5th and that Mother was sick .. So I came on home.   Fred Bassager came with me we got home at 10 in the evening

Saturday Aug 9th
 I went to town to day and telegraphed to Roxie so as to let her know that I received her telegram   Stopped in town

Sunday Aug 10th
 Came home about noon

Monday Aug 11th
 Washed some clothes this morning.. Went fishing in the afternoon caught 19

Tuesday Aug 12 the
 Worked in the garden most of the day   we had a fine rain this afternoon. Raining this evening.. I wrote a letter to Roxie to day trying to cheer her up

Monday Aug 18th 1890
 Started to Spring Creek to day with John Coll to do some surveying for him
 Camped this evening on Talyor Range at the Horse shoe..

Tuesday Aug 19th
 Got into camp at spring creek this evening

Wednesday Aug 20th
   Went fishing to day caught a nice lot

Thursday Aug 21 st
   Surveyed two claims to day

Friday Aug 22nd
   Raining most of the day we went fishing

Saturday Aug 23rd 90
   John Coll Fred Bassager and myself went to Crested Buttes this morning and while we were gone Mike Coleman blowed his right hand off with a giant Cartridge while trying to blow up a wood chuck hole.   Geo Coll brought him over to Cement Creek and sent for us We went over with a surveyor to Mr. Wallrods house where they were and amputated the hand

Sunday Aug 24th
   George Coll and I went back to Spring Creek to day to look after things

Monday Aug 25
   We went fishing

Tuesday Aug 26
   Went fishing

Wednesday Aug 27th 90
   Surveyed a claim to day

Friday Sept 5th
   We got back to Highland to day

Saturday Sept 6th
   Went to Aspen to day   got 45 dollars for my trip beside we made a location and surveyed it

Tuesday Sept 9th
   I came home this afternoon.   I pd Clark and Denman 20 dolls on a/c pd Slaven & McElvy 5 doll s on a/c Pd Clarendon Hotel 5 dolls on a/c

Wednesday Sept 10th
   I went up on the hill to day.. The park Lode next to the Rip has an engine on it and they are retimbering the shaft. The Little Anna is shipping lots of mineral and they are building a road up Lime Gulch. The outlook on the Richmond Hill is great for a big boom this winter..
   The frost cut the garden 3 days ago

Thursday Sept 11th
   I got up early this morning   mowed some of the hay in the field   blistered my hands.. In the afternoon caught some trout.. Rained all last night and this morning   above timber line was white with snow.. A little stormy all day.. Wrote a letter to Roxie this evening

Monday Sept 15th
Mowed grass in the field till about 4 oclock when John Coll Bush & Schlag came along and I went with them.   We camped in Ashcroft this evening

Tuesday Sept 16th 1890
We got into Spring Creek this evening

Wednesday Sept 17th
Bush and I caught 105 trout to day   John & Schlag prospected

Thursday Sept 18th
Bush and I fished all day but did not have very good luck

Friday Sept 19th
We all went fishing in a lake up Deadmans Gulch   caught a nice lot of big trout   I killed 4 grouse

Saturday Sept 20th
Rained most all day.   I went hunting part of the day but did not kill anything   the rest of the boys were fishing

Sunday Sept 21st
We started for home to day.   Fished some in Taylor River but with poor success. Camped in Bowman this evening

Monday Sept 22nd 90
Got home about 2 oclock had dinner and went to Aspen

Tuesday Sept 23
In Aspen all day

Wednesday Sept 24
In Aspen

Thursday Sept 25
Got home about 4 oclock   received a letter from home Roxie & Mother are well

Friday Sept 26th
Burt Fuller and I dug the potatoes in the garden to day

Saturday Sept 27
Dug potatoes in lower field

Sunday Sept 28th
Finished digging the potatoes

Tuesday Sept 30th 90
I went up to Foggs this evening to do some surveying

Wednesday Oct 1st 90
Surveyed a claim for Fogg to day. Rained quite hard last night and the mountains are white with snow this morning

Thursday Oct 2nd
Came home with Fogg this morning   the ground is covered with snow

Armstrong may have had something amorous on his mind when he sketched this woman and man (a self-portrait?) on the front inside cover of his 1890 journal. He frequently jotted down addresses, made calculations, and recorded dates on the inside covers of his journals. (Armstrong's journals)

Friday Oct 3rd

Burt Fuller & I went up on Richmond Hill to day   The park is looking lively. The Little Anna is building ore houses &c and are making great preperations for work

Saturday Oct 4th 90

Burt and I rode down with Fogg to Aspen.. I got some groceries and came home with him. Snowed all day and was very cold and disagreeable

Sunday Oct 5th

Snow about 10 inches deep this morning. I went out with the rifle this afternoon but saw no game.. quiet day

Friday Oct 10

Hunted bear all day fired at him but did not hit

Tuesday Oct 14th

Cold stormy day   I was in the house most of the day washing. Schlag here this evening also Burt Fuller   he has been here since last Friday.. Clay Higenbothom was here about a week before Bert came they seem determined to eat me up

Wednesday Oct 15th 1890

Snowing when I got up this morning but eased up and has been a fine day but cold. I wrote a letter to Robert Armstrong to day

Friday Oct 17th

Burt went to Aspen to day.   Cris Conn stopped with me last night

Saturday Oct 18th

Clear fine day.. But the roads are very bad.   I rode to Aspen with Fogg this morning stopped in town most all day   Did not accomplish much.. I have been about sick with a severe cold I wrote a letter to Roxie to day

Sunday Oct 19th

Fine day.. I killed a grouse this morning and cooked him for dinner Schlag here last night

Monday Oct 20th 90

Stormy

Tuesday Oct 21

Fine day I went up to the Jersey Lily to day and brought down our wheelbarrow

Wednesday Oct 22st

I gathered the beets in the garden to day.. Ed Higenbothom here this evening   He has been in Aspen the past 3 weeks on a drunk and this evening he is very sick and is swearing off very earnestly.   I wrote a letter to H. N. Wood

Thursday Oct 23rd

Gathered the cabbage and carrots to day. Ed went on the hill this morning.   The Puzzler Mine is working under a lease. Employ 4 men

Saturday Oct 25 90

Went to Aspen to day   fine day

Sunday Oct 26th

Got home this afternoon from town. Fine day   I stopped at the Clarendon Hotel for Lodging & breakfast. Pete Olsen was down from Conundrum Gulch I deeded him 1/16 in the Phoenix. I deeded it to him 2 years ago but he lost the deed so I have him a new one..

Monday Oct 27th

I packed up a lot of turnips and potatoes for Major Pickrel to day

Tuesday Oct 28th

Got up early this morning and surveyed 2 claims for Joseph Graham &c.   Got home after dark. fine day

Wednesday Oct 29th 90

Fine day.. I fixed up the old stable and arround the house

Thursday Oct 30th

Had Morse haul in the hay this morning.   There were 2 loads about 2 tons I think.. Schlag was here to dinner and packed 814 lbs turnips 75 carrots and 1000.. Potatoes up to Major Pickrels camp

I located 2 claims south of the Wilton Bell mine this afternoon. Abe Lee here to dinner

Friday Oct 31st

I was up to Careys camp to day. Took dinner at Pickrels.   I went up to take a look at the Grand Union Tunnel and Tom and Pete had quit work so I did not go in.. But saw some of the mineral that they got out of the Jessie vein it is heavy load ore and looks as though it would pay

I think I will have it assayed and see if it will pay.. Came home this evening... Fine day

Monday Nov 3rd 1890

I was up on the hill to day and did some work on one of the claims that I located a few days ago it shows about 2 feet of heavy spar

Tuesday Nov 4th

Election day.. I did not vote but worked on the claim Fine day

Wednesday Nov 5th

I rode down to Aspen with Fogg this morning   Collected 15 dollars for surveying that I did a while ago.   Paid the Clarendon $5 bot 5.50 worth of clothing, bot a watterberry watch for 2.50 paid Al Hopely $5 that I borrowed a while ago. Received a letter from home all well..

Thursday Nov 6th 90

Stopped in Aspen last night. Came home this afternoon. Tom Ogburn and Pete Olsen are stopping here with me.. Stormy day

Sunday Nov 9th 1890

Stormy weather we are having but this afternoon the sun is shining but the weather is cold.. Schlag came down from Conundrum this evening he and Jim here for supper

Monday Nov 10th 1890

Pete and Tom went to Aspen to day.   Schlag & Jim went down this afternoon. Pete Tom & Jim here for supper. fine day

Tuesday Nov 11th 1890

Pete and I went up on Richmond Hill to day. Things are looking fine up there and there is lots of work being done   Fine day   Jim & Schlag here to supper

Wednesday Nov 12th

Hauled up some wood for the house.   Fine sunney day   Sold the hay to Schlag for $25 00

Thursday Nov 13th

Went up to the Leavenworth tunnel this afternoon and did a little work   Splendid weather we are having

Monday Nov 17th

Worked on the Leavenworth

Tuesday Nov 18th

Worked on the Tunnel cleaning it out

Wednesday Nov 19th 1890
  Splendid fine day   I went to Aspen to day
  Paid Clark & Denman $700
  " Slaven & McEroy $5.00
  " Clarendon Hotel 10.00
  " Chas Boesch full 5.00
  Got another watch for $400.. paid 1.50 cash & my 2.50 watch
Bot 5# sausage 65cts
    1# candles 40 "
came home with Pete go here about dark

Thursday Nov 20th
  Got up in good season this morning.. Pete Olsen & Tom Ogburn
left for Utah & Idaho this morning.. They have a good outfit 4 ponies
good guns & tent & every thing that they need to camp out with..
Splendid nice morning clear and warm.. And I hope they will have
good luck..

Friday Nov 21st 1890
  Old Bush came up here last evening and this morning we went up
Conundrum Gulch and commenced work on the Phoenix.   Came
home this evening

Saturday Nov 22nd 1890
  Worked on the Phoenix to day.   Bush does nothing but shovel a
little dirt and stand around and watch me work

Sunday Nov 23rd 1890
  Worked on the Phoenix to day

Monday Nov 24th
  Finished work on the Phoenix to day.   I am working for Ben
Bonell.   I ran in about 6 feet the lead looks pretty good the work
came to 14 dollars

Tuesday Nov 25th /90
  Bush and I went up Castle Creek about a mile this forenoon
prospecting did not find anything.. Bush went to town this afternoon

Wednesday Nov 26th
  I went to Aspen to day. Got back this evening   Bot some groceries.
got a letter from home they are all well. Have got the insurance
money $2200. And have paid up all their debts and bought a house
and have $800 left which I am going to borrow at 10% per annum..
I answered the letter in town

Thursday Nov 27th 90
  Thanksgiving day. I was to the Milk ranch this afternoon visiting
Cap Dwyer.. Fine day.. I had a fine oyster stew this evening at home
Bob Donaldson spent the evening here visiting me..

Saturday Nov 29th

43 years old to day. Went to town. Got a letter from Roxy with a check for $800 dollars.   I paid my bill at Clark & Denmans $30<u>00</u> paid the Clarendon $12 Slaven 2.50 and dont owe any of the a cent now and dont propose to owe them any more

Sunday Nov 30th

In town all day. Got a 1/4 of beef from Al Hopely

Monday Dec 1st 1890

Came home this afternoon   rode up with an ore tram

Tuesday Dec 2<u>nd</u>

Arround the house all day   not feeling very well

Wednesday Dec 3<u>rd</u>

Got up in good season this morning.. Paid Morse 5 dollars owe him/7 more

Went up to the Leavenworth Tunnel this afternoon and did some work in the drift and struck some nice looking galena in blue lime.. The first sign of mineral in over 300 feet of work it makes me feel might good.. Stormy this evening.. Got home after dark as my watch stopped on me

Thursday Dec 4th 90

Snowing most all day.   I stopped home and chored arround the house. Wrote home this evening

Friday Dec 5th

Worked in the tunnel to day   fine weather again

Saturday Dec 6<u>th</u>

Walked to town this morning to attend to some business but things did not work very satisfactory

Sunday Dec 7th

Stopped in town last night and walked up home this forenoon

Monday Dec 8<u>th</u>

Jim Gordon and myself hauled up quite a bot of wood to day. Fine sunny day but cold

Tuesday Dec 9<u>th</u> 1890

Rode down to town with Fogg this morning. Very cold morning. Collected ten dollars of Jim Downing on last years assessment.. He owes me 55 dollars yet.. I got another assessment of him which will pay one $100

Wednesday Dec 10<u>th</u>

Stopped in town last night.. came home this afternoon walked up.. I got a letter from Tom Ogburn & Pete   They were in Greenriver Station on the 4th and expected to start for the Henry Mts. The next day.. They dont like Utah so far.. Say it is a god forsaken country

Thursday Dec 11th 90
    Worked arround the house all day. This evening went to Aspen
Friday Dec 12th
    Came up home this afternoon   walked up with Pete OReily
Schlag paid me $3 00 on a/c
Saturday Dec 13th
    Pete OReily and myself worked on the Little Jessie to day   we do
an assessment for an interest.. Fine day but cold
Sunday Dec 14th
    Worked on the Little Jessie this afternoon   finished
Monday Dec 15
    Pete and myself walked up to the Little Dick Tunnel   it is in about
1500 feet and is still in porphyry..
Tuesday Dec 16th 1890
    We packed a little grub and a few blankets on Croppie this
morning and went up to the Blue Lime Cabin.. Worked this afternoon
on the Queen of the Hills doing assessment for Jim Downing..
Wednesday Dec 17th
    Finished assessment this afternoon.. run in 15 feet and a 12 foot
face. Moved down home this evening
Thursday Dec 18th
    Stopped in the house all day   am somewhat under the weather
with diareah and a bad cough. Pete O.Reiley went to Aspen this
morning.. We are having splendid sunshiny weather.. The roads are
dry and dusty. splendid.
Friday December 19th 1890
    Rolled out of bed about 8 oclock this morning. Stopped arround
the house all day doctoring myself up a little.. Cloudy and threatening
snow.. But dont seem to snow much.
    Made out a deed to Mother on the Rip Van Winkle Lode
Saturday Dec 20th
    Worked on the Leavenworth a little to day but felt so bad that did
not do much
Sunday Dec 21st
    Was up to Russells and Ed Higenbothoms this afternoon fine weather
Monday Dec 22nd
    Went to town to day. Bought Pete OReiley's 1/9 in the Little Jessie
for $20 00   So now I own 1/3 interest in it. McMasters deeded it to
me and I put it on record
Tuesday Dec 23rd
    In town got the deed from the Argentum Mining Co for part of the
conflict on the Blue Lime & Pilot Knob

Wednesday Dec 24
    Sent up a sock of flour and some other stuff by Fogg

Thursday Dec 25
    Christmas day. Am in town Fine day

Friday Dec 26th
    Still in town have checked out of the bank 25<u>00</u> money
                                   20.00 "
                                 <u>23.50</u> Hotel

Paid Clarendon   68.50 full
$23.50 Collected $12<u>00</u> of
Bonnell " $5<u>00</u> of Jim Downing

Saturday Dec 27<u>th</u> 1890
    Came home to day

Sunday Dec 28th
    Went up to Sandy Gulch to show Watson some claims charged him
$5<u>00</u> got 3<u>00</u>
    Sunshiny day

Monday Dec 29th
    Schlag and I packed up on Richmond Hill to day to do assessment
on the Bear Lode.. I comenced

Tuesday Dec 30th
    Schlag hired a man in his place to work

Wednesday Dec 31<u>st</u>
    Finished the 10 foot that I agreed to do for an assessment to day
at noon   moved down this evening Very cold and stormy

Thursday Jan 1st 1891
    Clear sunshiny day.   I stopped in the house all day making good
resolutions and cooking and mending and reading.. Schlag here
with me..
    The Sioux indians under chief Big Foot had a fight with the 7<u>th</u> U.
S. Cavalry and killed and wounded 50.. dont know how many
indians were killed.. Dec 29th
    Old Sitting Bull was killed about a week ago

Friday Jan 2<u>nd</u> 1891
    Did nothing much to day   waiting for a surveyor from town.. But
he did not come

Saturday Jan 3<u>rd</u> 1891
    Baked some light bread and stopped in the house most of the day.
Schlag brought the mail up this evening   Fine day but cold

Sunday Jan 4<u>th</u>
    Fine sunney day   Washed some clothes.. Had roast duck for dinner
Wrote a letter to the Surveyor general regarding the Ranche also wrote
to Montgomery & Ward for reloading outfit for my rifle $3<u>00</u>

Monday January 5th 91

Went up to the Leavenworth and work 5 or 6 hours she still shows some galena. Fine day but cold

Tuesday Jan 6th

Snowed about 2 inches last night and storming this morning but cleared up and was a fine day. I went to Aspen and bought a few things.   Walked down and up got home 4.30 in the evening feeling good but tired.

Wednesday Jan 7th

At home all day. Schlag went up to the Cummings Mine to day they have cut the lead with their tunnel and have a lead 9 feet 8 1/2 inches wide with about 4 feet of ore.. Major Pickrel went up to day. Cold and windy day.. I made out 3 certificates for Pickrel

Thursday January 8th 1891

At home all day.   Baked some light bread & tinkered arround the house.. Cold and cloudy

The cover of Armstrong's 1891 - 1892 journal shows considerable wear. Miraculously, all twenty of Armstrong's journals survived. (Armstrong's journals)

Friday January 9th 1891

Was up Sandy Gulch doing some surveying to day for Blockman & Ellithorpe   charged them $10.00. Got home this evening   cold day but sunshiny

Saturday Jan 10th

Fine day but cold.   I walked to Aspen.. Collected $20.00 of Jim Downing and $5.00 of Chas Ellithorpe.. Lent $5.00 to John Watkins. Bought some groceries & other truck got home about 4.30 in the evening.. Got a letter from home and one from Surveyor General of Denver

Sunday Jan 11th 1891

Very cold day but clear.   I stopped in the house all day reading &c

Monday Jan 12th

Was up to the Leavenworth Tunnel and did some work Cold clear day

Tuesday Jan 13th

Worked in the tunnel   clear fine day   and somewhat warmer than it has been for the past week

Wednesday Jan 14

I walked to Aspen this morning. Went down for the purpose of settling with H.P. Cowenhoven and Van Hovenberg.. But of course Schlag was not ready and could do nothing so I had to stop in town

Thursday Jan 15th 1891

The U.S. Senate passed the Free coinage bill last night.. And Fritz Simmons from Australia whipped Jack Dempsy.. In New Orleans

I settled my share of the debt that we owed H. P. Cowenhoven & Co amounting to $37500 paid them the cash also paid VanHovenberg $122.40 my half of the bill we owe him.. Schlag could pay nothing.. But it lets me out anyway.. I came home this evening   got here at dark

Friday Jany 16th

Did not get up till 9 oclock this morning.. Baked some light bread and set arround the house all day reading &c.. Fine sunney day

Saturday Jany 17th 1891

Splendid sunshiny day.   I put in part of the day writing certificates and in the afternoon measured a line to see where the South line of the Ranche would come.. Wrote a letter home to day..

Sunday Jan 18th 1891

Clear warm day more like summer than winter.   Surveying arround the Ranche.. hardly any body on the road to day.. I am here alone but pass the time reading Ella Wheelers Poems of Passion some of the poems are hot enough to keep a fellow much warmer than the weather is now..

Monday Jan 19th

Washed clothes to day

Tuesday January 20th 91

Rode to Aspen with Mr. Morse.   Bought some things that I needed.. Received the Reloading tools for my rifle that I sent to Montgomery & Ward for they cost me $300 laid down here.. Walked home in the evening. fine day.. Town is rather dull.

Wednesday January 21st

At home all day moulding bullets for me rifle.. And choring arround fine day

Thursday January 22

When I got up this morning it was storming and the ground covered with about 2 inches of new snow.. And it stormed most of the day reloaded some cartridges and tried them they work first rate.. Baked bread to day..

Friday January 23rd 91

Clear and cold to day.. I stopped in the house all day shooting at a target and reloading cartridges and reloading &c.

Saturday January 24th

Clear fine day sun shone warm and thawed the snow some.. I went up to the tunnel this afternoon and worked 2 or 3 hours.

Sunday Jan 25th

Snowing a little when I got up this morning but cleared up and was a fine warm day   Stopped home all day wrote a letter to Surveyor Gen this even..

Monday Jan 26th 91

On the sick list to day my face is swolen and have a touch of toothache.. Fine day

Tuesday Jan 27th

Face swell up I think it is erecipelas.. Stormy day but warm reminds me of spring

Face better this evening

Wednesday Jan 28

Face bad this morning.. Snowing when I got up and has been snowing all day. the sleighing is quite good now.. Sent to town by Fogg and got 10 lbs pork of Al Hopely.. And the mail got a letter from home. the folks wells. answered it this evening

Thursday January 29th 91

Face better to day.. Fine weather but cold

Friday January 30th

Theadore Byxbee and Chas Jenkins came up from town about noon both pretty full.   Brought a turkey and oysters and we had a great feed.   Fred Basager came up in time for dinner.. They all left about 5 oclock.. Fred and his partner had bad luck their horse balked on the Red Hill and backed over the grade.. They tumbled out put the horse and sleigh went down the hill.. They came back and I went town with a lantern and we got the horse and got home about 9.30

Saturday Jany 31st 91

Fred and partner stopped with me last night.. Fogg passed about 6.30 this morning and the partner went to town with him.. Fred and I started to town about 11 with Mr. Morris the sleigh broke down, and while we were fussing with it Fred had a fit which frightened me most to death. I thought he was dead for a while.. but he came too allright and I got a chance to send him on to town.. I got as far as the Old toll gate with Morse when we met Fogg and I came back with him.. Stormy day..

Sunday February 1st 1891

Cold and stormy.. I stopped in the house all day.   Fogg came down this afternoon going to stop here to night

Monday Feby 2nd

Ground hog day.. Storming very hard this morning. I went to Aspen with Fogg. Bought some provisions and came home with Fogg.. Sent a deed to the Rip and a power of attorney to Roxie.. Paid McDonald $6.00 which payes him in full for Patenting the Rip.. paid 1.00 for box rent at Post Office

Tuesday Feby 3rd

Coldest morning of the season.   I got up at 9. Had quite a lot of company to day .. Bob Donaldson here to dinner clear sunny day but very cold

Thursday Feby 5th 91
   Road down to town with Mr Morris

Friday Feby 6th
   Stopped in town Snowed

Saturday Feby 7th
   Came up home to day   walked.   Bush came up with me.   I have leased the Rip again for 18 months at 20 pr cent $60000 bond

Sunday Feby 8th
   Sick to day very bad cold and bad cough

Wednesday Feby 11th
   I have been sick abed since sunday.. am a little better to day.   Bush went home to day.   Byxbee came up this evening and Chas Jenkins and had supper..

Saturday Feby 14th
   Signed the lease &c on the Rip to day   the parties were up here from town.. Schlag was here to day.. Fine weather we are having. I am much better but dont feel very will yet..

Wednesday Feby 18th 1891
   We are having plenty of snow.. it has been falling for the last 3 days about a foot of new snow now.. Got a letter from home to day they are all well.. I am about over any cold and am feeling very well again

Thursday Feby 19th
   Road down town this afternoon with Fogg.. Telegraphed to Roxy for her to send power atty at once cost me 75c

Friday Feby 20th
   Came home with Fogg about 2 oclock   snowing quite brisk   Fogg stopped with me... Man killed with snowslide on Aspen Mt. to day

Tuesday Feby 24th
   Very stormy this morning.   Snowed about 18 inches last night and is drifting badly this morning.. Schlag is here rounding up his jacks.. Sun shining this afternoon

Wednesday Feby 25
   Very Stormy

Thursday Feby 26
   Still stormy
   Bob Donaldson here to supper

Friday Feby 27th
   Went to Aspen with Fogg Roads are bad with snow.   Got Power of Atty from Roxy

Saturday Feby 28
   Recorded Power Atty to day. Bot smoking fob and sack flour at

Clark & Denmans.   Came up with Fogg head to shovel the road out considerable. Got home 1 oclock   Bob Donaldson here yet

Sunday March 1st 91
Bob went to town.. I wrote a letter home.. Still stormy Maj Pickrel came down the gulch

Monday March 2nd
Very stormy.. I washed up my clothes..

Tuesday Mar 3rd
Clear fine day.. I have two boarders came here for dinner.. charge them $100.   for day I put in the day baking &c

Wednesday Mar 4
Went to Aspen to get some grub. Could not get it up to day 1 more boarder to Supper

Thursday Mar 5th
Still in town.

Friday Mar 6th
Still in town.   Schlag packed up some supplies to day for me

Saturday March 7th 91
Came up with Fogg to day. Got home about noon   Got a letter from Tom Ogburn.   he and Pete are in Garfield Co Utah about 200 miles south of Salt Lake City   both well and enjoying themselves I answered it

Sunday Mar 8th
Have 4 boarders. Keeps me busy cooking rustling wood &c

Monday Mar 9th
Stormy

Tuesday Mar 10th
Very stormy snowy day.   Schlag here to dinner

Wednesday Mar 11th 99

Sunday March 15th 91
Splendid sunney day.. I put in most of the day baking.. Fogg stopped with me last night. I sent to Hopley s and got 10# sausage & 10# stake by him yesterday Schlag here to dinner.. The leasers on the Rip hauled their hoister by here to day bound for the Rip.. Got a letter from Roxie to day they are well.. I wrote to H. N. Wood this evening telling him how the Rip was prospering..

Monday March 16th
Fine warm day.. I cut down a tree and hauled it down to the house. Schlag here to dinner also Geo Triplet & 2 others.. Trip is going up to work on the Midnight.. Schlag brought up 1/4 beef for me & 10# onions

Tuesday March 17th 91
Storming when I got up this morning.. But cleared up till about 10 oclock.   A regular blizzard came up from the north.. And it stormed

most of the day.. Maj Pickrel went up the gulch.. The boiler for the "Rip" went up to day.

Friday March 20th
The worst storm of the season raged all day drifted the snow fearfully

Saturday Mar 21st
Fine day.. the snow settled very fast.. Geo Triplet stopped here last night.

Sunday Mar 22nd
Sun shone hot all day thawing the snow very fast

[Armstrong inserted the following note in the back of this journal.]

A few notes 1889 Nov 10th
There seems to be great demand for timber for mining &c There is a good chance to take up placar ground covered with timber up Ingleside gulch.   I must see Dave Brown and some of the mining men about it. In the Anaconda Mine Montana they use 80,000 feet of timber under ground daily or 30,000,000 feet a year and at the Anaconda smelter they use 180 cords of wood daily or 65,700 cords a year

[Now begins another journal.]

Monday March 23rd 1891
Another boarder here to dinner.   I have 5 now at a dollar a day

Tuesday March 24
Somewhat stormy to day.   I baked bread and pies and hauled in some wood

Wednesday Mar 25th
Fine warm day.. Toney Nugent and Tommy Leatherdale was here this afternoon.. I sent to town with Morse for some provisions

Thursday Mar 26th
Splendid day.. Snow is setling very fast

Friday March 27/91
Fine day.. Baked bread & pies to day.. Morse brought up 25# sugar 25# butter 20 lard 2 1/2 Baking powder & sack potatoes from Clark & Denmans to day.

April 1st 91 Wednesday
Jim Magee & Toney Nugent here to dinner.   I turned in my bill amount $114.76 to Thorene for board

Apr 3
Bixby stopped with me last night

April 4th Saturday
Splendid sunney day Maj Pickrel here to dinner on this way up the Gulch.. I got 10# pork 10# beef stake of Al Hopely to day.. The leasors on the Rip have steam up and are hoisting water

Apr 5th Sunday
Fine day.. Schlag here for dinner. He is going to pack coal for the Rip Vanwinkle

Monday April 6th 1891
Very warm spring day thawing.. I hauled in two good trees for firewood on the crush this morning

Tuesday Apr 7th
Went down and hauled in a fine tree this morning for wood.. Fine day..

Wednesday Apr 8th
Very stormy.. snowed about 6 inches

Thursday Apr 9th
Fine day.. Morse hauled up from C & D 1 case milk 2 hams & 100# flour

Saturday Apr 11th
Went to town and drew 114.75 for board from Thorene. Paid Clark & Denman and ordered more grub paid Al Hopely 13<u>00</u> on a/c

Monday Apr 13
Went to Glenwood with Bush & Ed Watkins cost me 20<u>00</u>

Friday Apr 17th
Came home this afternoon after making as big a fool of myself as possible

Saturday Apr 18th
Sick all day

Sunday Apr 20th
Stormy Baked bread & pies.   Two more sweeds came here to dinner have 6 here now on the Wilton Belle tunnel

Thursday Apr 23rd
Very warm day and the snow is going very fast   Wrote to Gurley for his Manuals cost 50c

Saturday Apr 25th
Fine day.. Got letter from Tom Ogburn & Pete they were in Salt Lake the 21<u>st</u> but were packed and were going to start the same day for Ketchum. Idaho

May 11th 1891
I went to aspen this afternoon to get pay for boarding the men on the Wilton Belle but did not get it.. Mr. Morse plowed the garden a few days ago and I have planted a few things..

May 12th Tuesday
Stopped at the Clarendon Hotel last night.. Did not get paid to day.. Got a letter from Tom Ogburn and Pete Olsen they were in Ketchum when they wrote but expected to pull out for Stanly Basin on Salmon River Idaho

Wednesday May 13th
Got paid this morning $13600   I paid Clark & Denman $73.15
Al Hopely $2000 Clarendon 400 Jerome $200 bot some clothes 500
and spent about 500 pd 200 for recording deed from Argentum
mining Co to conflict on Blue Lime Lode pd 200

Saturday May 16th 91
Got some groceries from Clark & Denman.. Morse hauled them
up yesterday.   Paid Morse $800 on a/c.   Schlag brought up 10lb
Beef Steak from Al Hopely for me to day.. I planted some potatoes in
the garden to day

Sunday May 17th
Fine day.. Had 5 extra here for dinner.. Baked light bread to day

Saturday May 30th 91
Walked to Aspen this morning.. Decoration exercises were good

Sunday May 31
Lodged at the Clarendon last night.   Was at the baseball game to day

Monday June 1st
Stopped at Clarendon last night

Tuesday June 2nd
Came home to day.   Old Bush came up with me

Wednesday June 3rd
Stormy rained good and hard

Thursday June 4th 91
Rainy.. Bush and I put in the time hunting mushrooms & fishing

Friday June 5th 91
Caught a small mess of fish to day

Saturday June 6th
Bush and I went to town to day walked down

Sunday June 7th
Stopped at Clarendon last night settled after dinner $200.. Was to
the Opera house to hear Mrs Rease the great Alliance politicion talk
she is fine.. Came home this afternoon.   Schlag and Jim Kinney
stopped here to night

Monday June 8th
Schlag and Jim went over to Italian Mt. this morning.   I washed
and did a little work in the garden   fine weather we are having

Tuesday June 9th
I went up on Richmond Hill to day to take a look at the countrey.
The first time I have been up there this year. It looks like business up
there now

Wednesday June 10th
I went to Aspen this afternoon to see about getting my money of the Red Jacket Co   did not get it

Friday June 12th 91
Stopped at the Clarendon last night in town all day

Saturday June 13
In town all day

Sunday June 14
Came home this forenoon.. Spent $15<u>00</u> in town and nothing to show for it
Rainy day

Monday June 15<u>th</u>
Was up Conundrum to day fishing   did not get one.   Planted some potatoes in the garden in the afternoon   Raining this evening

Friday June 19<u>th</u> 1891
Went to Aspen to day

Saturday June 20th
In town all day

Sunday June 21st
In town all day.   Was to the foot race Gorman beat .. 5 miles in 35"- 10"

Monday June 22<u>nd</u>
Settled with the Red Jacket Co to day for boarding the men the month of May.. Pd Clark & Denman in full over $40..
Pd Clarendon 20
" Slavens in full 3.50
" Gerome " 5.57
" Court Exchange 4.60
" Roxy by draft for interest for 6 months $40
came home this evening

Tuesday June 23rd 91
At home all day. Went fishing this morning but did not catch anything   Worked in the garden a little.. wrote to Pete and Tom

Wednesday June 24
Went to Aspen
Registered deed for conflict
on Blue Lime Lode 2<u>00</u>
Pd Jim Magee borrowed money 10<u>00</u>
" Elliot & Calabene 10<u>00</u>
" Clark & Denman for
bill of groceries 10<u>00</u>
Pd Phil Carbary in full 1.30
Came home this evening

Thursday June 25th
Very warm and very windy.   I took a walk up to the Milk Ranche Cabin this fore noon.. Jim Magee and Thorine were here to day

Friday June 26th 91
Washed some clothes to day.   Got lunch at noon for about 15 Big Guns of the Midland R.R. that Charlie Franklin and Jess Waters were taking up on Richmond Hill to look at the Park & Mamie Mine. The secretary of state of Colo was amongst them.. They were a nice sociable lot of men
Was talking with Maj Pickrel this evening   he has got to work on the Grand Union in good shape..

Tuesday June 30th
Bert Fuller and Mis Russell were married to day

Monday July 20th 91
Wrote a letter to Tom and Pete yesterday at Bonanza City Idaho. Wrote to Toney Nugent at Silver City Utah.. sent Tom some papers to day.. We are having very dry weather.. And need rain badly.. The fish are beginning to bite.. I caught a small mess to day.. The grand Union is looking fine I hear.. The "Rip" folks are down 200 feet and are drifting to the East have some low grade mineral.. John Coll went over to Spring Creek yesterday to show some people his property.. July 7 I got $2000 of Jim Downing he owes me $9000 yet

Tuesday July 21st 91
Surveying all day for Mr. Frantz about 1/2 mile above the house.. warm day

Monday Aug 10th 91
The Rip shut down to day for a while

Tuesday Aug 11th 91
Came home day before yesterday from Taylor River. Started over there the 28th of July with Bush fishing caught lots of trout.. Received a letter from Roxie yesterday all well.. We have had some fine rains since we left here.. having some small shower to day with cool weather..

Saturday August 15
Surveyed a Mill Site for Morse & Mead to day charged them $500. Did not get it

Sunday Aug 16th
Worked all day in the Phoenix Tunnel for Ben Bonell.. Old Bush helped me

Monday Aug 17th 1891
Walked to Aspen with Bush to day.. Pickrel pd me 500 for the surveying of the Osborn last spring.. Mr Cowen is in town I was trying to get him to patent some of our claims for 1/4 interest.. But

could not get him to do it.. I paid 2<u>00</u> for recording notice to leasers about holding the Rip for debts..

Tuesday Aug 18<u>th</u> 91
In town all day

Wednesday Aug 19th
In town all day

Thursday Aug 20th
Came home at noon rode up with John Coll   he is going over to Cement Creek.. Fred Bassager let me have 500 to day which surprised me very much

Friday Aug 21<u>st</u>
Had a tramp here for bed and breakfast. I went up Conundrum this afternoon and picked a few rasberries

Saturday Aug 22<u>nd</u>
Went up to the Rip this afternoon and posted a notice warming everyone that we are not responsible for leasers debts

Sunday Aug 23<u>rd</u> 91
Washed my duds to day. was out gunning a short time in the morning did not see any game.. caught a few fish in the evening

Monday Aug 24<u>th</u>
Went to Aspen to day. Sent one dollar for N.Y. Sun came home in good shape

Tuesday Aug 25th
Took the gun and went on the hill looking for grouse did not get any.   Was up to the Blue Lime   Cris Con and two others are in the cabin. they are working on the Unexpected. I stopped in to see the Leavenworth Tunnel   got home about 6 oclock.. very warm day..

Wednesday Aug 26th
Went up Conundrum after berries

Thursday Aug 27<u>th</u> 1891
Washed some dud this forenoon. walked to town in the afternoon to see Geo Nyce about some surveying

Friday Aug 28<u>th</u>
Stopped at the Clarendon last night and to breakfast and dinner. Rode Crop home in the afternoon.   Bush and Schlag went over to Taylor river to day.. I wrote a letter home to day

Saturday Aug 29<u>th</u>
At home most of the day fixing fish pole &c. Caught a mess of fish this evening

Sunday Aug 30<u>th</u> 91
Got up early this morning and went up to the Big Park up Conundrum after grouse   killed 7 gave 3 to Sam Selden who was here when I got home

Monday Aug 31st 1891

At home all day fussing arround   made a plat for Mr. Frank of the claims I surveyed for him

Tuesday September 1st 91

Was up to the Leavenworth Tunnel and cleaned it out.   Rained this afternoon

Wednesday Sept 2nd 91

At home most of the day

Thursday Sept 3rd

put in some track in the tunnel and cleaned it out beside doing some work in the breast

Friday Sept 4th

Rode Crop up to the Big Park up Conundrum hunting grouse   did not kill but one.

Saturday Sept 5th

Road down town with Mr. Morse. Got some groceries at Clark and Denmans got $3.00 of Ben Bonnell   he owes me 2.50 yet

Sunday Sept 6th

Stopped at the Clarendon last night.   Stayed in town all day

Monday Sept 7th

Raining very hard when got up this morning   slept at the Clarendon. Rained till about noon   I walked up in the afternoon

Tuesday Sept 8th

At home most of the day   not feeling very well

Wednesday Sept 9th

Went up Conundrum and picked 3 qts of Rasberries   there is plenty of them yet

Thursday Sept 10th

At home most of the day. Baked some raspberry pies in forenoon   went fishing in afternoon caught 3

Friday Sept 11th 91

Went up to the Leavenworth Tunnel   put in some track and took out some dirt got home at dark

Thursday Sept 17th

Was up to the Leavenworth Tunnel to day and did a little work on the Little Jessie

Friday Sept 18th

Sharpened and fixed up drills and picks to day

Saturday Sept 19th

Went to Aspen to day

Thursday Sept 20th 1891
In town all day. Pete started for here   Got letter from Tom Ogburn the 31 of August

Monday Sept 21st
In town all day Raining

Tuesday Sept 22nd
Raining very hard all the forenoon.. I came home in the afternoon

Wednesday Sept 23rd
At home all day We are having very wet stormy weather

Thursday Sept 24
Walked to town to see about some assessment work walked back in the evening

Friday Sept 25th
Rained most all day.. I did some washing

Saturday Sept 26
Ground covered with snow this morning

Tuesday Sept 29th 91
Went to Aspen to day to 4 paws show [traveling circus] Fine show

Wednesday Sept 30th
In town all day

Thursday Oct 1st
In town all day

Friday Oct 2nd
Came home to day   Bush and Don Kennedy came up with we

Saturday Oct 3rd
Arround the house all day

Sunday Oct 4th
Surveyed two claims for A. B. Morgan and L. H. Fullbright charged them $1000

Monday Oct 5th
Surveyed a claim for Morse up at the Tenderfoot charged $500

Tuesday Oct 6th 1891
Pete Olsen came home yesterday from Idaho.   Road horseback all the way Don Kennedy went to town yesterday.. Today Pete, Bush and myself went up to Engleside..
I am helping Bush do assessment work on the Phoenix. I am working for Ben Bonnell..

Wednesday Oct 7th
worked all day

Thursday Oct 8th
worked all day

Saturday Oct 10th
   Pete went to Aspen today

Monday Oct 12
   Snowed 6 inches last night

Tuesday Oct 15 91
   Finished work on the Phoenix this evening   10 days $35<u>00</u>
Bonnell owes me

Friday Oct 16th
   Bush went to Aspen this morning.   I cleaned out the trail to the
Jersey Lily and in the afternoon Pete and I moved down to Highland

Saturday Oct 17th
   Collected $3.00 from McClintock and $6<u>00</u> from Schlag Pete and
I rode the ponies to Aspen to day came home this evening

Sunday Oct 18th
   Stopped arround the house all day

Monday Oct 19th 91
   Pete and myself dug the potatoes and turnips in the garden to day
and put them in the cellar.. fine weather we are having

Thursday Oct 22nd
   Pete and I went to town to day to see about getting patent on the
Phoenix through.. came home this evening. got a letter from Roxie.
she is to marry Mr Sewell the 29th   sent me a specimen of the
material for her wedding dress

Monday Oct 26th 1891
   Went to Aspen to day to see about the patent.   Paid $2.10 for an
abstract and $10<u>00</u> fee to Rogers the attorney.   Got the plat and
notice to post on the claim got home in the evening. Ben Bonnell paid
me $20<u>00</u> cash owes me $17.50 more

Tuesday Oct 27th
   Pete and I rode up on the hill to day.   Got McCabe and George
Cline as witnesses and posted plat and notice on the Phoenix Lode

Wednesday Oct 28th
   Went to town to day with McCabe and George Cline to make
affadavit to postng plat and notice   Came home this evening.. Bill
Emery came up with me and stopped all night

Thursday Oct 29th 91
   Pete and I went up to Robinson Tunnel to day   they are 1200 feet
in the porphyry and are not through it yet

Friday Oct 30th
   Went up on the mountain to day and killed 6 grouse

Saturday Oct 31st

Fine day did some washing and choring arround the house. Wrote a letter to Dr Manders at Alamosa about lease on the Rip

Sunday Nov 1st 1891

Fine day Pete and I rode up Conundrum Gulch. Took dinner with Abe Lee and wife took a look at the Grand Union Tunnel on our way back

Tuesday Nov 3

Election of County officers to day.   We went to Aspen. Got a bill of Grub $23.00 paid $10.00 came home in the evening

Thursday Nov 5th

Pete went up to work on the claims to day. I baked some bread and pies.   Joe Packer brought our supplies up to day   I paid him 75c for it

Friday Nov 6th

Pete and I worked all day on the tunnel. fine day but snowing this evening

Saturday Nov 7th

We worked on the tunnel all day   snowed a little this afternoon

Sunday Nov 8th

Cold and stormy all day ground covered with snow   We stayed at home all day baked bread &c

Monday Nov 9th

Cold and stormy. We worked on the tunnel all day..

Friday Nov 13th 1891

Pete and I walked to town to day I got $22.25 of Tom Hunt for his share of assessment on the Little Jessie   Pete went home this evening I stopped in town got fine 1/4 beef of Al Hopely

Saturday Nov 14

In town all day

Sunday Nov 15

In town all day

Monday Nov 16

In town all day

Tuesday Nov 17th

Pete came down and I went home with him

Wednesday Nov 18th

I was sick all day

Thursday Nov 19th

Went to town this afternoon walked down and back

Friday Nov 20th

We worked on the tunnel to day

Saturday Nov 21st
Very stormy to day regular blizzard   We got up some wood for the house

Sunday Nov 22nd
Worked at the tunnel timbered it up in good shape   Cold & some snow falling

Monday Nov 23rd
Clear fine day, stopped at home and baked and washed, and fixed up arround the house.

Thursday Nov 26th
Thanksgiving Day at home all day .. we hauled up a lot of wood with the jacks

Friday Nov 27th 91
Rode to town with Morse. Got the mail and some medicine for Pete walked up in the evening stormy

Saturday 28th Nov..
Caught a martin this morning.. Babbit and his man was here to dinner   they are surveying the Wilton Belle tunnel

Sunday Nov 29th 1891
I am 44 years old to day. at home all day   Baked some bread &c clear warm day

Wednesday Dec 9th 1891
Pete and I moved up to Dyers cabin to day. so as to be nearer the tunnel.   Morse hauled our stuff for us

Thursday Dec 10th
We worked in the tunnel to day

Friday Dec 11th
I came down to the house this morning and moved the blacksmith outfit up to camp with Morse

Saturday Dec 12th
Rode to town with Morse. Got some groceries and a 1/4 of beef. Morse brought them up.   Ben Bonnell paid me 5<u>00</u> on a/c Jack & Mc paid me the rent 3<u>00</u>

Sunday Dec 13th 91
Worked at the tunnel

Monday Dec 13th [date repeated]
about 8 inches of new snow this morning   Worked all day.

Tuesday Dec 14th
Fine clear day.   we worked in the forenoon in the afternoon went down home

Wednesday Dec 15th 91
Went to Aspen to day

Thursday Dec 16th

Pete and I stopped at the Clarendon last night. Came home this forenoon. I got $10<u>00</u> of Al Hoply this morning paid Bixbee $5<u>00</u> bot me a pair of overshoes and 2 pr socks 2<u>00</u>

Friday Dec 17 1891

Wrote a letter to Tom Ogburn. He is in Carson City Nevada. Wrote to Roxie..

We went up to Camp to day helped Robinsons move their machinery.. they struck a great flow of water in their tunnel.. and it did much damage washed away part of the works and blockaded the road so teams can not get up or down from Ashcroft..

[Note: Armstrong is probably writing in response to the following letter which he kept with this journal.]

Oct 27/91

At Camp. Red Cannon <u>Nev</u>
Mr. C A Armstrong
Friend Charlie,

It has been a long time cince I wrote to you and am ancious to hear from Aspen and all the news I left Bonanza city on the 18<u>th</u> of Sept. the night of 17<u>th</u> it snowed 4 or 5 inches so I pulled south next morning via Deadwood Gold Hill Idaho City to Boise City I stoped 2 days at Deadwood one day at Gold Hill one at the sweet Mine 2 in Boise City the way I came was 235 miles from Boise to Silver City 100 then to De La mar then in to Oregon over the Old Silver City stage road to camp McDurmit to Winneamucca 210 m from their to Virginia city was their 2 day then to Carson City 200 miles from their to the Rich strike 30 miles south in Douglass Co. It was Rich in Gold but only a pocket I stoped one week and then moved to Red Cannon 10 miles south so I am just 40 miles south of Carson 45 south of Virginia City The formation is Lime Porhyry & Ironite dont know how long I will stay hear but until the first of Dec I think By the way I got on Dandy and wrode up to Lake Tahoe on the summut of the Sierra Nevada Mountains and I think it was the finest sheet of watter I ever saw 2/3 of the Lake is in California several steamers on the Lake I saw the deep Lake wheare no on ehas found bottom yet it has been sounded 1800 ft. it is the reverse of Salt Lake when one drowns in Salt Lake one never rises I saw the deep shaft and machinry it was something to look at I was only in one of the mines the Crown Point and then only down

1500 ft all of the mines are working on the 11 to 15 levels the Deep Shaft is not a work from a distance one would think it a Hot Spring to see the steam coming out of it the shaft is 9 x 28 ft. I was on the croppings of the Comstock it looks like the Grand Union blowout wall old Boy I wish you were hear to take a look at it I caught on to a vein that looks well carrys gold but how much I cant say will be in town soon and will have some assayed and will write you How is Pete and what kind of a trip did he have tell him to write me all about it tell him I have old Tintic and Dandy yet give him My kindest regards and write me all the new answer soon so long your friend

W T Ogburn Carson City Nevada

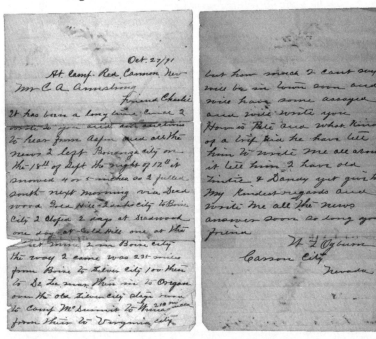

On October 27, 1891, Tom Ogburn wrote his "Friend Charlie" a lengthy letter from "Camp Red Cannon, Nev." The first and last pages are shown here. (Armstrong's journals)

Saturday Dec 18th
Pete went down to Highland this morning after the dogs.. I scared up a lot of wood for the house

Sunday Dec 19th 91
We got out timbers for the tunnel this forenoon and put in a set.. Fine day

Monday Dec 20th
   Worked in the tunnel all day Fine day

Tuesday Dec 21
   At work all day Fine

Wednesday Dec 22
   Worked at the tunnel   Came down to Highland this evening.
Stormy

January 15th 92. Friday
   Surveyed 3 claims for L. H. Fullbright   chg'd him $15<u>00</u> did not
get the pay

1892

January 20th 1892 Wednesday
   Fine day.   Pete and I came down from the tunnel day Sunday and
went to town Monday. stopped in town over night got home
yesterday evening.. I collected $22.25 of Mrs. Adair for assessment
on the Little Jessie.. and also $40<u>00</u> of Jim Downing.. he owes $50<u>00</u>
yet.. I sent Roxies $40<u>00</u> interest
   We stopped at the Clarendon $3<u>00</u> paid.. Got $16<u>00</u> worth of
grub at Clark & Denmans chgd.. Got $6<u>00</u> worth of meat paid..
Morse brought the stuff up..
   We are in 66 feet in tunnel

January 31st 1892
   Worked in tunnel part of the day. Moved down to H.land in the
afternoon. We are 80 feet under cover in tunnel.. We are having fine
warm weather for this time of year

February 1st
   At home all day.,. Lots of people going from here to the new camp
Creede.. in the souther part of the state

Saturday Feby 6th 1892
   Went to town to day. Got 5# apples & 5 of rice & bot of
horseradish 190 paid for them. I walked down and up got home
about 8 in the evening. Pd rent at P. O. 1<u>00</u>. Got letter from Roxie
and one from Toney Nugent

Tuesday February 9th 92
   Rode to town with Morse this morning.. walked back in afternoon
sent a letter to Roxie & one to Toney Nugent. Big strike of wire silver
in the Little Annie..
   Got a letter from Roxie today acknowledging the receipt of the
$4000 I sent her the 19th of January. Very cold weather..

Wednesday Feby 10th 1892
   Clear cool day.. at home all day

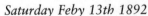

Saturday Feby 13th 1892

    Schlag came up with me with a cutter this evening and we went to town and sold the Ranch to B. Clark Wheeler for $6500. I got 2000 cash and notes for the rest due in 30 and 60 days at 1 1/2 per cent for month secured with 32000 shares Pontiac mining stocks.   I stopped at the Clarendon Hotel all night

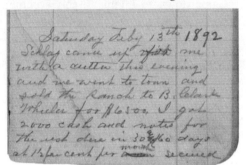

After Armstrong "sold the Ranch to B. Clark Wheeler," a prominent Aspen pioneer and mine owner shown above, he took up residence at the first-class Clarendon Hotel (below). Armstrong occasionally rode Little Annie ore wagons going to or coming from Aspen, since the cutoff to the mine was less than a mile below his cabin along Castle Creek. As indicated

by this stock certificate, B. Clark Wheeler also owned the Little Annie. (From left to right: Armstrong's journals; Aspen Historical Society; Courtesy of Ralph Kemper; Courtesy of the Lake County Public Library)

Sunday Feby 14th

Came up this morning and have been busy all day gathering up things that we want to take away

Monday Feby 15th

Pete and I went to town early this morning.. settled with Schlag and settled with the Clarendon Hotel $41 + 74.75 = 115.75 with Clark and Denman $67<u>00</u> Slaven $11<u>00</u> Mint $12<u>00</u> John Watkins 5<u>00</u> Al Hopely Aspen Times $20<u>00</u>

Deposited $1800.<u>00</u> in First National Bank. I hired a team and Pete & I rode up home. Took some grub with us

Tuesday Feby 16<u>th</u> 1892

We walked to town this morning.   I sent $200 home and $189.15 to Gurleys for a transit &c pd $11<u>00</u> for a tent

Thursday Feby 18<u>th</u>

Stopped at the Clarendon.   Got hair cut   Stormy day

Friday Feby 19th

In town all day

Saturday Feby 20<u>th</u>

Got $5000 of Jim Downing bal. on a/c Paid Cowenhoven & co $62.40 and took up note.. got a little grub and Pete and I came up home with Morse.. Paid Hotel bill 3<u>00</u> for Pete and 4<u>00</u> for me

Wednesday Feby 24<u>th</u>

Pete and I went down to Highland this morning and located the Spotted Tail Lode back of Highland

I settled with Morse this evening $5<u>00</u>

Thursday Feby 25<u>th</u>

I went to Aspen to day. Bought a 500 foot tape of Lee Hayes paid him $10<u>00</u> for it.. Went to lodge this evening   paid dues for the past two years $10<u>00</u>

Friday Feby 26th

In town all day

Saturday Feby 27<u>th</u> 1892

Got my instrument from Gurley to day   expressage came to $7.20 paid it

Sunday Feby 28<u>th</u>

In Leadville with Sam Selden.. left Aspen 11 oclock last night by D & R.G.R.R. Got here about 9 oclock. Took breakfast at the Saddle Rock Resteraunt.. looked over the town and surroundings till 5 P.M. We took the Midland train for home Got to the wreck about 7 oclock

Monday Feby 29th

We were delayed till 8 oclock this morning at Sellers station on the Frying Pan.. by an engine that was off the track arrived in Aspen 12.30   Fair over and back 9.70

Tuesday March 1st 1892
Came up home this forenoon with John Bolland

Wednesday March 2nd
Pete and I went up to John Boland s camp to day. Took dinner with him   Stormy this afternoon

Friday March 4th 1892
John Bolland was here this morning and Pete and I showed him our claims. Were up to the Blue Lime and over the hills   the snow is off so that it does not bother much.. John stopped with us for dinner

Saturday March 5th 92
Sold the blacksmith outfit and some tools to Morgan tice for $2000

Sunday March 6th
Went to Aspen to day. Received a letter from Tony Nugent he is in Bingham Cannon Utah.. Schlag left town to night

Tuesday March 8th
In town yet. Bought 508 shares of Little Anna stock at 21 cents $106.68

Wednesday March 9th 92
In town.   Pete came down this morning and got drunk

Thursday Mar 10th
Pete went up home to day.. I received a letter from Robert Armstrong Leavenworth.   I went to Lodge this evening wrote letter home

Friday March 11th
Settled Hotel bill and left town at 8 oclock. Rode up with Morses team got home about noon.. Very warm nice day and snow going very fast

Saturday Mar 12th
At home all day.. warm and pleasant

Sunday March 13th 1892
Pete and I went up on Richmond Hill for a walk and to see the folks. Took dinner with Mr. McCabe.. warm but cloudy day

Monday March 14
Paid Kinney of Ashcroft $200 that I have been oweing him since last summer

Tuesday March 15th
We went up to Robinson Tunnel this afternoon   called on the family and had quite a visit
They are cleaning out the tunnel and fixing up preparatory to resuming work..

Wednesday March 16th
About 8 inches of snow fell last night

St. PatrickThursday March 17th 92

Cold last night.. we did not get up till 8.30 oclock this morning.. has been clear and cold all day.. In the house all day reading &c..

Friday March 18th

Pete and I went to town to day.   Schlag got news that his father died to day.   he left for home this evening

Saturday Mar 19

Pete went up home to day I sent Bob Armstrong $10000 and Bought pair of boots $500.   Sent to Gurley $12.54 for books and prismate & eyepiece for transit

Sunday March 20th 1892

Very stormy this morning   In town all day

Monday March 21st

Arround town all day

Tuesday Mar 22nd

In town

Wednesday Mar 23rd

In town   Stormy   Wrote letter to Roxie and to Tony Nugent

Thursday Mar 24th

In town

Friday Mar 25th

In town

Saturday Mar 26th

Came up home this afternoon with Morse.   Brought up some meat 200 Clear but cold.. Settled hotel bill $12.50

Tuesday March 29th 1892

We went down to Highland this afternoon to see the boys and to take a little exercise.. Storming when we came back   Got some mackeral from town that I ordered a week ago

Thursday March 31st

Very stormy all day. Staid in the house all day

Friday April 1st 1892

Windy and stormy to day.. sun trying to shine.. but very feeble

Tuesday April 5th 1892

Rode to town with Morse to day. Received letter from Robert Armstrong acknowledging receipt of the hundred Dollars I sent him

Wednesday Apr 6th

Got the books and eyepiece from W & L. E. Gurley to day

Thursday Apr 7th

In town all day   Went to show at the Rink.. very good home talant   Sent up some grub by Morse this evening

Saturday April 9th 92

Lent A. L. Hopely one thousand dollars for 30 days at 1 1/2 per cent per month. Took his notes and gave him check on First National Bank for the amt.. Came up home road is very muddy.. Abe Lee came up and made a location.. Stormy this evening..

Sunday Apr 10th

Snowing and storming very hard this morning

Monday Apr 11th

Got up early this morning and Pete and I went down below Highland to do some surveying for John Nash & Geo Mowl but neither were there so we came home.. very warm nice day..

Friday Apr 15th 1892

Got up at 6 this morning and walked to Aspen.   B. Clark Wheeler paid me 625 dollars with interest for 60 days and 1 1/2 per cent per month amounting to $18.75.   I deposited it in First National Bank..

Saturday Apr 16th

Pete came down this morning his ponies came up from below this afternoon. I let Pete have $500 this evening Recd letter from Fred Bassiger today

Sunday Apr 17th

Let Pete have $2000 this morning to pay his Ranch bill.. I walked up home and Pete brought up the horses. I got 508 shares of Little Anna Stock No of certificate is 1465.. Apr 15th 1892

Monday Apr 18th 1892

Pete and I went down the road this morning early and surveyed a placer for John Nash and George Mowl   warm day and muddy and wet

Tuesday Apr 19th

At home all day doing nothing   Snowed about an inch last night but the sun took it all off to day

Wednesday Apr 27th 1892

Pete and I rode the ponies to Aspen this morning.. got some provisions and Pete came back this evening.   I stayed in town drew $10000 out of the bank and paid Clark & Denman $34.60 on a/c

Sunday May 1st 1892

I went down to Carbondale this morning with Sam Selden and Bush to look at an iron lead.   It did not amount to anything.. tried fishing but the river was to muddy so we stopped in Carbondale till about 11 oclock in the evening and came up on the train

Tuesday May 3rd

Gave John Coll a check on the bank for $15000 and took a bill of sale on his team harness and wagon as security.. I walked up home to day

Wednesday May 4th
Stormy and cold all day.   Jap Frost stopped with us for dinner & supper

Thursday May 5th
Jap Frost stopped with us over night and pulled out early this morning to go over Pearl Pass

Friday May 6th
Pete and I survyed a placer for Johyn Bolland to day

Saturday May 7th 1892
Pete and I rode the ponies to Aspen this forenoon.. Geo Triplett was up to look at our claims this morning and went to town with us.. I bought 2000 shares of Little Annie Stock to day for 20 1/4 cents a share gave check on the bank for $465 00 to A. J. Peck also drew $50 00 out of bank for myself.

Sunday May 8th
Pete and I surveyed a placer claim for Ben Ellithorpe to day charged him 8 00 for it   got the cash

Monday May 9th 1892
Geo Triplett and a Mr. Cooper was here for dinner to day.. They took a look at our property this afternoon and went up to Mrs. Russells to stop all night

Turesday May 10th
Was up to Ellithorpes to correct some coerners this forenoon Triplett and Mr. Cooper here to dinner

Wednesday May 11th
Pete and I went down near Highland to survey some claims for Thorine

Thursday May 12th 92
Surveying for Thorine four claims.. did not quite finish them.. I was so sick that I could hardly get home

Friday May 13th
Sick in bed all day

Saturday May 14th
Sick in bed all day

Sunday May 15th
Up to day but not feeling very good

Monday May 16th
Pete and I rode the ponies to town to day.. stormed so that we stayed in town all night

Tuesday May 17th 92
Came home this afternoon

Wednesday May 18
  Sick from a cold all day Fine weather

Thursday May 19
  Still on the sick list Fine day

Friday May 20th
  Still under the weather

Tuesday May 24th
  Pete and I surveyed a placer claim for John Bolland to day

Wednesday May 25th
  We rode to Aspen to day on the ponies. came home this evening
fine day..
  got some groceries and meat and some cough medicine

Thursday May 26th
  Rainy day.. staid at home

Friday May 27th
  Stormy all day and the ground white with snow this evening

Tuesday May 31st
  Snowed quite a bit this morning   About 2 inches on the ground
when we got up this morning

Wednesday June 1st 92
  We went to Aspen to day came home this evening fine day.. I sent
$81.00 to Montgomery and Ward of Chicago for a lot of things..
Wrote to Roxie..
  We got some grub and came home

Thursday June 2nd
  I caught 3 trout to day
  Fine day

Friday June 3rd
  Ground covered with snow this morning and it snowed steady all
day

Monday June 6th 1892
  Fine warm day.. I surveyed two claims for Wm Dougherty to day
got the cash for it $10.00

Tuesday June 7th
  Fine warm day surveyed a claim for Mr. Frantz.. very warm and
we suffered from thirst very much

Wednesday June 8th
  Warm fine day washed clothes and stayed arround the house all
day. Triplett and Mr. Cooper were here this afternoon.. they are still
looking for property to lease.. People are going over Taylor Range
most every day now but there is plenty of snow up there yet..

Thursday June 9th 92
We went to town to day.   I paid Clark & Denman in full.. Pete came home but I stopped in town to see about some biz

Friday June 10th
Rode John Coll s horse up Bush came up with me.   We are going over on Taylor river and Spring Creek to make some locations and catch some fish. lent John Watkins $400 for a year

Saturday June 11th
At home all day   not felling well

Sunday June 12th 1892
We got out early this morning and struck out for Taylor river. Got on top of the range about 9 oclock and down to Bowman about 11.   Tried the fishing but did not catch any. moved down to Red Mt. Ranch and stopped for the night

Monday June 13th 1892
Pulled out early and got over to Spring creek about 11 oclock. Tried the fishing this afternoon but had no success.   located 2 placer claims

Tuesday June 14th
Surveyed the Springtime Placer to day

Wednesday June 15th 92
Moved over to Taylor river to day. Stopped all night a Bowman

Thursday June 16th
Got home at noon.   Bush went on to town

Friday June 17th
Went to town today

Saturday June 18th
In town all day waiting on John Coll..

Sunday June 19th
Came home very warm day..

Monday June 20th 92
At home all day choring arround very warm day and the creek is very high..

Tuesday June 21st
Surveyed a mill sit for John Bolland to day   Pete helped me. very warm

Wednesday June 22nd
Washed some clothes today and chored arround the houses

Thursday June 23.
We rode the ponies up Conundrum to day.. and got some specimens from the Jersey Lily. to have assayed.. The Democrats at Chicago nominated Cleveland on first ballot

Saturday June 25th 92

We went to Aspen to day.   I paid 3<u>00</u> for assaying.. Gave Schlag 5<u>00</u> this evening.. We stayed in town   I got letter from Nugent

Sunday June 26th

We came home this afternoon   very warm and dusty

Monday June 27th

I went to town with Morse.. got my things from "Montgomery and Ward.. paid $8.84 freight Got some groceries at Clark & Denmans.. Got 5<u>00</u> of John Coll.. lent Jule Baily 1<u>00</u>

Tuesday June 28th 92

Surveying all day for Chas Boyd & Co.   Pete helped me, very warm

Wednesday June 29th

Surveying all day

Thursday June 30th

Surveying all day

Friday July 1st

Surveying all day finished 8 claims for 40<u>00</u>

Saturday July 2nd

Resting up to day

Sunday July 3rd

At home all day filling out certificates &c

Monday July 4th 92

We were down to Highland to see what improvements are going on.   B. Clark Wheeler has started his tunnel to cut Richmond Hill and is setting up an air compressor to do the work by machinery..

Tuesday July 5

We went to town today got some groceries & things.   Pete came home this evening and I stopped in town to see to some business. Got a letter from home all well

Wednesday July 6

Collected 35 dollars for locating and surveying placer claim on spring creek. Collected 20 dollars on the surveying I did last week.. lent $20<u>00</u> to John Watkins this evening.   hired a rig of Al Hopely and Ed Watkins drove me up home.

Thursday July 7th 1892

Rained all day so I stopped in the house.

Friday July 8th

Rained all day

Saturday July 9th

We went to town to day.. Got some groceries &c came home this evening by moonlight

Sunday July 10th
At house all day

Monday July 11th
At home all day

Tuesday July 12th
We packed up early this morning and got over to Red Mountain

Thursday July 21st 1892
At house all day resting.. ought to have gone over to Spring Creek but did not feel able..

Friday July 22nd 1892
Pulled out for Spring Creek this morning. Met Besser on the range.. We arrived in camp just before dark Rainy day..

Saturday July 23
In camp all day rainy

Sunday July 24th
Surveyed the ditch and did some work on it

Monday July 25th 1892
Fishing all day we caught 24 between us.. Rained all the afternoon and evening

Tuesday July 26th
We dug 100 feet of ditch this forenoon.   Rained very hard about noon and was at it all the after noon & evening

Wednesday July 27th
Rained all night.. We went fishing to day caught a good mess

Thursday July 28th
Mets, Peter & I went over to the Doctor Mine this forenoon and fished some in the afternoon.. no rain to day

Friday July 29th 1892
Out prospecting this fore noon. Pete in helping Besser to day..

Saturday July 30th
Surveyed three claims for Geo Besser to day.   Pete helped Besser to day

Sunday July 31st
Surveyed 2 claims for Paddy Reilly to day.   Pete helped

Monday Aug 1st 92
Surveyed one claim for Reilly to day

Tuesday Aug 2nd
Surveyed two claims for Reilly to day

Wednesday Aug 3rd 1892
Surveyed three claims for Geo Besser to day

Thursday Aug 4th
   We pulled out for home this morning. Came by the way of Cement Creek and the head of Taylor River got home about 5 P.M.

Friday Aug 5th
   At home all day writing up certificates

Saturday Aug 6th
   We went to Aspen to day got some grub and Pete went home. I loaned Jim Kinney $75⁰⁰ got check of Al Hopely for $75⁰⁰

Sunday Aug 7th 1892
   Pulled out for Denver this morning at 7.45 A.M. On a special train of Knight Templers
   Got into Denver about 11.30 P.M. Stopped at the Markham Hotel. They charged 3⁰⁰ a day for a room..

Monday Aug 8th 1892
   Taking in the sights to day.   I bought $6.35 worth of clothes We changed our room hired one for 2⁰⁰ per day in the Hallet Block

Tuesday Aug 9th 1892
   The great parade of Knights Templer at the 25th Triennial conclave.. They presented a fine appearance.. There were about 20,000 in line.. From all the states in the union and Canada

Monday August 15th 1892
   We pulled out for home this morning at 8.05 with a long train crowded.. Had a fine ride over the MidLand R.R.   Had dinner at Woodland Park .. Supper at Leadville and arrived in Aspen about 11.30 P.M.   I stopped at the Clarendon

Tuesday Aug 16th
   In town all day   My trip to Denver cost about $75⁰⁰

Wednesday Aug 17th
   Rode up home with Joe Parker got home about 1 P.M.
   Bear was at home to welcome me

Thursday Aug 18th 1892
   Pete came home from Spring Creek this afternoon.. I washed my clothes today..

Friday Aug 19th
   We took a walk up to Robinsons Tunnel to day and up to the Blue Lime.. picked some rasberries for dinner

Saturday Aug 20th
   We went to Aspen to day.. I got a note of Jim Kinney for $87.50 for one year at 10 per cent interest.   Money I loned him for his trip to Denver
   We got home about 9 oclock

Sunday Aug 21st 92

At home all day.. Sam Selden & mother & sister called her to day.. John Bolland and Bill Rose were here to dinner. fine day.. John Coll here this evening   he is going over to Spring Creek with us

Monday Aug 22nd

We pulled out for Spring Creek about 6 oclock. Got into Camp about 4 oclock   caught a mess of fish for supper

Tuesday Aug 23rd

John Coll and I went fishing and Pete went over on Cement Creek after Johns wagon.   I caught 22 & John 1 fishes..

Wednesday Aug 24th 92

I took the gun and went hunting for grouse this morning   did not find any.   Marks the surveyor came in this even

Thursday Aug 25th 92

Surveying all day on the placer claim

Friday Aug 26th

Surveying all day

Saturday Aug 27th

finished the surveying this forenoon.   Marks left about 2 P.M

Sunday Aug 28th

We hitched John & Dick to the wagon and drove over to Taylor River   Caught some fine fish this evening

Monday Aug 29th 92

Fished till 2 P.M had poor luck.. hitched up and drove home by 6 oclock

Tuesday Aug 30th

John Coll left for Aspen about 8 this morning..

Wednesday Aug 31st

Worked on the ditch

Thursday Sept 1st

worked on the ditch

Friday Sept 2nd

worked on the ditch

Saturday Sept 3rd

Surveyed claim for John Coll

Sunday Sept 4th

Surveyed the Fountain Lode to day.. got 37.50 of Mr. Walsod on a/c of wagon sold him the wagon for 75.00

Monday Sept 5th

Packed up and pulled for home to day.. by way of Italian Mt.. camped on Taylor this evening caught a mess of fish

Tuesday Sept 6th
  Got home about dusk. Got 3<u>00</u> worth of provision of Kinney at Ashcroft paid him

Wednesday Sept 7<u>th</u> 92
  Washed up some clothes to day

Thursday Sept. 8<u>th</u>
  We went to Aspen to day

Friday Sept 9<u>th</u>
  In town all day

Saturday Sept 10<u>th</u>
  Came home this evening late..

Sunday Sept 11<u>th</u>
  Home all day

Monday Sept 12th
  At home all day

Tuesday Sept 13<u>th</u> 1892
  We rode to Aspen to day. Came home this evening Fine day.. but the roads are very dusty

Wednesday Sept 14<u>th</u>
  Went up on Richmond Hill this afternoon.. to see the big strike on Copper Hill on the Topliff claim.. fine showing.. got home about 5 oclock.. fine day..

Thursday Sept 15<u>th</u>
  Washed my clothes to day.   This afternoon surveyed tunnel for Mr Morgan

Friday Sept 16
  Took the gun and dogs and went up Tola [?] Gulch to hunt grouse did not see a grouse.. got home about 3 oclock fine day

Saturday Sept 17
  Hunting grouse this forenoon   In afternoon helped Pete get out house logs fine day

Sunday Sept 18th
  hunting in forenoon at house   the rest of the day visiting with some of the neighbors. fine day

Monday Sept 19<u>th</u> 1892
  We went to Aspen to day.. I got $10<u>00</u> of John Coll... pd livery bill $5<u>00</u>.. bot 2<u>00</u> beef and other things so I had 70 cents left.. Received a letter from Roxie they are all well.. We got home in the evening..

Tuesday Sept 20<u>th</u>
  I put in the forenoon loading shells and experimenting with the gun   In the afternoon helped Pete on trail to our new cabin site..

Wednesday Sept 21st

Worked a little on the cabin this forenoon.. fished a little in the afternoon   did not see a fish..

Sunday Sept 25th 92

We rode up Conundrum to the Big Park. Hunted about 3 hours for grouse but did not see any.   Got home about 5 oclock

Monday Sept 26th

Surveyed a claim for Z. T. Carson.. And let it go toward paying him for assessment work for last year on the Little Jessie Lode..

Tuesday Sept 27th

Worked on the Cabin

Wednesday Sept 28th

Worked on the cabin

Thursday Sept 29

Worked on the Cabin.   Pete helping Morse this afternoon

Friday Sept 30th

Worked on the cabin.. Pete helping Morse get in hay.. Very warm dry weather

Saturday Oct 1st 1892

We road to town to day.   I stopped in town and Pete came home

Sunday Oct 2nd

Bush and I went to Glenwood Springs to day. Came back about midnight had a fine time swiming in the Big Pool. Saw John Watkins

Monday Oct 3rd

Pete came down with the horses and we came home in the evening

Saturday Oct 8th

I took the gun and dogs went up Sawmill Gulch and over in to Sandys Gulch and down home   was after grouse but did not get any

Sunday Oct 9th

Washed my clothes in the forenoon worked on the cabin the rest of the day

Monday Oct 10th

Rainy I was after grouse in the afternoon   did not see one

Tuesday Oct 11th

Worked on the cabin in the forenoon.. Got 500 feet of lumber of B. C. Wheeler to day for roofing.. got the roof partly on and it began to snow so we had to quit.. About 4 inches of snow this evening

Wednesday Oct 12th 92

12 inches of snow this morning.. Snowed all day.. We stopped in the house

Thursday Oct 13th
Cloudy but warm.   Put the roof on the cabin to day..

Friday Oct 14th
Worked at the cabin

Saturday Oct 15th
Daubed the Cabin to day

Sunday Oct 16th 92
Went up on Richmond Hill and got a door off the Rip VanWinkle

Monday Oct 17th
Went to Aspen to day Collected 20 dollars.   Bought a stove of B. Clark Wheeler $500 let Pete have $6.50 bought a window lock hinges &c $1.75 got some meat $1.50. Came home in the evening very cold.. The Grand Lodge of Odd Fellows paraded to day. fine turnout

Tuesday Oct 18th 92
Working at the Cabin all day   clear and cold

Wednesday Oct 19th
Working at the cabin

Thursday Oct 20th
Rode to town with Morse this morning.. Got a bill of groceries and some other things.. and saw about getting the stove up..

Friday Oct 21st
Moved into our new cabin to day.. She is a daisy. Put up the stove &c.. eat supper in the new cabin

Saturday Oct 22nd 92
Fixing things in shape to day.. fine day but threatens a storm this evening

Sunday Oct 23rd
We went up to Sandy Gulch and picked out some slabs

Monday Oct 24th
Mr. Morse hauled our slabs this morning

Tuesday Oct 25th
We worked on the Little Jessie Lode to day doing assessment

Wednesday Oct 26th 92
Worked on the Jessie

Thursday Oct 27th
Went to Aspen to day.   I was on a jury to try a man by the name of Lee for insanity. Found him insane.   Pete came home with the horses and a 1/4 of beef.   I went to Lodge this evening working on the 1st

Friday Oct 28th
In town all day stormy

Saturday Oct 29th
Came home this afternoon with Fogg Stormy

Sunday Oct 30th
Snowed all day   working around the house

Monday Oct 31st
Washed my clothes   Stormy day

Tuesday Nov 1 st 92
Stormy day   did nothing

Wednesday Nov 2
Stormy.. At home all day

Thursday Nov 3rd 92
We worked on the Little Jessie fine day

Friday Nov 4th
Worked on the Little Jessie fine day

Saturday Nov 5th
Got up at 6.30 and did some surveying for Mr. Gent this morning.. Worked on the Jessie the rest of the day.. Triplett took supper with use Fine day..

Sunday Nov 6th 92
Storming this morning and stormed most of the day.   I stopped in the house all day

Monday Nov 7th
We worked on the Jessie all day   Fine but cold

Tuesday Nov 8th
Stormy this morning.   We went up to Ashcroft and voted the Peoples ticket to day

Wednesday Nov 9th
We hitched the ponies to a buckboard and went to Aspen to day.. Stopped in town all night

Thursday Nov 10th 92
In town all day.. got some supplies at Clark & Denmans.. Pete drove the outfit home this evening.. Cleveland and the democrats swept the country by an over whellming majority

Friday Nov 11th
In town today

Saturday Nov 12th
In town all day.   Pd W W Corley tax on Rip 2 50

Sunday Nov 13th
Walked up home this forenoon.. Fine warm day

Monday Nov 14
At home all day

Tuesday Nov 15th 1892

Pete and I saddled the ponics and started for Spring Creek to post the notices for patent onthe Springtime Placer.. We got to Frank Stewarts camp on Italian Mountain about 4 oclock.. Storming furiously this evening   Posted 3 notices on his claims

Wednesday Nov. 16th

Storming hard this morn but we pulled out down Spring Creek and posted our notices and pulled for the R.R. at Almont Station. Got in about 4 oclock and put up the ponies & dogs got supper and at 7.30 took the train for Gunnison City. Arrived there about 8 stopped at the La Veta hotel   the finest in town

Thursday Nov 17

Fixed up our business at the Land Office and took the train at 4.30 P.M. for Almont.. dark when we arrived.. Fisher's the people here could not keep us so wc saddled up and rode up Taylor River 6 miles to Stevense's Ranch.. got supper about 7 oclock

Friday Nov 18th

Had a good nights rest and supper and breakfast and they would not take any pay for it.. I gave the little girls a dollar and we pulled out about 8 A.M.   Got to Stewarts Camp early   Very fine sunny day

Saturday Nov 19th

We pulled out about 9 this morning and got home about 5 this evening   Fine sunny day..

Sunday Nov 20th

At home all day resting   fine sunney day

Monday Nov 21st

Fine sunny day.. We went to Aspen. Got some supplies.   I Rode home with Fogg.. He paid me the $4000 that he borrowed last month

Tuesday Nov 22nd 1892

We worked on the Little Jessie today.. Fine day

Wednesday Nov 23rd

Fine day.. We worked in the Little Jessie Lode

Thursday Nov 24th 92

THANKSGIVING DAY

Cold and windy   We did not work   Took dinner with Morgans.. had roast turkey &c.. good dinner

Friday Nov 25th

Worked on the Little Jessie

Saturday Nov 26th 92

Worked on the Little Jessie.. cold dissagreeable day.. We opened the contact but it dont show any mineral.. brought our tools down to the house

Sunday Nov 27th

Fine day. I took a walk with the dogs down to Highland took a look arround. it made me think of old times.. but glad that I had sold out and got the money.. And was not compeled to stay on the ranch all the time.. Pete took the ponies to town and turned them out for the winter to day

Monday Nov 28th 1892

Pete got back to day pretty drunk. Fine day

Tuesday Nov 29th

I am 45 years old to day   at home all day

Wednesday Nov 30th

At home all day.. Chas Miller was here to dinner

Fine weather we are having.. I wrote Roxie and to Ben Bonnell at Indianapolis a dunning letter for the balance that he owes me for working in the Phoenix $13.50

Thursday Dec 1st 92

Went to Aspen to day   fine weather

Friday Dec 2nd

In town all day

Saturday Dec 3rd

In town all day

Sunday Dec 4th

Went to Glenwood springs with Bush took a sweat in the Caves.. got back to Aspen about 11 oclock in the evening

Monday Dec 5th

Arround town all day

Tuesday Dec 6th 92

Snowing all day

I leased the Rip to Chas Franklin to day for 2 1/2 years 20% royalty and 60 thousand bond

Wednesday Dec 7th

In town all day not feeling well on account of cough. Cold and stormy all day

Thursday Dec 8th

Murcury at zero this morning   In town all day not feeling well on a/c of bad cough

Friday Dec 9th

Pete came down town to day to see what had become of me

Saturday Dec 10th

Received a letter from Roxie to day. They are all well and looking for me.. Pete and I came home with Fogg this afternoon

Sunday Dec 11th
   In the house all day doctoring my cold.. Fine weather

Monday Dec 12th
   In the house all day.   Fogg was here for a while this morning fine day

Tuesday Dec 13th
   Looks stormy.. I stopped in the house all day

Wednesday Dec 14 92
   At home all day

Thursday Dec 15th
   Went to Aspen with Fogg. Got home in good season   Got some oysters &c.. Very cold day.. Chas Miller here for supper.

Friday Dec 16th
   In the house all day

Saturday Dec 17th
   At home all day   Fine sunny weather but cold

Sunday Dec 18th
   At home all day

Tuesday Dec 20th 1892
   Cold and snowing
   Old bear seems to be sick wont eat and dumps arround the house.. Chas Hubbard took dinner with me. he came from Italian Mt

Wednesday Dec 21st
   Poor faithfull Old Bear lay on the floor dead this morning.   He must have got a dose of poison night before last.. I have been mourning over him all day.. I raised him from a puppy. he was born in 1883.. and there has hardly been a day that we have not been together in all that time.   I rode down to Aspen with Fogg to day the first sleigh ride of the season

Thursday Dec 22nd
   Walking arround taking a little exercise.. Fine sunny day.. I feel very lonesome and sad about Old Bear dieing.. He has been such a faithfull old comrad all these years..

Friday Dec 23rd
   Washing clothes to day fine sunny day.. cut a lock of hair off of Old Bears tail to remember him by.   I had no idea that I loved the old dog so.. till he died, now I miss him and cant help mourning about him all the time..

Saturday Dec 24th 92
   Pete & I rode to Aspen with Fogg to day

Sunday Dec 25th
   Celebrating Christmas all day

Monday Dec 26th
  In town all day

Tuesday Dec 27
  Still in town

Wednesday Dec 28
  Came up with Fogg to day

Thursday Dec 29th
  Very stormy.. at home all day sick

Friday Dec 30th 92
  At home all day feeling sick

Saturday Dec 31st
  Stormy this morning but cleared off fine in afternoon.. Mr. Gent was here most of the day talking mining and prospecting

Sunday January 1st 1893
  No more treating nor drinking in Aspen. no more smoking but business and rational pleasure..

  Splendid weather I have been in the house most of the day.. and am feeling pretty well my cough is getting much better and by taking care of myself.   I think will be all right soon

Monday January 2nd 93
  Splendid day.. I took a long walk down toward Highland.. Put in part of the day fixing up my mineral specimens and gun material.. preparatory to packing my trunk to go back home on a visit..

Like most people, Armstrong repeatedly made New Year's resolutions that he did not keep. (Armstrong's journals)

Tuesday Jan 3rd
  Rode to Aspen with Fogg to day. Splendid sleighing and fine weather

Wednesday Jan 4th 93
  In town all day.. Saw Frank Neubauer and had a long visit with him he has been ranching over on Eagle river for the past 7 years but has not got rich yet..

Thursday Jan 5th
  Splendid warm nice day.. Walked up home this afternoon.. Fogg came up with me..

Friday Jan 6th 93
Fine warm day.. Washed my clothes

Saturday Jan 7th 93
Pete and I went to town today walked down.. a fine day

Tuesday Jan 17th
Paid Chas McBride bar bill $3000
He owes me now $35.55
I lent Fogg $2000 to day

Wednesday Jan 18th
Came home with Morse fine day.. I have been in Aspen since the 7th trying to get settled with different parties. stopped at the Clarendon Hotel.   I dont owe anybody in town a cent..
Settled with Cris Bow & John Wall on Springtime Placer.   They paid me $187.67. Paid Clark & Denman $101.35 in full of a/c

Thursday Jan 19th 93
Splendid day.. I have been in the house all day reading and repairing old clothes..

Friday Jan 20th 93
We started to work on the tunnel to day.   I got 130 feet of iron rails of L. Fullbright to apply on what he owes me Splendid day

Saturday Jan 21st
Worked at the tunnel a little this forenoon.. and wrote a letter home
Was down the road and got some straw for my bed.. Splendid day

Sunday Jan 22nd 93
Splendid springlike day Pete and I took a walk down toward Highland this forenoon. Dave Allan took dinner with us.

Monday January 23rd
Fine day. We worked on the tunnel all day.

Tuesday Jan 24th
Splendid Weather. Worked in the tunnel

Wednesday Jany 25th
Warm and springlike this morning. We are having the finest winter I ever saw in this countrey.

Thursday Jany 26th 93
Rode to Aspen with Morse.. Sleighing is poor all the hillsides are bare.. Stopped at the Clarendon for Supper Bed & Breakfast Went to Lodge this evening

Friday Jan 27th
Got some things at Clark & Denmans this morning and sent them up home by Morse
Stopped in town.. Stormy James G. Blaine died this morn at 9 oclock

Saturday Jany 28th
  Snowing hard this morning

Sunday Jany 29th
  Rode home with Morgan   Got home about noon

Monday Jany 30th 93
  Very windy to day and the snow is drifting badly.. At home all day

Tuesday Jany 31st 93
  In the house all day baking bread &c.. Snowing all day

Wednesday Febuary 1st 93
  About 2 feet of new snow on the ground and more coming
Worked in the tunnel in the afternoon

Thursday Feby 2nd
  Stormy day about 3 feet of new snow on the ground   Washed
some of my clothes

Friday Feby 3rd 93
  Clear today.. Got the mail there were two men killed near Aspen
Wednesday by a snow slide.. this seems to have been a general storm
all over the western countrey
  We did not work to day but set arround the house.. and read
the papers..

Saturday Feby 4th 93
  Rode to town with Mr. Morse.   Roads are heavy and snow deep
Stopped at Clarendon for Supper.. Collected $93.34 of C. M. Stillson

Sunday Feby 5th
  Still in town had dinner with Sam Selden folks

Monday Feby 6th 93
  About 6 inches new snow this morning

Tuesday Feby 7th 93rd
  Clear sunny day

Wednesday Feby 8th 93
  Rode up home with Mr Morse this morning.. Got some butter at
Clark & Denmans and fore 1/4 of beef at Chas Marshalls pd him 5
1/2 c per lb $6.50.. The Sleighing is fine. Received a letter from
Roxie.. She had a daughter Christmas and is sick yet.. So I am uncle..
Storming hard this evening

Thursday Feby 9th 93
  Snowed all day.. No body on the road. We stopped in the house
all day..

Saturday Feby 11th 93
  Settled with Pete to day.   I owe him $61.50 to balance all a/c..
Rode to Aspen with Mr Morse this afternoon   stopped at
the Clarendon

Sunday Feby 12th 1893
Warm nice day..

Tuesday Feby 21st
Rode up home with Mr Morse this morning very cold but clear.. washed my shirts

Wednesday Feby 22nd
Stormy day.. packed my trunk preparitory to starting for home.. was up to the tunnel. It is in fine black shale full of iron pyrites looks good..

Thursday Feby 23rd
Clear & cold this morning

Friday Feby 24th
Went to Aspen to day. Rode down on an ore wagon cold stormy

Monday Feby 27th
Hired an express team and went up home after my things. Left transit & compass with Sam Seldens folks..

Tuesday Feby 28th 93
Pete came down to day
I took the evening train for Denver.   Stopped at Glenwood Springs over night   slept with Geo Triplett

Wednesday March 1st
Left Glenwood Springs at 1.30P.M. on the Denver and Rio Grand R.R.
took a bath this fore noon.

Thursday Mar 2nd 93
Got into Denver 5.30 A.M.   Put up at the Markham Hotel.   Saw Abe Lee to day.   Went to Tabor Opera this evening

Friday Mar 3rd
Knocking arround town   Bought a 30 dollar over coat & a 4.50 hat

Saturday Mar 4th 93
Knocking arround town   Stormy & cold

Sunday Mar 5th 93
Still in town

Monday Nov 6th 93
Knocking arround town with Abe Lee

Tuesday Mar 7th 93
Left Denver this evening at 8.30 P.M. on the Burlington & Missouri R.R.

Wednesday Mar 8th 93
Got into Kansas City about 9 P.M.

Thursday Mar 9th 93
Stopped at the New Albany Hotel opposite Union Depot Kansas

City last night.   pd bill. L & B 2_00_ and took train for Leavenworth. Took dinner at Continental Hotel.. Ordered suit of clothes made at Eckarts

Friday Mar 10th 93

Knocking arround town all day. wrote letter to Roxie. I dont find many of the Old Timers arround town so I am getting sick of the town allready

Saturday Mar 11th 93

Fine day.. Met Don Roberts.. an old timer that used to be on surveys with us years ago.. Also met Diefendorf and old surveyor and put in the afternoon visiting and talking over old times.

Went to Crawfords Opera House to see the Danger Signal   a spectacular Rail Road Play   it was pretty good..

Sunday Mar 12th 93

Cold and windy.   Was arround the Hotel most of the day.   Saw Hackbush this evening and had quite a pleasant chat with him   He is a member of the legislature now..

Monday March 13th 93

Cold and windy   Did not go out much.

Tuesday March 14th

Cold wind but clear weather   The old missouri is up and booming. Saw Ed Burwell this afternoon

Wednesday March 15th 93

Cold and windy to day.   The Missouri is full of floating ice.. Was over to the soldiers home this afternoon with Mike Pzybylowicz and also to the funeral of John Brown from Kansas City a very prominant mason.. at Mount Muncie Cemetery.. Got a suit of clothes of Mr. Eckart. Paid him $36_00_ for them.

Thursday Mar 16th

Snowed all day.. I stopped arround the hotel.. Was to the opera house to the Show   8 Bells   very good show.

Friday March 17th 93

St Patericks day.. Stormy and cold

Saturday March 18th 93

Put in most of the day spreeing arround with a sewing machine man by the name of Healy and a Mr deuridquist[?] a tobacco man. We kept it up till 3 oclock in the morning..

Sunday Mar 19th 1893

Arround town all day working off the effects of last night's round up

Monday Mar 20th

Was around most of the day with Elisha Diefendorf

Wednesday Mar 22nd 93

Was up to Fort Leavenworth today.. Called on Albert Schlag who is boss of the Tailor Shop at the Military Prison. He showed me through the shops &c and I took dinner with him at the guards mess..

He called on me at the Continental this evening and we had a long chat.. While walking arround town this evening I came across Ikes the Post Master at the Fort.   He knew me but I would never have known him if he had not spoken to me Thunder storm this evening..

Thursday Mar 23rd 93

Loafing arround town all day

Friday Mar 24th 93

Loafing arround town. Went to the Opera House this evening to see Modjiska in As You Like it

Saturday Nov 25th

Went to Jake Schwaglers to day. Had dinner there and drank a lot of wine   got back home at dusk

Sunday March 26th 93

Fine day.. Somewhat sleepy.. drank a little to much stuff yesterday With Haley the Sewing machine man..

Monday March 27th 93

Snowed hard all day   flakes as big as a silver dollar. about 8 inches of snow this evening. Was arround with Healy but he got to drunk for any good..

Tuesday Mar 28th

I bought a ticket for Kansas City and left Leavenworth on the 4 P.M train.. bought a ticket in Kansas City for New York for $2500 and left Kansas City at 8.40 P. M.

Wednesday Mar 29th

Got into St. Louis over the Chicago & Illinois R. R. at 7 oclock this morning and have been prancing around town all day.   Went to a Matinee at Popes Theatre this afternoon very good show..

Have been down on the Levee looking at the River Craft.. Left at 8.05 - P.M. over the Ohio & Mississippi

Thursday Mar 20th 93

Arrived in Cincunatti at 7.10 this morning. Stopped at the Palace Hotel corner of 6 St. & Vine   charge $200 a day.   Put in the day walking arround the city   Find it a very nice city.   Went to the Walnut Street theatre this evening   the play was a countrey circus   it was first class

Friday Mar 31st

Arround town part of the day but my feet got sore and I set arround the hotel a great part of the time

Saturday Apr 1st 93

Rained hard most of the forenoon   Sun came out in the afternoon
I paid my bill at the hotel $5<u>00</u> and took the Erie R.R. for home

Sunday Apr 2nd

Arrived in Hornellsville about 11 A.M. Took breakfast on the train
charged 1<u>00</u> but had a good breakfast.. Put up at the Page house here
in Hornellsville

Monday Apr 3rd 93

Settled at the Page House after dinner at the rate of $2<u>00</u> per day
took the 4 P.M. train for Arkport.. the first person I struck that I
knew was Mrs. Colgrove and rode up with her on the train.. found
Arkport greatly changed.   I did not recognize the place hardly.. got
home and found the folks all well *[This does not mesh with William
Hurlbut's description of Mrs. Roxie Armstrong's poor physical
condition in 1891. See pages 23, 24]*

Tuesday Apr 4th 93

Have been home all day visiting and reading the Aspen papers that
have accumulated for the past month.. has been a nice day but
somewhat windy..

Wednesday Apr 5th

At home most of the day

Sunday April 9th 93

Went to church to day the first time in many a year. Stopped at
Sunday School and went to church in the evening.. Saw quite a lot of
people that I know

Tuesday Apr 11th

Was arround the corners and up to Charley Smiths.. most all of the
old boys and girls that I knew years ago are married and have families
arround them

Saturday April 22nd 1893

Went to Hornellsville on the 11 oclock train with brother in law
Sewell.   Bought a Baby Carriage for Roxie paid 17.50 for at
Deposited $300<u>00</u> in Col Cranes bank subject to check got home on
the 5 oclock train

Monday April 24th 1893

Left Arkport at 11 oclock.   Got one hundred dollars out of
Cranes bank at Hornellsville.   Had quite a talk with Ed Crane and
his son Sidney.   They are relatives of S. I. Hallet of Aspen..

Took the 11.55 train for New York City for $7<u>00</u>. Got into NY
about 9 oclock put up at the Cosmopolitan Hotel at the corner of
Chambers St and West Broadway

While touring New York City, Armstrong witnessed an impressive International Naval Review. On April 25, 1893, he watched thirty-five of the world's premier warships steam up the Hudson River, including the U.S. Steamer Dolphin, part of the "Great White Squadron." In 1896 the Pepsin Gum Company produced buttons (above) commemorating this memorable event. (Author's collection)

Tuesday Apr 25th 93

Got up at 7 oclock this morning. Took breakfast in the restaurant at the hotel   cost 70 cts..   Raining this morning and has rained more or less all day.. I put in the most of the forenoon on the battery and along the North River.   The first curiosity I struck was a diver who was at work in 25 or 30 feet of water I should judge from the length of the rope and tube that they employed..

The next big thing was three Spanish Men of war towing the Caravels Santa Maria the Nina & the Pinta up the Hudson The guns at the Godess of Liberty fired a salute which was answered by one of the Spanish ships

Then the U. S. Steamer Dolphin hove in view and steamed on up the Hudson saluted by the guns at the Governors island. After that I

On April 25, 1893, Armstrong also walked over the Brooklyn bridge, then one of the modern technological wonders of the world. (Author's collection)

walked along the docks up East River to the Brooklin Bridge and walked over that to Brooklin then crossed back on the Fulton Ferry boat. Took dinner at the South Lerry Hotel had shad potatoes bread and coffee cost 30 cts.. then took the Elevated R.R. and went up to Central Park. Did not walk in the park as it was raining hard but I had an umbrella so I kept dry.. Was in the Plaza Hotel looking at the pictures they have some fine ones and have a fine hotel to.. had to hunt quite a while to find Broadway but finaly got there and walked down it till I got tired and took the horse cars and got back to the Hotel about 4.30 with blistered feet..

Armstrong rode on New York's elevated railroad, a far cry from the rickety stage coaches that rumbled by his cabin along Castle Creek. (Courtesy of Joann Leech)

A portion of Central Park as it looked when Armstrong strolled through it. (Author's collection)

SCENE IN CENTRAL PARK, NEW YORK.

Wednesday Apr 26th 93

Got up 6.30 this morning clear and fine.. Took an excursion boat and went down to the narrows and saw all the men of war.. had a nice trip.. The Sweeds had a great day to day unveiled the Statue of Ericson on Battery Park

After I got back from the excursion I took the cars up Broadway to Central Park.. walked arround there all the afternoon   Was in the Art Gallery a long time   It is a grand thing.   Saw Cleopatras needle. Got back to the hotel and took a doz raw on the half shell cost 35 cts.. In the evening Went up to the Acadmy of Music to see the Black Crook   cost 50cts had to stand up.. Splendid piece.. the finest costumes I ever saw

Thursday April 27/93

Raining hard when I got up this morning and kept it up all day more or less.. I took a walk after breakfast down on the dock and arround back to the hotel.. Then took the Elevated R.R. to 80 Street.. walked down that to the west to the river.   The English flagship Blake and the U. S. flagship Philadelphia lay off the fort of 88 st there was a big crown all along the bluffs of the river.. I stood arround in the rain from about 10 till 5 oclock.. the grandest sight of all was the tugs and excursion boats.. the great cannonade that the papers were blowing about did not ammount to much they used the little guns.. did not fire a big gun in the whole shooting watch..

Friday April 28th 1893

Clear fine day.. The great street parade came off about noon.   I got a good view of it on a stand on the corner of Washington square. Paid $1<u>00</u> for the seat.. President Cleveland dashed by ahead of the procession and I caught a glimps of the bald spot on the back of his head.. all the big guns of the fleets rode by in carriages also governor Flower.. The sailors of all the man of wars and the marines marched by beside a big lot of Militia regiments   so I got the worth of my dollar over and over. In the evening went to Union Square Theatre to see the Froth of Society play'd   very good whore house play..

Saturday Apr 29th 93

Rainy to day.. did not accomplish much today. Was at Hepners museum on Union Square   eat dinner at the Morton House. Had shad and shad roe coffee and potatoes cost 60 cts.. got ticket to Black Crook $1.50 went to Acadamy of Music to see the Black Crook   Great Show

Sunday Apr 30th 1893

Am at the Cosmopolitan Hotel corner of West Broadway & Chambers St. N. Y. City.   Did nothing much today

Monday May 1st 1893

Rainy day.. took an excursion boat up the Hudson around the fleet

Tuesday May 2nd 1893

Took one of the Iron Steam Boats from the Battery of the Hudson around the fleet to accompany a Mr Rogers from Baltimore that I got accquainted with.. was arround with him all day.. in the evening we went up too Thesis concert hall on Union Square a great place to catch snaps

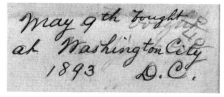

As witnessed by the above notation, Armstrong purchased one of his journals on May 9, 1893, in "Washington City, D.C." (Armstrong's journals)

Wednesday May 3rd 1893

Feeling bad to day. walked arround in afternoon with Rogers. was at the exchange on Wall St. and had lunch at the Delmonica Restaurant.. I went to bed early in the evening.

Thursday May 4th

Did not get up till late this morning. Rogers left last night. I went to Eden Music 23st near 6 ave.. good. went to Worth's museum 30st 6 ave good.. in evening was up to Thusis Thesis [?}and Hotel Europa.

Friday May 5th

Was over to Statue of liberty. Was over the Cainpania of the Cunardea Line

Saturday May 6th

Was up to Central Park to the Hotel Waldorph & Imperial..

Sunday May 7th

Took walk over Brooklin Bridge. rode back on cable cars.

On May 8, 1893, Armstrong toured the Capitol Building, shown here in an 1892 souvenir booklet from Washington, D.C. The booklet boasted: "To interest and instruct the visitor there is first the Capitol—the Nation's Palace—which has cost $20,000,000 and within which are stores of art in historical paintings, statuary, bronze panels and doors, etc. The view from the central dome of this structure is the finest in the world." (Author's collection)

Monday May 8th 93

Paid my bill at the Hotel and took the 8 oclock A.M. train over the Pennsylvania R.R. for Washington. Got into town in good season and stopped at the St. James Hotel on Penn Ave.. Walked over to the Capitol building and went through that and also through the Botanical Gardens..

Tuesday May 9th

Started out early this morning. Walked over to Washington Monument and then up to 1623 16th N.W. and called on H. B. Denman. Stopped with him to lunch at 1 P.M. saw his wife and son.. had a fine visit. The Col is nicely fixed. Was through part of the National Museum this evening

Wednesday May 10th 93

Was through the Museum and The Smithsonian Institute very fine. Went to the Lyceum Theatre this evening to see the London Gaity Girls a leg show.. Was to Albaughs Opera House last night to see Said Pasha. good

Thursday May 11th 93

Took a trip to Mount Vernon to day on the Steamer McAlister. Splendid trip fore 75 cts round trip.. left at 10 A.M. returned 2.30 P.M. Rode arround town on street cars after my return.. with a Dr. Keen and his father..

Went into a restaurant this evening and who should come in but John Davenport an old-timer that was in Aspen in 80.. He left there in 1882 and went to New Mexico and this is the first I had heard or seen of him since.. we walked around town all the evening talking over old times..

Friday May 12th 1893

John Davenport, his pard Ed.. Oakley and I went down to the Navy Yard to day.. and saw them building big guns   They have a big lot of them finished and a lot of them on the way.. Saw a lot of Old guns that were captured from the rebels and some that were captured from the English at Yorktown during the revolution and 1812 war..

Went through the Corcoran Art gallery this evening.. 25cts admission

Saturday May 13th 1893

Went up to the top of the Washington Monument 500 feet. This forenoon and walked through the War Navy and Treasury Departments.. But the biggest thing I saw was the panorama of the battle of Getisburg.. cost 60 cents and it was well worth it..

Went to the National Theatre this evening.. the play was Twelfth Night it was very good

Sunday May 14th 93

We took an excursion boat down the Patomac to Marshall Hall a pleasure resort where the great dish is Planked Shad.. The way they cook these is to nail several dressed shad on a plank back to the blank and set them up before an open fire out of doors.. and let them broil.. We got back about 2.20 P.M.

This evening at 7 oclock we took the Steamer Norfolk to Norfolk cost 4.50 and had to buy our meals.

Monday May 15th 93

Waked up at 5.30 this morning and turned out found ourselves out on the Chesepeak Bay with very little land in sight.. Stopped at Fortress Monroe about 6.30 and unloaded a lot of stuff.. then eat breakfast.. Got into Norfolk about 8 oclock.. after a very pleasant ride..

We went over to Portsmouth and visited the Navy Yard. Boarded the Cruiser Charleston and went through her.. The Texas, a big line of Battle Ships.. is building here   also the cruiser Raleigh and Monitor Amphitrite. The Concord.. another cruiser is here also the training Ship Portsmith a big sailing vessel.. Warm weather here. We are on the Old Dominion Steamer Roanoke bound for New York City.. left Norfolk about 8 oclock P.M. Did not go to bed till late sat on the deck and watched the different lights & light house

Very dark night

Thursday May 16th 93

Got up 6.30 this morning and found we were out of sight of land Rained most all day.. had a very pleasant sail to me

Got into N.Y about 6.30 P.M.   We put up at the Cosmopolitan Hotel.. Went to the Acadamy of Music to see the Black Crook this evening

Wednesday May 17th

Was up on the dome of the New York World building   3751/2 feet High grand view of the City

Was in the press room in the cellar. After coming out of there went up to the Hoffman House to see the baroom kept by Ed. Stokes.. Walked down Broadway to the Hotel   I got 20 dollars of Davenport

The boys took the Lackawana R.R. for Cortland N.Y.   I took the Erie for home at 8.30 P.M

Thursday May 18th 1893

Arrived in Hornellsville about 8 this morning. Stopped at the Page House to B & D. Took the Lackawana Train at 2.30 P.M for Arkport.. found the folks all well..

Friday May 19th 1893

Got a letter from Jim & Jeff Armstrong. They live at Foreman Lake Co Mich.. Got a letter from John Bollan of Aspen.. he wants to lease the Phoenix of us.. with a bond of $30,000 for 1 1/2 years..

I wrote to Jim & Jeff to day.. The weather is clear but cold..

Saturday May 20th 93

Put in most of the day reading the Aspen papers that have accumulated since I have been away

Sunday May 21st

Went to church and sunday school in the forenoon and to church in the evening

Monday May 22nd

Fine warm day. I wrote a letter to John Bolland and one to Sam Selden.. Set arround the corners in the afternoon.. went fishing after supper. set some hooks for eels..

Tuesday May 23rd 1893

Got up early and went to look after our eel hooks.. not an eel.. Willie Sewell was with me

Sunday May 28th

Went to church and Sunday School this forenoon and to Methodist Meeting in the evening   Fine weather we are having

Monday May 29th

Fine day.   Helped Sewell work at the improvements on the church in the forenoon

Tuesday May 30th 93

Decoration day.   I stopped a home all day..

Tuesday June 6th

We have been having very warm weather for the past week.. but I stand it well..

Monday June 12th

I went to Hornellsville Saturday and stayed in town till this morning.   I came up on the 9.45 train

Tuesday June 13th 1893

Cool pleasant day

Monday June 19th

Took the train for Buffalo at 8.15 this morning. Arrived about 11 oclock.. Chas Smith came up with me. He is after a woman to work for him.. I stopped around Buffalo till 9 15 P.M. then took the Mich Central for Reed City Mich fare $9.55   Very hot day

Tuesday June 20th

Arrived in Detroit about 4 this morning. Stopped arround town till 8.50 and took the Flint & Pere Marquette R.R. to Saginaw City. Arrived there at noon looked over the town till 4.45 P.M and took the train for Reed City. Arrived here at 8.30   Stopped at the Sweet Hotel to S. L. B.

Wednesday June 21st 93

Took the train for Forman at 10-25 A.M. fare 45c. Arrived there at 11 A.M.   There is no Agent there so I had to leave my trunk with a private family. Walked over to Uncle Rials 2 1/2 miles out in the woods and like to have melted from the intense heat.   Found Aunt Leydin Uncle Rial Jeff and Jim at home Uncle and Aunt. Arrived here from Cedar Spring yesterday.   They are farely well.   Uncle is quite feeble.. he is 79 years old, they have 240 acres of land here on a nice lake. but it is very poor sandy soil

Monday June 26th 93
    I took the 11 oclock train for Ludington. Arrived at that place about 12-30 had dinner.. I have put in the time rowing on the lake in Jeffs' boat and visiting. They seemed to be glad to see me but they live very poor and I could hardly get enough to eat and there were lots of bed bugs to eat me..

Tuesday June 27th 93
    Took the F & Pere Marquette boat no 4 for Milwaukee last nigh at 10 oclock. Slept in a cot in the cabin. Arrived at Milwaukee 7 A.M. Took the 8 A.M. boat for Chicago. Arrived there 3 P.M.   stopped at the Rockisland house on sherman St.. Took the Illinois R.R. out to the Worlds Fair this evening   Grand Electric display   I got back home at 10 P.M.
    The fair is emence the trouble is there is so much that a person is confused.

Combine the immense 1893 Chicago World's Fair Grounds with crowds like the one shown above and it is understandable why Armstrong felt overwhelmed during his first day at the fair. (Courtesy of Joann Leech)

Wednesday June 28th 93
    At the Fair most of the day. Walked till I was tired.. got back to town early. Stopped at the Atlantic Hotel B.&B 1 00

Thursday June 29th 93
    Hunted up a room this morning near the fair grounds at the Albion Hotel 5463 & 5465 Kiniback Avenue 50 cts a day.. after dinner went to the fair and staid till 10 at night.. went through the California Building the Womans building and the Transportation Building.   Great display of fireworks on the lake front this evening

Friday June 30th 1893

Took the street cars for down town this forenoon. Called on Arthur Woodcock. Got my value at the Atlantic Hotel.. got a shave and come up home. Wrote a letter to Pete Olson and to Roxie.. went to the fair in the afternoon

Saturday July 1st 93

Went to the fair this morning Viewed the Midway Plaisance and invested in a souvenir spoon for Roxie and in beer and lunch for myself.

In the afternoon went through the fisheries building and the Sweadish building

Paid for room $3.50 for a week.. Splendid fire works on the lake front this evening.. I got back to the hotel at 10 oclock.. took a bath and went to bed

Sunday July 2nd 93

Went to the fair   Was in the art gallery most of the day.   Saw the Old De Wit Clinton Locomotive and coaches used on the Hudson & Schnactada R.R. in 1831.. Fir mast at the door of the Washington Building 215 ft high and only 3 1/2 ft diameter

In the late nineteenth and early twentieth century, Americans and Europeans could not seem to get enough of Buffalo Bill Shows and comic books. (Author's collection)

Monday July 3rd

Walked through the Illinois Building, the Government Bldg and Krups exibit and the Leather Exibit. Saw leather belt 12 ft wide. another 2 miles long. Saw Red Wood plant in Forestry building 16 ft & 5 in wide & 5 inches thick. Eat lunch in the Big Tree Restaurant. They use the Big Tree for a counter it is 4 ft square & 111ft long & weighs 92000 lbs & is 442 years old.. Went to Buffalo Bills show this evening

Tuesday July 4th

An immense crowd on the fair grounds to day. The celebration did not amount to much.. Big fireworks in the evening.. I got home 12.45. Saw Charley Fields from Aspen and was arround with him in the evening. Saw the Persian Dancing girls on the Midway Plaisance &c

Wednesday July 5th 93

Got up at 10 this morning. Went to the fair after dinner and walked arround to different exhibits. Saw a big load of logs from Ontonago River Michigan white pine 18 ft long on the bobsleds containing 36055 ft of lumber.. Was in to see the Turkish dancing girls on Midway Plaisance and also saw James Corbit & Prof. Donaldson box a bout in the Natatorium Music Hall..

Thursday July 6th 93

Was at the fair to day. Saw a silver fialagree model of the Horticultural Hall made in Monteray Mexico using 110lbs of silver. 11 ft 2 in long 3ft 2 1/2 inches wide.. represents the labor of 12 men 13 months at 18 hours a day.. Took in the Ferris wheel 50c   .. also the Streets of Cairo 15c.. also the English soldiers tournament 50c all good..

On July 6, 1893, it cost Armstrong fifty cents to ride this giant Ferris wheel. (Courtesy of Joann Leech)

Friday July 7th 93

The Caravels came in this afternoon and they received quite an ovation.   The parade was good.. U.S. Soldiers, English soldiers & sailors.. Indians South Sea Islanders, Excamo Dahomans. Bedouins &c &c.   I was up on the prominade on Manufacturers Building 140 ft high and 1/2 miles arround.. fine view cost 25c..

Saw a Tarpon from Florida.. 7ft 2in long weight 205lbs..

Saw a Tiffany diamond worth $100,000. Also Gormans silver statue of Columbus value $50,000.. was in the Libby glass works this evening 10c..

Saturday July 8th 1893

Went to fair this afternoon.   Took in the Bedouin encampment also Old Vienna.. saw the fire works this evening. They were first class.. stopped afterwards to hear the Cincinnati Band play they are fine.. Got a letter from Roxie this evening they are all well..

Sunday July 9th
   Wrote at letter home to day

Monday July 10th
   At the fair   Saw a chunk of pure native copper weight 8500lbs another weight 6200lbs from Central Mine Mich.. Saw the Kimberly South African diamond exibit.. diamond washing and rough diamonds also cutting the stones.. Was in the Iowa state building.. it is fine.. was in the English building.. was on the Caravel Santa Maria. Saw and had quite a chat with E. P. Cowan.. was introduced to his wife and her sister. Great fire in cold storage bldg.. 21 lives lost..

Imagine how this World's Fair scene must have impressed Armstrong, who lived in a one-room cabin along Castle Creek above remote Aspen, Colorado. (Courtesy of Joann Leech)

Tuesday July 11th
   Was down town. Had a long talk with Arthur Woodcock.. Was in Libby Prison this afternoon.. 50c addmission.. lots of relics of the War. The bed that Lincoln died on the sheet soaked with his blood.   Trees full of bullets & shells. two mini balls that met in mid air and were flattened out and welded togather.. &c &c Well worth the money..

Wednesday July 12th
   In Blarney Castle refreshment room getting away with a bottle of beer and a cheese sandwich - 25c.. admission 20c .. did not kiss the Blarney stone.. it is only a piece about 6 by 8 in.. costs 10c to Kiss it. It looks as though a million people slobbered over it.   Bought 2 linen hand kerchiefs 40c. 52 ton gun in Govt building.. 1000lbs shot 450lbs powder for a load.. Max in gun fires 750 shots a minute. Was in the diving bell show 10c.. & Colorado mine 10c

Thursday July 13th 93
   Did not go to the fair.   Set arround the house till about 4 P.M. and paid my bill and went down town. Went to see the great play of America at the Auditorium paid 100 Great show.. Very hot this evening.

Friday July 14th

Bought a ticket for Denver $10<u>00</u> over the Chicago & Alton & U.P.R.R. Stopped at the Atlanta Hotel last night. Left Chicago 2 P.M. Very hot weather.

Oddly, Armstrong did not mention seeing Aspen's Silver Queen (above) at the World's Fair. It was meant to remind the world that silver's worth and appeal equaled gold's. The message failed. (Courtesy of Joann Leech)

Saturday July 15<u>th</u> 1893

Arrived in Kansas City 8.15 this morning.. called at E. P. Cowans office in the Keith & Perry Building cor of 9<u>th</u> & Walnut. He was not in. Took the 4.35 P.M. train for Leavenworth. Arrived about 5.. Put up at the Continental.   Saw Schlag.. he has been here since May.. came home to his mothers funeral.. Weather very warm.

Sunday July 16th

Set arround the Hotel all day   very warm

Monday July 17th

Stopped arround the house all day.

Tuesday July 18

Rained all the forenoon. Was arround with Schlag all afternoon

Wednesday July 19th 93

Warmer to day.. Went to the Show this evening with Nora one of the dining room girls

Sunday July 23<u>rd</u>

Hot day.. I got full this evening..

Monday July 24

Warm day.. Went buggy riding with Nora this evening.   Up set and had a duce of a time.. tried my best to get there but she would not.. Paid for the use of the rig 2.25 was in big luck that we did not smash things all to pieces. Got home about 11 oclock from Jake Schwaglers

Thursday July 26th 93
Settled Hotel bill $13.75. Took 8.00 A.M. train for Kansas City.. Took 10.45 train for Denver

Friday July 27th
Arrived in Denver 10 A.M. Stopped till 7.30 P.M. and took the D & R. G. for Aspen.   Saw John Boland

Saturday July 28
Arrived in Aspen this afternoon   town very dull

Tuesday July 31st
Stopped with John Coll 3 nights.   Came up home with Bob Long Nobody at home. I got in and got supper. Pete is on Texas Creek prospecting

Thursday Aug 2nd
Pete came home this evening

Friday Aug 3rd
We went to town today

Saturday Aug 26th 1893
I have been laid up with eresiphelas in the leg but it is about well

Tuesday Aug 29th
We went to Aspen this morning. Got home about midnight.   Got some groceries of Clark & Denman

Wednesday Aug 30th
We packed up to go over to Taylor River fishing but the weather threatened rain so we did not go

Thursday Aug 31st 93
Rained all day
John Coll went by going over on Taylor river with his family fishing

Friday Sept 1st
Pete and I packed up and went over to Red Mountain Ranch on Taylor River. I caught a trout this evening

Saturday Sept 2
We went over to Spring Creek

Sunday Sept 3rd
fishing no good here caught a few.. Was out with the gun but did not see any game

Monday Sept 4th 1893
Pete and I moved over on Taylor River.. John Coll stopped on Spring   we caught a few fish this afternoon

Tuesday Sept 5th
Fished most of the day.. caught very few

Wednesday Sept 6th

Moved down the river 4 or 5 miles. Caught a good lot of fish Saw Al Hopely he has been over to Tin Cup with some passangers

Thursday Sept 7th 93

Caught very few fish to day. to windy for fishing

Friday Sept 8th

Moved up the river to day.   I killed 3 grouse and Pete caught 3 trout.. we have a splendid camp this evening

Saturday Sept 9th

Moved over home.   John Coll caught up with us. he did not have very good luck fishing or hunting

Sunday Sept 10th 93

Arround the house all day.. had a fine rest and sleep last night.. fine weather we are having

Monday Sept 18th

Pete went to work on the Little Anna Mine 2.50 a day & board

Tuesday Sept 19th

Walked to Aspen this forenoon got 400 of John Coll.. the town is very quiet

Wednesday Sept 20th

Arround town all day.   Stopping at the Clarendon Hotel

Thursday Sept 21st

Set up all night with a brother mason by the name of Geo Williams.. he is sick with Eresipelas in the head.. Settled with the hotel 2.25 and came home on John Robinsons horse.. Got some groceries at Clark & Denmans..

Friday Sept 29th

Took the gun and went up Foly Gulch. Gone all day and caught 1 grouse

Saturday Sept 30th

Snowing all day. About 10 inches fell.. about 6 in on the ground this evening

Sunday Oct 1st

Cold and cloudy most of the day.. L. N. Fullbright here most of the day

Monday Oct 2nd 1893

Stormy.. I did my weekly washing.. Jim Kenney & Tom Bowen came over from Italian Mountain where they have been for a month doing assessment work.. They stopped here for a while and eat lunch and rested..

Tuesday Oct 3rd
Pete came down from the Little Anna this afternoon. Brought down some fine specimens of native silver.. I got a letter from Roxie and one from E.P. Cowen.

Wednesday Oct 4th 1893
Worked on the Jessie this afternoon   snowing this evening

Thursday Oct 5th
Snowed about 2 inches last night.. I took the gun and hunted after rabbits this forenoon but did not see any.   Worked on the Jessie this afternoon

Friday Oct 6th
Fine day. I hunted rabbits a while this forenoon but did not see a rabbit   caught 2 trout in the afternoon

Saturday Oct 7th 1893
Fine day.. fished most of the day and did not catch one.. Frank Bixbee clerk of the Clarendon burried to day. He died day before yesterday.. of dropsy.. Good fellow.

Sunday Oct 8th 1893
Was up to Bert Fullers and took dinner with them. Had grouse & a fine dinner. had a good visit. left about 5 in the evening..

Tuesday Oct 10th 1893
Walked to Aspen this morning. fine day   Very still in town

Wednesday Oct 11th
Stopped at the Clarendon Hotel. in town all day snowed about 2 inches last night.. fine day to day

Thursday Oct 12th
Fine day.   Came home with Bob Long.. Got $15.00 of John Coll to day paid Clark and Denman $10.00 bot sugar & salt.   Got piece of venison of John Coll. Pd Hotel bill $3.00 and 1.00 to Rogers for making out some papers

Wednesday Oct 18th 1893
Pete & I and Chas. Boyd & George Seebree struck out for Taylor River this morning on a fishing & hunting trip. Camped at Red Mt. Ranch with Mike Fox of Aspen who is camped there doing some assessment work.   I shot 3 grouse on the way..

Thursday Oct 19th
Got into camp at the mouth of Taylor canyon about 1 oclock.. caught a few small fish

Friday Oct 20th 1893
Caught a few fish to day but the fishing is very poor. All that we get are out of one deep hole.. I was down the Canyon 3 or 4 miles hunting but did not see any game

Saturday Oct 21st

I went up the river this morning with the gun. Killed 3 ducks and a jack Rabbit.. fished in the afternoon with poor success

Sunday Oct 22nd

Very windy dissagreeable day   poor success fishing

Monday Oct 23rd 93

Ground covered with snow this morning.. We broke camp and pulled for home. Arrived there about 8.30 in the evening.. snow about 12 inches deep on the Range

Tuesday Oct 24th 93

Fine day resting up after the trip

Wednesday Oct 25th

Snow falling most of the day. Got a letter from John & Jeff to day

Thursday Oct 26th 93

Snow about 8 inches deep this morning. Baked bread and cooked most of the day. Pete getting in wood in the snow

Thursday Nov 2nd 1893

Pete and I rode to town this morning. I got a fix 1/4 of beef 50lbs potatoes 6lbs butter and 10lbs beets of Al Hopely. charged.. Pete packed them home and I stopped in town.. sent a letter home today..

Friday Nov 3rd

Walked up home this evening. Very pleasant.. got home about 7.30

Saturday Nov 4th

Washed my clothes today.. fine weather

Sunday Nov 5th

Fine weather.. was arround the house most of the day

Monday Nov 6th 1893

Morgan and I went hunting on the mountain west of Highland after bear. Did not find any but killed 3 grouse.. It was a hard trip.. Stormy this afternoon & evening

Tuesday Nov 7th

Stormy day.. Pete and I walked up to Ashcroft to vote this afternoon. Got home after dark

Wednesday Nov 8th

Arround the house all day loading shells cleaning gun.. cutting wood &c fine day

Friday Nov 10th 1893

Wrote a letter to Jim & Jeff and sent some papers to Sewell Stormy

Saturday Nov 11th

Stormed a little to day.   Pete went to Aspen The Republicans swept the countrey.. Pitkin Co elected the Peoples ticket

Sunday Nov 12th

Fine sunny day.. Chas Straus was here for dinner. Geo Seebree & son were here in the afternoon.. Pete. Straus & Morgan & I played Cribbage till 11 oclock at night

Monday Nov 13th 1893

Chas Straus stopped here last night after breakfast. He struck out for the head of Difficult Creek.   Stormy this morning but clear most of the day.. Pete has gone up on Richmond Hill to see what is going on

Tuesday Nov 14th

At home all day.. Seebree & Son here & Chas Straus got back from Difficult Creek

Fine day.   Burt Fuller was here most of the day.. We put in the most of the time playing cribbage

Wednesday Nov 15th 93

Pete & I rode to town this morning & back in the evening.. fine day. I got a letter from Roxie the folks are all well

Thursday Nov 16th

Fine day. I sawed wood & chored arround the house

Friday Nov 17th

Stormy day. Pete went up Conundrum Gulch to see Major Pickerel.. Morgan got up from town with a load of Provisions.. he is going to put in the winter here.

Tuesday Nov 21st 93

We moved to Aspen to day.   Bob Long hauled us down charged 2.50 Pete paid him. We are in John Coll house

Saturday Nov 25th 1893

John Coll and I took the Midland train for Hartsel the new gold camp. Fair $8.85.. arrived at Hartsel in the evening. quite a lot of Aspen boys here

Sunday Nov 26th 93

Rode over to Camp this morning. Put up tent and after dinner took a walk over the Camp.   Cost 100 from R.R. to camp

Monday Nov 27th

Out prospecting all day.   Did not see any gold and dont believe there is any

Tuesday Nov 28th

Prospecting all day. Located 13 claims   Storming like blazes when we got into camp

Wednesday Nov 29th 93

I am 46 years old to day.. John Coll pulled for home. To day I moved over to the Sheep Ranch with McConnell and Chris Conn.. cost 50c

Thursday Nov 30th
   We started a hole to day and dug it about 7 feet

Friday Dec 1st 93
   Went over to work on the hole but a storm came up and we went to camp

Saturday Dec 2nd 1893
   Stormy did nothing

Sunday Dec 3rd
   Surveyed claim and did a little work

Monday Dec 4th
   Did nothing

Tuesday Dec 5th
   I went to Buffalo Slough to the New town of Balfour. Bot some potatoes and can of Peaches 45c
   Mc & Chris finished the 10 foot hole on the Sunshine Lode

Wednesday Dec 6th 1893
   I pulled out for Aspen this morning. Cost 1 50 to get to the R.R. had dinner at Hartsel 50c. Got into Aspen about 12 oclock at night

Thursday Dec 7th
   Roxie sent me the babies picture.   Pete and I rustled a stove to day. Storming and plenty of snow

Friday Dec 8th
   Storming.. I paid 1 00 for Stove pipe 15c for Key & 60c for lamp burner. Got a letter from Jim Armstrong

Saturday Dec 9th 1893
   Bought 4 chairs 50c a piece. Got a ton of coal 5.50   Started a fire in our stove.. it goes first class. Stormy

Sunday Dec 10th 93
   Fine clear day. Chored arround the house most of the day..

Monday Dec 11th 93
   Fine day.. was down to the court house hunting abstracts

Tuesday Dec 12th
   Took a walk with Ed Higenbothom.. fine day
   Got 5 00 cash of John Coll

Wednesday Dec 13th 1893
   Was over to see Geo.. Seebree with Pete.. I bought a table to day cost 1.25
   Lou Brown was burried to day. he died of pheunonia over at Cripple Creek.. I got a quart of beer of John this evening

Saturday Dec 23rd 93
   Splendid weather we are having.. I have been fooling away the past 3 days with Don Kennedy. He came to town from Tourtlolles Park

Tuesday and has been drunk ever since.. he stopped with me 3 nights but I hope I have got rid of him till he sobers up..

Sunday Dec 24
   Had roast goose & apple sauce & Oyster stew for dinner to day

Monday Dec 25th
   Took dinner with Sam Seldon to day

Monday January 1st 1894
   Fine sunney day   Did nothing much..

Tuesday Jany 2nd
   Fine day. Pete started for New Mexico to a new gold camp.. Major Pickrel sent him.. I saw him off on the 6.40 D & R.G. Train this evening

Wednesday Jany 5th
   Fine day. But about 6 inches of snow fell last night.. I patched up my britches this fore noon. Eat rabbit with Bailey this evening

Saturday Jany 6th 94
   Thermometer was 18° below Zero this morning

Sunday Jany 7th 1894
   Very cold weather we are having
   I got a statement of John Coll to day. He has a book a/c against me of 131.75   I guess it is all right.   Walked arround with Ed Higenbothom in the Afternoon. was at the Keely Club Room and played two games of whist

Wednesday Jan 10th 94
   Received a letter from Roxie. They are all well.. I took dinner with Geo. Seebree

Thursday Jan 11th
   Fine sunney day. Took a walk with Ed Higenbothom
   Was to Lodge this evening short session.. sent some papers home

Saturday Jany 13th 1894
   Worked all day helping John Coll to put up ice

Sunday Jany 14th
   Putting up ice all day

Monday Jany 15th
   Fine warm day

Tuesday Jany 16th
   Put forfature notice on record.. on the Blue Lime property & Leavenworth against Schlag pr Al Hopely

February 7th 1894
   Fine day. Took a walk with Ed Higenbothom. Made a horn for gold washing.. Played cards all the evening with Bailey. Bush & Gorge Seebree

Wednesday Feby 21st 1894

Snowing hard this morning.. Weather is warm and the past two day has been thawing.. There is nothing new in the camp.. silver keeps going down it is 63 1/4c for oz now.. I am very much afraid that it will go so low that the mines will shut down..

There is a gold excitement below Aspen Junction *[present-day Basalt]* and quite a number went down night before last to see what it amounted to.

Thursday March 1st 94

Fine sunny day

Monday Mar 5th

Sat up with Mcfee last night. He is sick with pneunomia.. he is at Geo. Allisons house

Tuesday March 6th

Stormy day.   I put in most of the day at home

Thursday Mar 8th

Fine sunny day. Water running down the streets.   I called on Mrs. Selden this forenoon and returned one of Coopers novels.. Went to lodge this evening.   Work in the 3rd a Mar. A. J. Davis

Friday Mar 9th

[no entry]

Monday March 19th

Bought a pair of boots to day. Cost 4 dollars. Frank Campbell moved in with me to stop a while

Tuesday March 20th

Stormy and snowing.   Got a letter from Chris Conn at Balfour no good news

Wednesday March 21

Stormy last night.. about 6 inches of snow this morning   Was playing cards in John Colls all the afternoon.. did not get stuck once

Friday March 30 1894

Warm and cloudy   We have had two or three days fine weather. I recd a letter from Pete Olson last week he has been helping Ballard sink a shaft. Sayes it shows up good in gold.   I washed my clothes this morning. Recd a letter from Roxie this afternoon. All well

Saturday Mar 31

8 inches of snow when I got up and still snowing.. stopped about noon. About 12 inches of snow fell..

Sunday Apr 1st 1894

Fine day. very sloppy

Monday Apr 2nd 1894
Fine sunny day

Monday Apr 9th
Considerable stormy weather the past week.   I got 10 dollars of John Coll and have been buying grub &c with it. To day is fine but somewhat chilly. I got up at 6 this morning Mox was arround after an all night spree. I went up town and took breakfast with him at the restaurant had ham and eggs.. Eggs are 15cts a doz now..

Saturday Apr 14th 94
Got up at 5.15 oclock this morning. Started up to Highland fine morning and the roads are not bad.   I met Morgan and Lard just this side of Coal Kilns and turned back with them. I was going up to see about the cabin as I had heard it had been broken into but Morgan said it was all right.. had got belated and went in for the night.. Abe Lee went up Conundrum this morning with Bert Seymour as company.. Raining this evening

Monday Apr 16th 1894
Got up at 6 after breakfast. Frank Campbell and I and the gun went up Roaring Fork to see if we could kill any ducks.. did not see a duck had a pleasant walk got home near noon..
Snowing this evening

Tuesday. Apr 17th
about 6 inches of snow this morning.. snowed all day

Sunday April 29th 1894
Ground covered with snow this morning
Two mass meetings to day to form auxiliary corpse to Coxies Army.. I was to both

Monday Apr 30th
About 10 inches of snow this morning and still snowing

Monday May 7th 1894
Went up to the cabin this morning rode up to the Anna road with an ore train and packed my plunder over on my back

Tuesday May 8th
Located the Little Jessie to day.. called it the Industrial Lode

Friday May 11th
Moved the most of my things up home to day.   Morse hauled them for me

Saturday May 12th
Fussing arround

Sunday May 13th 1894
Was up to Tenderfoot Ranch with Morgan calling   We had a heavy rain this afternoon

Monday May 14th
Worked on the claim to day

Tuesday May 15th
Sick all day. caught cold

Wednesday May 16th
Not feeling well

Thursday May 17th
Worked on claim

Friday May 18th
Worked on claim.. walked to Aspen this evening

Saturday May 19th 94
Not feeling well.. got $25.00 of John Coll this evening

Sunday May 20th
Warm nice day

Monday May 21st
Petes ponies came up this evening and I had to pay $25.00 Ranch bill on them. Rode them up home this evening

Saturday May 26th
Went to Aspen to day. Got 10.00 of John Coll. Bought some groceries & a gold pan and packed up home in the evening

Sunday May 27th 94
Arround the house fixing up to go prospecting

Monday May 28
Geo Kleinhans and I packed over Taylor Range and camped at Bowman. Had quite a time on the Range. We missed the trail and lost about 2 hours

Tuesday May 29
Hunted horses all the fore noon and found them in camp.   Rained in the afternoon tried fishing but could not catch any

Wednesday May 30th 94
Rained all day stopped in camp

Thursday May 31st
Rained most of the day.. prospected a little in afternoon

Friday June 1st 94
Baked Bread this morning

Saturday June 2nd
Moved camp down the river

Sunday June 3rd
Fished most of the day.. caught 2 fish

Monday June 4th

Packed up this morning and moved over to Illinois creek. Got into camp about 2 oclock

Tuesday June 5th 94

Panning in the old placers all the forenoon. Got some good prospects.. Geo Mayce is hidraulicing just below our camp

Wednesday June 6

Prospecting the foot hills all day.. came in tired and in a rain storm

Thursday June 7th

3 inches of snow this morning. In camp all the forenoon.. in the afternoon were panning near camp. Got about a dollar in gold out of 7 pans of dirt out of a hole in the bed rock that was left by the old miners.. The gulches were worked here in the 60s

Friday June 8th 94

Ground covered with snow this morning   Arround the camp most of the day

Saturday June 9

Out along the foothills all day. Hungry looking countrey all granite

Fine day

Sunday June 10th

Fine day Packed over to Red Mountain in forenoon. Fished all the afternoon.. did not raise a fish   Very windy

Monday June 11

Got home about 6 this evening, over to Morgans and played crib in evening

Tuesday June 12 94

Fine day George Cline, Ed Higenbothom Fogg & Andy Buckmaster here to dinner

Wednesday June 13

Walked to Aspen this morning. The town full of Old Veterens G A.R Encampment of Colorado & Wyoming

Thursday June 14

G.A.R. parade to day.. End of encampment.

Friday June 15

Got 50 dollars of John Coll to day

Saturday June 16

Paid taxes on Phoenix for Pete & myself $4.90

Sunday June 17th 94

Walked up home this evening.. got home about 9 oclock

Monday June 18

Washed my clothes to day

Tuesday June 19

Got up 4.30 this morning. Walked up Conundrum to the Jersey Lilly Lode and located it for Pete & myself. Brought down a lot of rock to test for gold

Wednesday June 20

Pounded up & paned several pieces of the rock that I got yesterday.. but could not get a color.   Ed Higenbothom & Andy Buckmaster here for dinner on their way to Dificult Creek.

Thursday June 21

Prospecting above the Puzzler.. did not find anything. very hard traveling. got bucket of milk at Tenderfoot Ranch and had Bread & Milk this evening.   Fine weather we are having

Friday June 22

Finished work on the Little Jessie to day

Saturday June 23

Rode to Aspen with Fred Griswold.. Got 5<u>00</u> of John Coll

Sunday June 24<u>th</u> 94

Got 5<u>00</u> of John Coll today. Came home this Afternoon. Got $10.30 worth of groceries of Putnam

Warm day   Sent $35<u>00</u> draft to Roxie today

Monday June 25

Fixed fence arround the pasture to see if I cant keep the horses home. Worked arround the house in afternoon

Tuesday June 26

Washed my clothes and baked bread. Was fishing in afternoon but did not catch any.   Bill Rose here for supper.. has his jacks with him.. has been over to Stevenses on Taylor River for them

Wednesday June 27

Bill stopped for the night & Breakfast. Cold and snowing a little to day

Pete Olson got back from Amizette New Mexico this evening.. he did not find anything..

Thursday June 28<u>th</u>

Pete was cobbling and fixing up to day

Friday June 29th

We surveyed the Industrial Lode to day. That used to be the Little Jessie and established some of the corners to the L & H.. *[Leavenworth & Hornellsville]*

Saturday June 30<u>th</u> 1894

Fixing up to go prospecting on Difficult Creek

Sunday July 1<u>st</u> 94

Moved up to the head of Difficult Creek and went into camp near Higenbothom & Buckmasters Camp

In the early 1890s almost every gulch and hill in the Aspen region seemed to sprout a small mining "camp," like the one shown above. (Armstrong's journals)

Friday July 6th 94
   We located a claim today named in the Golden Gate
   Snowed some and was very cold part of the day.   It has rained most every day since we have been here.. some of the ore here pans first rate

Saturday July 7th 94
   Pete went to Ashcroft with the ponies and got some grub. I worked a little on the claim

Sunday July 8th
   In camp most of the day

Monday July 9th
   We located another claim to day and named it the Golden Morn

Saturday July 14th
   We packed down home to day.. Rainey.. got home about 3 P.M.

Sunday July 15th
   Took a bath & changed clothes to day

Tuesday July 17th
   Caught 4 trout this evening

Wednesday July 18th 94
   Rained all the day. Got some grub from Town $8.40 worth. Got a letter from home all well. got a letter from E.P. Cowen.. also one from H. N Wood Denver.. about taxes on Grand Union & Rip..

Thursday July 19th
   Caught 8 nice trout this afternoon

Friday July 20th
   Pete & I rode to town. I paid the Taxes for 93 on the Rip 3.29 & on the Phoenix 2.62. Bought 6 cans milk 90c got $500 of John Coll.   We got home about 8 in the evening.   Got Frank the dog today from John

Saturday July 21st

Morgan & Fred went to Aspen with their Camp outfit. They have closed down on their Tunnel.. I caught 9 trout this afternoon & Pete caught 3

Sunday July 22nd

Had more fish for breakfast than we could eat. Bill Rose & Steve Burdick took dinner with us Fine day

Monday July 23

Wrote to H. N Wood about taxes on Rip.. caught 5 trout this afternoon & Pete 3

Fine day

Tuesday July 24th 94

Morgan brought up 5 gal oil for us. I paid him 1 55 for it.. Pete went to Aspen this afternoon and got Putnams mare and some bacon & beef.. I have him 82 00 for it

Wednesday July 25th

We packed over to Cement Creek to day.. Pete rode the mare.. we put up at Geo Seebrees cabin

Thursday July 26th

Prospecting arround to day. I saw and shot at a deer but did not get him.. he was to far away for buck shot..

Friday July 27th

Found Seebrees claims to day they are no good .. Misquitoes plenty

Saturday July 28th 94

Packed over to Bowman to day. Fishing in afternoon.. I caught 15 nice ones and Pete 7 rainy

Sunday July 29th

Packed down the river about 5 miles and camped in a splendid place. I killed 3 grouse and caught a few fish.. rained some in fore noon..

Monday July 30th

Not very good success fishing

Tuesday July 31

We packed down to Taylor Cannon as we hear the trout are very large and plenty. Got into camp about 11 oclock.. fished in after noon no luck.. Rained very hard and we got wet

Wednesday Aug 1st 1894

Fished all day with poor success. Saw Taylor & Stillson fishing.. they had very good luck above here. Rained some in the evening

Thursday Aug 2nd

Heavy fog this morning. Fished all day but with poor success. in the evening I caught a fine mess.. they seemed to bite better just at dark.

Friday Aug 3rd
    We packed out at 15 to 7 this morning and got home at 3 P.M Fine war day

Saturday Aug 4
    At home all day fixing our broken tackle. I helped Mr Morse measure some land

Sunday Aug 5th 94
    I was out with dog & gun looking after grouse.. did not find any. Was up to Morses this evening got some milk and had quite a visit.

Monday Aug 6th
    Washed my clothes to day. Shot 3 grouse in the afternoon.. the young ones are 1/2 as large as full grown ones. Pete caught 20 trout to day.

Tuesday Aug 7th
    Had fried grouse for breakfast. We went to town. I got 4.05 worth of grub and 1.25 of hardware. Got a letter from E. P. Cowen dated July 24. He was in Aspen July 30th I got 1500 of John Coll. We got home 6 oclock P.M   fine day

Wednesday Aug 8th
    We started to clean out the Tunnel to day

Thursday Aug 9th
    Worked at the tunnel to day

Friday Aug 10th
    Worked at the tunnel to day

Saturday Aug 11th
    I went out with dog and gun this morning and killed 2 grouse Worked at tunnel.. got one grouse this evening

Sunday Aug 12
    Killed 3 grouse this forenoon and caught 10 trout this evening Pete caught 16 trout to day

Monday Aug 13th
    Worked in tunnel

Tuesday Aug 14th 94
    Worked at tunnel.. Chas Hubbard and Paul Swanson here for dinner.   John Coll went over to Taylor fishing.. We join him tomorrow.
    I wrote to E. P. Cowen today.

Wednesday Aug 15th
    Packed over to Taylor River to day.. camped at Red Mountain Ranch. We caught quite a lot of fish

Thursday Aug 16th
    We were up Red Mt. Creek to day.. did no good

Friday Aug 17th 94
    Moved over to Texas Creek

Saturday Aug 18
Camped in Texas Creek.. fishing no good

Sunday Aug 19
Moved down to Taylor Cannon. Got into camp about noon.. Caught quite a lot of fish

Monday Aug 20
Fishing most of the day very good luck. Rained and turned cold which spoilt the fishing

Tuesday Aug 21st
I caught a fine lot of fish to day

Wednesday Aug 22nd 94
Rained hard most of the night. We moved up to Red Mt. Ranch and in afternoon went over to Forest Hill and to the lake.. rained hard all the afternoon

Thursday Aug 23rd
Moved up to Bowman fine day. I shot 1 grouse

Friday Aug 24th
Moved over home. I shot 2 ducks on the lake on the Range.. we got home about 2 P.M.   John & the rest took dinner with us and went on to Aspen.. Lost Frank the dog

Saturday Aug 25th 94
Geo Coll brought up a telegram from Dr. Walker at Leadville wanting me to meet him at Glenwood Springs at 10 today.. of course it is to late now. We got some track at the Billhart Tunnel and hauled up to our tunnel

Sunday Aug 26
Did nothing to day

Wednesday Aug 29th
We went to Aspen to day. I got 7.15 worth of grub. Pd for recording location certificate on Industrial Lode.. 100 NY Sun for one year 100.. Ammunition 130 haircut 35. Magazine 30 got cash of John Coll 1500

Thursday Aug 30th 94
Worked on tunnel made 3 feet

Friday Aug 31st
I put in the day hunting grouse.. did not get any but killed 3 teal duck on Castle Creek

Saturday Sept 1st
Pete went to Aspen this forenoon.. took Putnams mare down. I gave him 100 to get meat & green corn. I put in the day fixing my gun and training the dog..

Monday Sept 3rd 1894

Wrote a letter to L. H. Fullbright at Raton N. M.   Pete and I packed up and went over to the head of Difficult Creek. We got into camp about 2 P.M.   I killed a duck on one of the little lakes here

Tuesday Sept 4th

Worked on our claim.. put it down 10 ft.   I was down the gulch 2 or 3 miles to some lakes but did not see any game

Wednesday Sept 5th

Surveyed the Golden Morn Lode.. our gold mine.. I was out with the gun & dog this evening but did not see anything

Thursday Sept 6th 1894

We moved down home this afternoon. I shot two Ptarmagans or mountain quail on Gold Hill and two Grouse on Grave Yard Hill

Friday Sept 7th

Chored arrround the house all day. paning rock &c

Saturday Sept 8th

We worked in the tunnel

Sunday Sept 9th

Took gun & dog and went up to Grave Yard Hill.. killed 5 grouse but lost one

Monday Sept 10th 1894

Worked in tunnel

Tuesday Sept 11th

Worked in Tunnel. Got N.Y. Sun today

Wednesday Sept 12th

Worked in Tunnel

Thursday Sept 13th

Worked in Tunnel

Friday Sept 14th

Took dog & gun and went up Robinson Gulch after grouse.. but did not see any. Very cold morning ground frozen and snow above timber line.

Arket McMillen & Stewart have started work on the Et Cetira Lode.. going to work it all winter. Fine day. We moved L. H. Fullbrights stove into our cabin this evening. it is larger & better than ours. I washed my clothes this afternoon

Saturday Sept 15th 94

We went to Aspen to day. I got 10.40 worth of grub Recorded the Golden Horn Lode 1.10 more. Got 15.00 of John Coll. We got home about 6 P.M. got 75c shot

Sunday Sept 16th
Took dog & gun and went up the creek hunting.. but did not see anything

Monday Sept 17th
Worked in tunnel

Tuesday Sept 18
Worked in tunnel

Wednesday Sept 19
Worked in tunnel. Blacked the stove

Thursday Sept 20th 94
Worked in tunnel. this evening took dog & gun out for a couple of hours did not get anything. We are having splendid weather..

Friday Sept 21st
Worked in the tunnel

Saturday Sept 22nd
Took dog & gun and went up Saw Mill Gulch after grouse.. did not find any. Pete killed two with my 22 cal pistol

Sunday Sept 23rd
I caught 7 fine trout this evening. they bite the best after sun down. Sent to town with Mr Morse for 100 dollars worth of beef

Monday Sept 24th 94
Worked in tunnel in afternoon. Washed my clothes in forenoon

Tuesday Sept 25th
Worked in tunnel. Got beef.. Got the two last numbers of the N. Y. Sun   Fine to day

Wednesday Sept 26
Getting out timbers to day   We will have to do some timbering in the tunnel

Thursday Sept 27th
I baked bread in forenoon   Worked in tunnel in afternoon and caught 5 fish after quit work

Friday Sept 28th 94
Worked on tunnel all day timbering. Raining and snowing most of the day

Saturday Sept 29
About 4 inches of snow this morning. Fine clear day. Worked in tunnel timbering

Sunday Sept 30
Finished timbering tunnel

Monday Oct 1 st
Went to Aspen to day. Got 4.85 worth of grub for gloves 50c Overalls 50c.. Got cash of John Coll $1000   Stormy day

Tuesday Oct 2nd
Stormy & snowing. I taped my boots to day

Wednesday Oct 3rd 94
Worked in the tunnel

Thursday Oct 4
Worked in tunnel

Friday Oct 5
Worked in tunnel

Saturday Oct 6
I killed a grouse this morning.. a hawk had him and I scared Mr hawk away and the dog captured the grouse

Sunday Oct 7
Took dog and gun and went up to the Blue Lime cabin. Hunted across to the Etcetera and took dinner with the boys that are working it. did not get any game.   Pete was up on Richmond Hill to day. The ground was white with snow this morning

Monday Oct 8th
Worked in tunnel

Tuesday Oct 9th
Worked in tunnel

Wednesday Oct 10th
I went to Aspen with the horses and got some grub $11.75 worth
Paid Bill Rose for 2 sacks of potatoes 2 00 and Mr. Morse is to bring them up for me. Bought 10# giant 1.50 and 1#wood powder 1 00   Got 5# butter of Al Hopely 35c a lb 1.75   I got home about 8 in the evening fine moonlight. got an Outing Mag. 25c

Sunday Oct 14th 94
Have been at work in tunnel every day.. I got out early this morning with dog & gun and went up Foley gulch.. shot 6 grouse and a hen hawk got home about 4 P.M.

Sunday Oct 21st 1894
Have been at work in tunnel all the week. Struck plenty of water last Friday and are getting some lime boulders that come down from above in the water course
Morgan and Fred are back here and are cutting mining timbers. They are talking of running a new tunnel on their property. Yesterday it snowed all day.. about 5 inches fell. but the sun today has taken it about off. I have been arround the house most of the day

Thursday Oct 25th 94
Went up Foley Gulch to day. Killed 2 grouse.. Pete is working on his contract grading Morgan road

Friday Oct 26th
Washing & choring round the house

Saturday Oct 27
Very nasty day.. I went to Aspen. Got 10.50 of John Coll.. Paid Putnam for groceries $5.35   Went to Republican Meeting at Opera House this evening.   MacEntgie *[McIntire]* candadate for Gov spoke & several others.. no good

Sunday Oct 28th 94
Round town all day.. Very stormy & bad

Monday Oct 29th
In town all day. Went to hear J. Warner Mills candadate for Supreme Judge on Populist ticket this evening.. first rate speaker & first rate speech..
Got a letter from Roxie and some photographs.

Tuesday Oct 30th
Came home with Mr. Morse this afternoon. Got meat of Al Hopely.. 4.00 worth box of grapes 45c Mag 30c

Wednesday Oct 31st 1894
Stormy. I was arround the house all day. Pete is working on his contract

Thursday November 1
Ground covered with snow this morning

Monday Nov 5th
I helped Pete finish his bridge & cut wood

Tuesday Nov 6th
Election day. Pete & I rode the ponies to Ashcroft and voted the Populist ticket.. Fine warm day.   I sent a letter home

Wednesday Nov 7th 94
Fine day.. we hauled up our winters wood
The news is that the Republicans carried the state

Thursday Nov 8th
We worked in the tunnel all day. Cloudy & threatening a storm, but it is clear and cool this evening

Monday Nov 12th 94
Pete went to Aspen and got some provisions of Putnam
I went up Foly Gulch and killed two grouse

Tuesday Nov 13th 94
We worked in the tunnel

Wednesday Nov 14
We worked in the tunnel

Thursday Nov 15th
   Worked in tunnel.   W<u>m</u> Rose and partner were here this evening
Friday Nov 16th
   Worked in tunnel till noon
Saturday Nov 17
   We went to Aspen with the ponies. I got 8.72 cts worth of meat of Al Hopely and 2.10 cts worth of groceries for cash.. bought 2 suits of underclothes & 2 pr socks of Neirburg pd cash. Left my watch at Hawkins to be fixed.. I got 22.50 of Tom Hunt on the Little Jessie. Pete went home with the ponies.. I stopped in town. Sent a letter to Tom Ogburn at Boise City Idaho

5573. Aspen, Col. U. S, A.

By November of 1894, a year and four months after the silver crash, Aspen's mining activity had slowed to virtually nothing. Its streets (above) now eerily vacant. Yet in the mountains above, Armstrong kept searching for that pot of gold, or silver, at the end of the rainbow. (Author's collection)

Sunday Nov 18th 94
   I staid with Bush last night. got 25c worth of grub towards our breakfast   I got 25 dollars of Jim Kenney to day to apply on note. I walked up home this afternoon
Monday Nov 19
   We worked in the tunnel to day.. fine sunny
Tuesday Nov 20
   Was up to Tenderfoot Ranch all day. Steve got hurt in a runaway yesterday and Morse had to go to town today after his wife so I stopped with Steve. Made him a crutch and did the chores for him.. got home at dark
Wednesday Nov 21st
   Worked in tunnel in fore noon. packed up timbers in the afternoon

Thursday Nov 22<u>nd</u>

About 6 inches of snow this morning. Washed some of my clothes in fore noon.. in afternoon surveyed Morgans Tunnel. Very cold this evening. Pete got up some rails from L. H. Fullbrights tunnel

Friday Nov 23<u>rd</u> 94

Pete is helping Morgan cut timer to day. I am choring arround the house   Very cold this morning..

Saturday Nov 24th

I did some surveying for Fred Griswold on Morgans tunnel.. got 5<u>00</u> for the job. fine sunny day

Sunday Nov 25th

Fine day. I set a trap this evening for a beaver.   Pete is helping the boys.. I did a little work in the tunnel.

Monday Nov 26<u>th</u>

Caught a fine large beaver this morning. Put in most of the day skinning and fixing up the hide. set the trap again this evening.. this has been a warm pleasant day..

Tuesday Nov 27th 94

Fine day. John Nash was here this morning to borrow my gum boots. After he left I visited the trap and found nothing in it. Put iron track in the tunnel in place of about 40 feet of wooden rails. Then worked at building a road up to tunnel.

Wednesday Nov 28th

Taking observations on the sun with the transit in forenoon.. in afternoon worked on road Fine warm day. We are having a splendid fall

Thursday Nov 29th 94

Thanksgiving. Fine day.   I am 47 years old to day

Friday Nov 30<u>th</u>

Stormy. Ike Fullbright was here to supper.. he is after Lon's blankets

Saturday Dec 1st

Ike stayed here till after breakfast and then left for town. John Nash brought my gum boots back to day. in afternoon I went down to Highland to see if there was any beaver. Did not see any sign.. Snowing hard this evening

Sunday Dec 2

About 6 inches of snow this morning. Fine sunny day

Monday Dec 3<u>rd</u> 94

Very cold morning. I took a bath and changed clothes. and put in most of the day sawing stove wood. Fine clear day but cold..

Tuesday Dec 4<u>th</u>

Choring arround.   Caught the dog in trap this evening

Wednesday Dec 5
   Caught a fox this morning in the trap. a gray one

Thursday Dec 6th
   Got a pound of Tobacco & 2 cobpipes of Putnam to day.. Fred brought them up. Snowing most of the day. Pete did not work today.. I got a letter from Roxie to day all well. Got the Sun

Friday Dec 7th 94
   about 8 inches of new snow this morning and blowing a blizzard when we got up.. stormed all day. Was over to Morgans in afternoon and played cards a while

Saturday Dec 8th
   Pete went to town with the horses, I sawed wood most of the day fine
   Morgan hurt his leg today log fell on it.. The mail went by on a sleigh.. also Mr. Morse went to town on runners. The sleighing is good

Sunday Dec 9th
   Stormy in morning but cleared up and was warm & fine the rest of the day. Sawed wood.. Pete returned this afternoon. He sent the horses down on Cattle Creek with a man by the name of Harvy payes 10.00 a piece for wintering them till first of May.

Monday Dec 10th 94
   Stormy.   At home all day sawed some wood.

Tuesday Dec 11th
   Fine sunny day but cold.. Sawed wood

Wednesday Dec 12th
   Fine sunny day but cold. Morse went up with the hay press. wants Pete & I to come up this evening to help him. I baked some bread & sawed wood

Thursday Dec 13
   Helping Morse cooking   Cold weather

Friday Dec 14th 94
   Cooking for Morse

Saturday Dec 15th
   Cooking. Stormy day

Sunday Dec 16th
   Got through baling hay at noon Fine day

Monday Dec 17th
   Went to Aspen with Morse on a load of hay. He paid me for cooking 5.25. I got 5.00 of John Coll. Got my watch at Hawkins.. he cleaned it. Paid him 2.00 & 1.00 that I owed him. got Petes watch paid 4.50 for it. Bought 4 martin traps 1.00 & one beaver trap 1.00   Sent Roxie $25.00   Got Tinc of Iron 25c

Tuesday Dec 18th 94
Got bill of grub at Putnams $19.05 and some meat at Al Hopelys. Came up with Morse.. got home at 1 P.M.

Stopped for supper last night at Ed Higenbothoms. Stayed with Bush all night & breakfast. Brought up 2 chairs & my trunk.. Fine day   Helped Morse weigh hay in afternoon

Wednesday Dec 19
Helped Morse with hay in forenoon.. set 2 traps this evening. Very warm to day some snow & some rain

Thursday Dec 20
Worked in tunnel a while in Afternoon. Weather warm & stormy

Friday Dec 21st 94
Very nice day. warm as spring ought to be. Sawed wood

Saturday Dec 22nd
Nice day. Sawed wood

Sunday Dec 23rd
Fine day   Sawed wood

Monday Dec 24
Stormy. Snowing hard this evening.. Baked some mince pies

Tuesday Dec 25th
About 4 inches of new snow this morning.. Had roast chicken & oysters for dinner. Cold day   Lay arround the house all day

Wednesday Dec 26th 1894
Clear and Cold this morning.. Very cold night. the creek is frozen over.

Thursday Dec 27th
Caught a fox in the trap and he broke the chain. The dog & I followed him. had a long chase but I finaly shot him. Cold day.. but clear

Sunday Dec 30th
Stormy. about 6 inches of new snow this morning.   Washed my clothes and took a bath

Monday Dec 31st
Very cold night. clear & sunshiny this morning.. Worked in tunnel. Pete went to Aspen this afternoon

O bviously, Charles Armstrong did not quit writing in his journals on December 31, 1894. In fact, he faithfully kept his journals for another *thirty-two years.* Toward the end of the twentieth-century, he watched America become more of a player, albeit a reluctant one, on the world stage. During the first quarter of he twenty-first century, he witnessed the steady decline of Aspen's economic fortunes. And from the first automobile chugging into town to the first airplane soaring overhead— advances in technology fascinated him.

In 1911, at the age of 64, he moved from his cabin down to a small house on West Hopkins Street in Aspen. The first flickering motion pictures mesmerized him. In 1917 he ruefully watched many of Aspen's young men march off to fight in the "war to end all wars." During 1919 Armstrong survived a horrible pandemic that depleted Aspen's already dwindling population. Until the early 1920s, he enjoyed summer life in his comfortable cabin along bubbling Castle Creek. There he continued to write about all that transpired in his world, and sometimes beyond.

He penned his last entry on May 8, 1926. According to *The Aspen Times,* Charles died on November 20, 1928, "following an extended illness over the past year." A portion of his obituary which appeared on the front page read:

> *Charles S. Armstrong was born in New York state on Nov. 29, 1847, and lacked but 9 days of being 81 years of age at the time of his passing.*
>
> *When a young man of 20 years, he served as one of the crew to survey the route across the plains for the Union Pacific railroad, and was in many battles with Indians, who opposed every step of the surveyors.*
>
> *He came to Aspen in 1879 and had lived in this district since that time. He had been a member of the Masonic fraternity for the past 44 years and a member of Hiram lodge at his death. He has served this county as county surveyor for the past several years and held that position at the time of his death. A sister living in Akron, Ohio survives him.*

Helped survey the Union Pacific Railroad? Fought Indians? Came to Aspen in 1879? Armstrong's obituary is instructive about the accuracy of historical accounts. As any research historian knows, one must be cautious about believing what one reads, especially in newspapers. I wonder, however, where the person who wrote Armstrong's obituary obtained such inaccurate information. After all, we *know* that Charles neither worked for the Union Pacific Railroad nor fought Indians. And we *know* that he came to Aspen in 1880. Had Charles, somewhere along the line, perhaps in a saloon, embellished his past? Or had the local rumor mill spiced up Armstrong's early years as a night clerk in Leavenworth, even though that was several years after the completion of the transcontinental railroad in 1869?

I do not believe that Charles S. Armstrong told anyone he surveyed the Union Pacific Railroad, let alone fought Indians along every step of the way. That was not Charlie. He neither exaggerated nor felt any need to be someone he was not. His journals tell us so.

BIBLIOGRAPHY

Abbott, D. (1989). *Colorado Midland Railway, Daylight Through the Divide.* Denver, Colorado: Sundance Publications.

Ambrose, S. E. (2000). *Nothing Like It in the World: The Men Who Built the Transcontinental Railroad 1863 - 1869.* New York, New York: Simon & Schuster.

Athern, R. G. (1962). *Rebel of the Rockies, A History of the Denver and Rio Grande Railway.* New Haven, Connecticut: Yale University Press.

Atlas of Steuben County New York. (1873). Complied by D. G. Berrs & Co. [1997 reproduction by the Steuben County Bar Association]. Steuben County Historian's Office (Magee House): Bath, New York.

Buys, C. J. (1986). "Power in the Mountains: Lucien Nunn Catapults the San Juans into the Age of Electricity," *Colorado Heritage,* 4, 25 - 37.

Buys, C. J. (1997). *Historic Leadville in Rare Photographs and Drawings.* Ouray, Colorado: Western Reflections Publishing.

Buys, C. J. (1998: Summer). "Henry M. Teller: Colorado's 'Silver Senator,'" *Colorado Heritage,* 29 - 36.

Buys, C. J. (1999). *Historic Telluride in Rare Photographs.* Ouray, Colorado: Western Reflections Publishing.

Buys, C. J. (1999). *Illustrations of Historic Colorado.* Ouray, Colorado: Western Reflections Publishing.

Buys, C. J. (2001). *Historic Aspen in Rare Photographs, Featuring the Journal of Charles S. Armstrong.* Ouray, Colorado: Western Reflections Publishing.

Canfield, J. G. (1893). *Mines and Mining Men of Colorado.* Denver, Colorado: John G. Canfield Publishing.

Centennial Anniversary (1852 - 1952) of the Presbyterian Church at Arkport, New York. (1952). Centennial Committee.

Child, H. (1868). *Gazetteer and Business Directory of Steuben County, N.Y., for 1868 - 9.* Syracuse, New York: Journal Office.

Clayton, W. W. (1879). *History of Steuben County, New York.* Philadelphia, Pennsylvania: Lewis, Peck and Co.

Coleman, J. T. (1997). *The Skeletal Shell Game: A History of a Colorado Ghost Town, 1880 - Present.* Unpublished master's thesis. University of Colorado, Boulder, Colorado.

Colt, N. F. (1977: 2nd ed.). *The Bonds of Womanhood: "Woman's Sphere" in New England, 1780 - 1835.* New Haven, Connecticut: Yale University Press.

Crofutt, G. A. (1881). *Crofutt's Grip-Sack Guide of Colorado.* Omaha, Nebraska: Overland Publishing, Co.

Early Arkport, 1797 - 1830. (1981). Canisteo Valley Historical Society, New York.

Fredrick, L. (2001). Personal communications and archival files.

Graves, M. (Editor). (1982). *From Arks to Celery.* Canisteo Valley Historical Society, New York.

Hornellsville Tribune. (January 12, 1877).

Hornellsville Weekly Tribune. (August 12, 1867).

Johnson, S. L. (2000). *Roaring Camp: The Social World of the California Gold Rush.* New York, New York: W. W. Norton & Company.

Knoll, C. K. (1977). *Memories Worth Saving: The Story of Ashcroft, Colorado.* Unpublished master's thesis. Western State College, Gunnison, Colorado.

Leavenworth City Directories. (1875 - 1881). Leavenworth County Historical Society (Carroll Mansion).

Pokagon, S. (1893). *The Red Man's Rebuke.* Hartford, Michigan: C. H. Engle.

Postman, N. (1985). *Amusing Ourselves to Death, Public Discourse in the Age of Show Business.* New York, New York: Viking Penguin Books.

Roberts, M. F. (1891). *Directory of Steuben County, New York. 1891.* Syracuse, New York: Press of John Single Paper Company.

Rohrbough, M. J. (1986). *Aspen: The History of a Silver Mining Town, 1879 - 1893.* Oxford, New York: Oxford University Press.

Steuben County Census. (1860). Steuben County Historian's Office (Magee House): Bath, New York.

Steuben County Gazetteer and Business Directory, 1868 - 1869.

Stuart, W. M. (1935). *Who's Who is Steuben County.* Dansville, New York: F. A. Owen.

The Compact Oxford English Dictionary. (1998: 2nd edition). New York, New York: Oxford University Press.

The Leavenworth (Daily) Times. (Selected issues: 1877 - 1880). Leavenworth Public Library. Leavenworth, Kansas.

The Steuben Courier. (August 15, 1890; December 20, 1895).

Unrau, W. E. (1979). *Tending the Talking Wire.* Salt Lake City, Utah: University of Utah Press.

Wilson, J. (1999). *The Earth Shall Weep.* New York, New York: Atlantic Monthly Press.

INDEX